A Chaste Maid in Cheapside

THOMAS MIDDLETON

EDITED BY

R. B. PARKER

THE REVELS PLAYS

METHUEN & CO LTD
11 NEW FETTER LANE · LONDON EC4

This edition first published 1969 by Methuen & Co. Ltd
11 New Fetter Lane, London EC4
First published as a University Paperback 1973

Printed in Great Britain by
The Broadwater Press Ltd, Welwyn Garden City, Herts
SBN 416 77710 4

Distributed in the USA by

HARPER & ROW PUBLISHERS, INC.
BARNES & NOBLE IMPORT DIVISION

THE REVELS PLAYS

General Editor: Clifford Leech

A CHASTE MAID IN CHEAPSIDE

A
CHAST MAYD
IN
CHEAPE-SIDE.

A
Pleaſant conceited Comedy neuer before printed.

As it hath beene often acted at the Swan on the Banke-ſide, by the Lady ELIZABETH her *Seruants*.

By THOMAS MIDELTON Gent.

LONDON,
Printed for *Francis Conſtable* dwelling at the ſigne of the *Crane* in *Pauls* Church-yard.
1630.

The title-page of the 1630 Quarto

To

DOROTHY, BRONWEN, AND MATTHEW

General Editor's Preface

The Revels Plays began to appear in 1958, and in the General Editor's Preface included in the first few volumes the plan of the series was briefly sketched. All those concerned in the undertaking recognized that no rigid pattern could be proposed in advance: to some extent the collective experience of the editors would affect the series as it developed, and the textual situation was by no means uniform among the plays that we hoped to include. The need for flexibility is still recognized, and each editor indicates in his introduction the procedures that have seemed best in relation to his particular play.

Nevertheless, we were fairly convinced that in some matters our policy would remain constant, and no major change in any of these respects has been made. The introduction to each volume includes a discussion of the provenance of the text, the play's stage-history and reputation, its significance as a contribution to dramatic literature, and its place within the work of its author. The text is based on a fresh examination of the early editions. Modern spelling is used, archaic forms being preserved only when rhyme or metre demands them or when a modernized form would not give the required sense or would obscure a play upon words. The procedure adopted in punctuation varies to some extent according to the degree of authority which an editor can attribute to the punctuation of the copy-text, but in every instance it is intended that the punctuation used in a Revels volume should not obscure a dramatic or rhetorical suggestiveness which may be discerned in the copy. Editorial stage-directions are enclosed in square brackets. The collation aims at making clear the grounds for an editor's choice wherever the original or a frequently accepted modern reading has been departed from. Annotations attempt to explain difficult passages and to provide such comments and illustrations of usage as the editor considers desirable.

When the series was planned, it was intended that each volume should include a glossary. At an early stage, however, it was realized that this would mean either an arbitrary distribution of material between the glossary and the annotations or a duplication of material. It has therefore become our practice to dispense with a glossary but to include an index to the annotations, which avoids duplication and facilitates reference.

Act-divisions are employed if they appear in the copy-text or if the structure of the play clearly points to a five-act division. In other instances, only scene-numbers are inserted. All act- and scene-indications which do not derive from the copy-text are given unobtrusively in square brackets. In no instance is an editorial indication of locality introduced into a scene-heading. When an editor finds it necessary to comment on the location of a scene, this is done in the annotations.

The series continues to use the innovation in line-numbering that was introduced in the first volume. Stage-directions which occur on lines separate from the text are given the number of the immediately preceding line followed by a decimal point and 1, 2, 3, etc. Thus 163.5 indicates the fifth line of a stage-direction following line 163 of the scene. At the beginning of a scene the lines of a stage-direction are numbered 0.1, 0.2, etc.

The Revels Plays have begun with the re-editing of a number of the best-known tragedies and comedies of the later Elizabethan and Jacobean years, and there are many such plays to which the techniques of modern editing need to be applied. It is hoped, however, that the series will be able to include certain lesser-known plays which remain in general neglect despite the lively interest that an acquaintance with them can arouse.

It has always been in the forefront of attention that the plays included should be such as deserve and indeed demand performance. The editors have therefore given a record (necessarily incomplete) of modern productions; in the annotations there is, moreover, occasional conjecture on the way in which a scene or a piece of stage-business was done on the original stage. Perhaps, too, the absence of indications of locality and of editorial scene-headings will suggest the advantage of achieving in a modern theatre some approach to the characteristic fluidity of scene and the neutrality of acting-space that Shakespeare's fellows knew.

CLIFFORD LEECH

Toronto, 1963

Contents

Illustrations

Preface

This edition tries to present an accurate text of *A Chaste Maid in Cheapside* based on the 1630 Quarto, with appropriate textual notes, commentary, introduction, and appendices. A special effort has been made to provide information which may be of value to actors and directors of the play, including detailed discussions of the play's first production and of its most recent professional revival.

I am grateful to the Canada Council for a Senior Fellowship during the latter half of 1966, when most of the work on the edition was completed at the British Museum, and to the University of Toronto for a research grant in the summer of 1964 and grants towards typing and a research assistant. I should also like to thank the various libraries which allowed me to consult their copies of the original edition, either directly or by photostats, and their librarians who answered my queries.

I am personally indebted to A. C. Sprague for a hint about the 1912 production; to Desmond Conacher, Alec Dalzell, and George Grube for help with classical references; to Patricia Brückman, Catherine Cox, Sally Kaplan, and Shirley Kenny for checking details of research; to David Carnegie, Alexander Leggatt, and Alan Somerset for letters discussing the Royal Court production; and to Martin Short and William Gaskill for lending their promptbooks and discussing their productions with me. I also count myself privileged to have attended the rehearsals and performances of William Glassco's production in Toronto.

To David George, who generously shared the results of his own research on Middleton, to John Cutts, who provided the appendix on the play's music, to Clifford Leech, for his unfailing thoroughness and patience as General Editor, and to my wife, who did much of the most intricate typing but did not forget that the play is a comedy, go my especial thanks and gratitude.

BRIAN PARKER

Toronto, August 1967

Abbreviations

In addition to abbreviations for the previous editions of *A Chaste Maid in Cheapside* (see Intro., pp. xix–xxi), the following are also used.

(A) WORKS OF REFERENCE, ETC.

Abbott	E. A. Abbott, *A Shakespearian Grammar* (1879).
Arber	Edward Arber, *A Transcript of the Register of the Company of Stationers of London, 1554–1640.* 5 vols. (1875–94).
Barker	R. H. Barker, *Thomas Middleton* (1958).
Bartley	J. O. Bartley, *Teague, Shenkin and Sawney* (1954).
Bentley	G. E. Bentley, *The Jacobean and Caroline Stage.* 7 vols. (1941–68).
Chambers	E. K. Chambers, *The Elizabethan Stage.* 4 vols. (1923).
Cotgrave	Randle Cotgrave, *A Dictionarie of the French and English Tongues* (1632).
Douce	Douce Collection of Broadsides in Bodleian Library.
ELH	*English Literary History.*
E.S.E.A.	*Essays and Studies of the English Association.*
E.C.	*Essays in Criticism.*
Farmer and Henley	J. S. Farmer and W. E. Henley, eds., *Slang and its Analogues.* 7 vols. (1890–1904).
Greg	W. W. Greg, *A Bibliography of the English Printed Drama to the Restoration.* 4 vols. (1939–59).
J.E.G.P.	*Journal of English and Germanic Philology.*
Kökeritz	H. Kökeritz, *Shakespeare's Pronunciation* (1953).

Libr.	*The Library.*
M.L.N.	*Modern Language Notes.*
M.L.R.	*Modern Language Review.*
M.P.	*Modern Philology.*
Nares	R. Nares, *A Glossary of English Authors*, ed. J. O. Halliwell [-Phillipps] and T. Wright. 2 vols. (1888).
N. & Q.	*Notes and Queries.*
O.E.D.	*Oxford English Dictionary.*
Partridge	Eric Partridge, *Shakespeare's Bawdy* (1947).
P.Q.	*Philological Quarterly.*
P.M.L.A.	*Publications of the Modern Language Association of America.*
R.D.	*Renaissance Drama.*
R.E.S.	*Review of English Studies.*
Sh.A.B.	*Shakespeare Association Bulletin.*
Sh.Q.	*Shakespeare Quarterly.*
Sh.S.	*Shakespeare Survey.*
S.F.Q.	*Southern Folklore Quarterly.*
Stow	John Stow, *Survey of London*, ed. H. B. Wheatley (1965 ed.), unless otherwise cited.
S.B.	*Studies in Bibliography.*
S.P.	*Studies in Philology.*
Sugden	E. H. Sugden, *Topographical Dictionary to the Works of Shakespeare and his Fellow Dramatists* (1925).
Tilley	M. P. Tilley, *A Dictionary of the Proverbs in England in the Sixteenth and Seventeenth Centuries* (1950).

(B) TEXTS

Middleton's works (including some on occasion attributed to him) are abbreviated as follows:

A.F.Q.L.	*Anything for a Quiet Life.*

B.B.	*The Black Book.*
B.M.C.	*Blurt, Master Constable.*
C.	*The Changeling.*
C.M. in C.	*A Chaste Maid in Cheapside.*
F.Q.	*A Fair Quarrel.*
F. of L.	*The Family of Love.*
F.H.T.	*The Ant and the Nightingale; or Father Hubbard's Tale.*
G. at C.	*A Game at Chesse.*
G. of L.	*The Ghost of Lucrece*, ed. J. Q. Adams (1937).
H.K.K.	*Hengist, King of Kent; or the Mayor of Quinborough.*
H.E.	*Honorable Entertainments*, ed. R. C. Bald (1953).
I.T.M.	*The Inner Temple Masque; or Masque of Heroes.*
M.W.M.M.	*A Mad World, My Masters.*
M.T.	*Michaelmas Term.*
M.C.	*Micro-Cynicon.*
M.D.B.W.	*More Dissemblers Besides Women.*
N.W.N.H.	*No Wit, No Help like a Woman's.*
O.L.	*The Old Law.*
Peace.	*The Peacemaker.*
P.	*The Phoenix.*
Pur.	*The Puritan; or The Widow of Watling Street*, ed. C. F. T. Brooke, *Shakespeare Apocrypha* (1908).
R.T.	*The Revenger's Tragedy*, ed. R. A. Foakes (1966).
R.G.	*The Roaring Girl.*
S.M.T.	*The Second Maiden's Tragedy*, ed. W. W. Greg (Malone Society, 1909).
S.G.	*The Spanish Gipsy.*
T.C.O.O.	*A Trick to Catch the Old One.*
Wid.	*The Widow.*

W.S.P.	*The Wisdom of Solomon Paraphrased.*
Wit.	*The Witch.*
W.B.W.	*Women Beware Women.*
W.T.T.	*The World Tost at Tennis.*
Y.F.G.	*Your Five Gallants.*

Unless otherwise noted, the references are to A. H. Bullen, *The Works of Thomas Middleton*, 8 vols. (1885–7). The titles of Shakespeare's plays are abbreviated as in Onions, *Shakespeare Glossary*, p. x; their line-numbering is that of Peter Alexander's edition (1951). Jonson's works, including *Eastward Ho !*, are cited from the Herford and Simpson edition (1925–52); Webster's *White Devil* and *Duchess of Malfi* are cited from the Revels editions by J. R. Brown, other Webster texts from the collected edition by F. L. Lucas (1927). Chapman is quoted from *Chapman's Works: The Comedies*, ed. T. M. Parrott (1914). The manuscript versions of the songs in IV. i and V. i are referred to in the collation collectively as MSS.; when a particular manuscript version needs to be distinguished, the shelf numbers recorded in Appendix II are used. Q^a indicates an unrevised state of the 1630 Quarto, Q^b a revised state.

Introduction

I. THE TEXT

History of Editions

A Chaste Maid in Cheapside was entered in the Stationers' Register by Francis Constable on 8 April 1630:

> Mr. Constable Entred for his Copie under the handes of Sr Hen: Herbert / and Mr Bill warden A play called *The Chast Maid* [*of Chepside added*] . . . vjd.[1]

The Register also records two transfers of copyright: on 17 February 1648 Francis Constable's widow transferred the play to Richard Thrale, and on 11(?) April 1681 Thrale's widow transferred it to Benjamin Thrale. It is also included in the catalogue of plays appended by Richard Rogers and William Ley to *The Careles Shepherdess . . . by T.G. Mr. of Arts*, 1656, and in Edward Archer's catalogue appended to Philip Massinger's *The Old Law*, 1656.[2] There seems, however, to have been only one early edition (STC 17877), a quarto put out by Constable in 1630 as 'neuer before printed'. The following copies were collated for the present edition[3] (the abbreviations in the left-hand column will be used for reference; the state of copy and provenance, where ascertainable, are put in parentheses):

BM 1 British Museum, *162. d. 30* (t.p. defective).

BM 2 British Museum, *C. 34. f. 9* (once Garrick's copy; sheet K from another copy).

BM 3 British Museum, *Ashley 5353* (T. J. Wise's copy; K1 from another copy).

[1] See Arber, IV. 198; Greg, II, no. 433. [2] Greg, III. 1322, 1331.
[3] In addition, there are some separate versions of the play's two songs; see Appendix II.

Scot. 1 National Library of Scotland, *H. 28. 1. 6(5)* (t.p. and K4 defective; margins cropped).

Scot. 2 National Library of Scotland, *Bute 371* (date cropped and '1620' written in).

Scot. 3 National Library of Scotland, *Bute 372*.

Bod. 1 Bodleian, Oxford, *Douce MM 465*.

Bod. 2 Bodleian, Oxford, *Malone 245(8)* (date cropped).

V. & A. Victoria and Albert Museum, London, *Dyce 6562* (Heber's copy, consulted by Gifford).

Worc. Worcester College, Oxford (possibly Gerard Langbaine's copy).

Eton Eton College, Windsor (lacks sheets A and K).

Bost. Boston Public Library, Massachusetts.

Harv. Harvard University Library (lacks sheet K).

Chap. Chapin Library, Williamstown, Mass. (from the Huth Library).

Cong. Library of Congress, Washington, D.C.

Folg. Folger Shakespeare Library, Washington, D.C.

Morg. Pierpont Morgan Library, N.Y.

Pforz. Carl H. Pforzheimer Library, N.Y. (Mostyn-Clawson copy).

Hunt. Henry E. Huntington Library, San Marino, California.

The following later editions have also been collated:

Dyce Alexander Dyce, *The Works of Thomas Middleton*, vol. IV (London, 1840).

Lamb Charles Lamb, *Specimens of the English Dramatic Poets, including Extracts from the Garrick Plays* (London, 1854) —extracts with interesting emendations.[1]

[1] In the collation Lamb's readings are supported by a later editor's wherever possible, since 'extracts' are not strictly an edition.

Bullen A. H. Bullen, *The Works of Thomas Middleton*, vol. v (London, 1885–7).

Ellis Havelock Ellis, *The Best Plays of Thomas Middleton*, vol. I (Mermaid, London, 1909).

Fisher Margery Fisher, *A Critical Edition of Thomas Middleton's 'A Chaste Maid in Cheapside' and 'Women Beware Women'* (B.Litt. thesis, University of Oxford, 1937).

Wall Richard J. Wall, *A Critical Edition of Thomas Middleton's 'A Chaste Maid in Cheapside'* (Ph.D. thesis, University of Michigan, 1958).

George David F. George, *A Critical Edition of Thomas Middleton's 'A Chaste Maid in Cheapside'* (M.A. thesis, University of Manchester, 1962).

Although most of the basic modernizations and relineations derive from Dyce, Bullen's edition has been used for reference because his is the only full edition with line numbering. A new edition of Middleton's works is being prepared by G. R. Price and Samuel Schoenbaum; the latter is also editing *A Chaste Maid* for the *Regents Renaissance Drama* series; and the play is announced for inclusion in an anthology of Elizabethan drama to be edited by Richard Hosley. Alan Brissenden's edition in *The New Mermaid* series (London, 1968) appeared while the present edition was in proof.

This Edition

The present text is based directly on the 1630 quarto. Spelling and punctuation are modernized silently, unless they affect meaning or metre. They are then recorded in the collation, along with the readings of subsequent editions which have been adopted or offer important alternatives. Crucial readings are also discussed in the commentary. Conjectures, as distinct from emendations, are indicated by '*conj.*' 'So' indicates an arrangement of text which is not a substantive change. Square brackets are reserved for editorial additions to stage-directions, additions within the text or in speech-headings being noted in the collation but not in the text itself. Added stage-directions are not collated except where clearly distinguishable alternatives have been offered or where a change, as distinct from an insertion, is made.

Punctuation and lineation pose special problems. Middleton's pointing is notably light, relying mainly on commas. Since this leads to frequent obscurity, the present edition has sacrificed raciness to clarity at the risk of seeming to punctuate too heavily. Lineation is more controversial. From *A Chaste Maid* on, Middleton's verse is remarkably loose in metre, full of triple and quadruple feminine endings, extra (often emphatic) syllables within the line, slurrings, anapaests, and occasional half-lines. The result is a flexible style which can range from the tragic to the farcical, but which it is sometimes hard to distinguish from prose, particularly since Middleton's prose seems always to have the rhythm of blank verse behind it. The problem is further complicated by Middleton's manuscript habit of beginning verse lines with lower-case letters and carrying long lines over into the beginning of the lines which follow, with a visual effect indistinguishable from prose.[1] The very erratic lineation of the 1630 quarto seems to derive primarily from these manuscript habits. Much of the 'prose' is quite certainly verse, and the apparent alternations between verse and prose lack any rationale, indicating neither the rank of the speaker nor the seriousness of what he says. Since it will be argued later that *A Chaste Maid* is not 'realistic' but a highly artificial structure which depends for some of its most important effects on ironic parallelism and modulations of tone, it has seemed more appropriate to line throughout as verse than to bow to the modern caution about relining. It is assumed, however, that musical regularity is less important here than the sense of imaginative consistency, of an autonomous 'world of the play' set off by the verse form. Accordingly, the temptation to regularize the lines has been resisted. Their occasional roughnesses of metre are no worse than those accepted in *The Alchemist*, where verse form is played off against colloquialism for some of the same effects. Such a thorough relining necessitates a separate 'Lineation Appendix', as in the Revels edition of *The Changeling*.

[1] See R. C. Bald's comments on the Trinity MS. of *A Game at Chesse* in his edition (1929), p. 35.

Lastly, the two foreign languages in the play have different treatments. The Latin has been regularized because, though a case can be made for deliberately bad Latin to match the bad logic, it seems more probable that the mistakes originated from the compositor. Middleton certainly knew Latin. On the other hand, it is unlikely that he knew Welsh. The Welsh phrases in the play seem to have been transcribed phonetically; and, since their meaning is obscure, they have been rendered precisely as in the copy text.

Printer

Variants between the nineteen copies of the first edition are few and unimportant; apart from the confusion in lineation, the text is very clearly printed, arguing a skilled printer and a clear manuscript. No printer is mentioned in the 1630 quarto or the Stationers' Register, but it seems likely that *A Chaste Maid* was printed by the brothers Thomas and Richard Cotes. The ascription must remain tentative, however, because it depends on identifying rather nondescript type ornaments, of a sort which were exchanged quite freely among Elizabethan printers. The fleurons and ornamental rectangles on sigs. A2v and B1 of Q turn up in the work of no less than four of the five printers who worked for Francis Constable around 1630: the Coteses, William Stansby, Elizabeth Allde, and Augustine Matthewes; only Nicholas Okes appears not to have used them. However, these ornaments are used by the Coteses more frequently than by the other three put together, in a ratio of about seven to one. More significantly, the ornamental initial H on sig. B1 of Q turns up in two other Cotes' books: on sig. A3 of Thomas Fuller, *David's Hainous Sinne*, 1631 (STC 11463), and on sigs. Nnn 6 and Ooo 5 of Part I and (upside down) on sig. b2v of Part II of Helkiah Crooke, *A Description of the Body of Man*, 1631 (STC 6063). This initial occurs in none of the British Museum books put out by the other Constable printers around 1630.

If the Coteses printed the quarto, its clearness is understandable. They took over the flourishing business of Isaac Jaggard in 1627, and by 1630 had the most prolific printing-house in London, only excepting the King's printer. It was with their imprint that the second Shakespeare folio and many of the later Shakespeare quartos appeared.[1] Compared to *Pathomachia or the Battell of the Affections* (STC 19462), however, a play they certainly printed for Constable in 1630, Middleton's play is presented very unelaborately. It gives an impression of skilled but casual execution, which is borne out by an analysis of the press-work. *A Chaste Maid in Cheapside* seems to have been printed on a single press in pauses between some more urgent or demanding work.

Only one skeleton forme was used for most of the middle of the play, and the copy was 'cast-off' (that is, divided into approximate page lengths in the MS. to allow the compositors to work on pages out of sequence). Martin lamp examination shows that the outer forme was printed first in most sheets (a sign of casting-off), and this is borne out by an analysis of the transference of damaged type.[2] The 'cast-off' nature of the copy is also confirmed by irregularities in page length—though a run of long pages at the beginning of gathering K suggests that the final sheet at least was composed seriatim, with the compositors trying to save a leaf to turn back for the title-page but abandoning the attempt after K3^{v}.[3] Perhaps it was the shortness of two pages on E (outer) which enabled the compositors to get just far enough ahead of the press to reintroduce skeleton II briefly in F (outer), and its second reappearance at H (inner) has light thrown on it by the transference of types within sheets G and H and the substitution of ordinary italic capital Ms for the usual swash italic Ms on H (inner). G (outer) was evidently distributed before G (inner) was composed, since they share

[1] See H. R. Plomer, *Dictionary of Printers . . . 1641–1667* (1907), p. 53; Arber, III. 700, IV. 182, 242; W. A. Jackson, *Records of the Court of the Stationers' Company, 1602–1640* (1957), p. 194.

[2] The sequence of formes and skeletons works out as follows: B (outer), skeleton I; B (inner), skeleton II; C (outer), an aberrant, composite skeleton; C (inner), skeleton I; D (inner), skeleton I; D (outer), skeleton I; E (outer), skeleton I; E (inner), skeleton I; F (outer), skeleton II; F (inner), skeleton I; G (outer), skeleton I; G (inner), skeleton I; H (inner), skeleton II; H (outer), skeleton II; I (inner), skeleton I; I (outer), skeleton II; K (inner), skeleton II; K (outer), skeleton I. When skeleton II was reintroduced in H (inner), it still had the page numbers of F (outer) in it; so, in uncorrected copies of Q, H1^{v} is numbered 36 instead of 50; H2, 33 instead of 51; H3^{v}, 40 instead of 54; and H4, 37 instead of 55.

[3] A similar change from forme to seriatim composition is discussed by G. W. Williams, *S.B.*, XI (1958), pp. 39 ff.

type, and this should have released enough type to have enabled the compositor to set up H (inner) without substituting for its swash italic Ms. The fact that he did substitute for them suggests that H (inner) was composed *before* G (outer) was distributed, that is, before G (inner) was composed; and the curious sequence of skeletons in these sheets confirms this. The sequence at this point was most probably G (outer), skeleton I; H (inner), skeleton II; G (inner), skeleton I; H (outer), skeleton II. Then, after a normal alternation of skeletons in sheet I, the seriatim composition of sheet K would slow down the compositor(s) so that he could use skeleton II again in the first forme of that gathering in spite of the fact that it had been used in the second forme of the previous sheet.

There is clear evidence that more than one compositor was engaged on the play,[1] but they seem to have worked in sequence, one after the other, not simultaneously. The different compositorial habits of spelling, abbreviation, and spacing do not fall into any pattern of regular alternation, and without such a pattern the statistics for individual pages are too meagre and contradictory to identify particular compositors' characteristics or stints.

Copy Text

The 1630 quarto reveals clear traces of Middleton's writing habits,[2] which makes it likely that the copy text for the edition was either a Middleton holograph or a copy closely derived from his MS. Like *A Game at Chesse* it is divided into acts but not scenes, and extra

[1] There are variant spellings of Allwit/All-wit, Yellowhammer/Yellow-hammer, Dahumma/Dahanna; different speech-headings for Davy/Dau.; and different habits of punctuating abbreviations and contracted speech-headings. Note, moreover, that in Allwit's long verse speech on sigs. B4^v and C1, the lines on B4^v begin with lower-case letters, then suddenly on C1 go into capitals.

[2] For specimens of Middleton's handwriting, see W. W. Greg, *English Literary Autographs* (1932), Part 3, no. XCIV. His MS. habits are discussed by R. C. Bald, ed., *A Game at Chesse* (1929), pp. 32 ff.; by G. R. Price in 'The MS. and Quarto of *R.G.*', *Libr.*, 5th ser., vol. XI (1956), 180 ff., and 'Authorship and Bibliography of *R.T.*', *Libr.*, 5th ser., vol. XV (1960), 262–77; and by Cyrus Hoy, 'The Shares of Fletcher and his Collaborators in the Beaumont and Fletcher Canon (V)', *S.B.*, III (1960), 77–96, 104. Previous evidence is summarized and new statistical data are added in Peter B. Murray, *A Study of Cyril Tourneur* (1964), pp. 144 ff.

material such as the songs is marked off from the text by a preliminary rule and heading—e.g., 'The Song'.[1] Some of the minor characters, such as the servants at I. ii. 57–63 or the watermen at IV. iii. 13–22, are merely given numbers for speech-headings.[2] The punctuation is characteristically light, relying on commas, not periods, and on sig. B4^{v} there is a passage of blank verse beginning with lower-case letters as in the MS. of *A Game at Chesse*. Moreover, the text is full of Middleton's preferred spellings.[3] The analyses of Hoy and Murray show a small difference in statistics, however, which distinguishes the *Chaste Maid* quarto from average Middleton usage; and, though this is perfectly explicable as the result of his own inconsistency or of compositorial intervention, when it is combined with other factors it may also indicate a scribe.

For instance, the text is so clearly printed that we must assume that it was set up from fair copy, not foul papers, yet the copy apparently was not revised for either production or printing. There are, indeed, a few details which might seem to point to copy which had been marked for theatrical use: there are several early entrances (three lines early at II. i. 114.1, II. ii. 16.1; two lines early at I. i. 90.1, 115.1, I. ii. 101.1, II. i. 61.1; one line early at V. iv. 79.1), but the interval in each case seems too short to be of much practical use; the dashes at III. iii. 113 and IV. i. 209, 213 (and possibly also the blank at IV. i. 243) suggest censorship, but this may well have been for printing, not performance; the imperative mood usually associated with prompt-books appears in the stage-directions '*Kiss*' (III. ii. 154, 157), possibly in '*Both draw and fight*' (IV. iv. 55), and in '*set them down . . . while all the company seem to weep and mourn*' (V. iv. 0.8–9); and, lastly, there are several stage-directions which are theatrically technical: '*enter . . . at one door . . . at the other door . . . a sad song in the music-room*' (V. iv. 0.1 ff.), '*a shop being*

[1] The songs were probably kept on separate sheets from the rest of the script, as was customary. This might explain how the 'Welsh Song' promised in IV. i was apparently replaced by another Middleton song: see Appendix II, p. 128, n. 2.

[2] Other examples of this characteristic can be found in *P.*, *Y.F.G.*, *T.C.O.O.*, and *R.T.* See Price, 'Authorship . . .', p. 265, and R. C. Bald, 'The Foul Papers of a Revision', *Libr.*, 4th ser., vol. XXVI (1945), 39.

[3] See the statistical tables at the end of Hoy's article and Murray's book.

discovered' (I. i. 0.1), '*A bed thrust out upon the stage, Allwit's wife in it*' (III. ii. 0.1), and '*Kix to his Lady within*' (III. iii. 41). None of these is beyond the scope of a man as versed in theatre as Middleton, however, and they are outweighed by evidence which points to copy *not* prepared for theatre use. Except for the three directions in the imperative (and one of them doubtful), the other directions are in the indicative mood; several of them have a rather 'literary' quality, e.g., '*Enter a Wench with a basket, and a child in it under a loin of mutton*' (II. ii. 127.1–2); and there are two 'permissive' directions: '*Enter three or four* Watermen' (IV. iii. 13.1) and '*attended by many in black . . . attended by maids and women*' (V. iv. 0.3, 0.6–7). More important, however, are the inconsistencies and omissions which a bookholder would surely have cleared up: the confusion between '*Moll*' and '*Mary*' (I. i. 25, 115.1), for instance; the sudden introduction of '*Susan*' by name (V. ii. 85.1) when she has been merely '*Maid*' throughout; the mute unnecessary '*Midwife*' who enters in II. iv and has no exit; and the confusion about the number of gossips, *two* entering in II. iii but *five* speaking in II. iv. In the latter scene, moreover, Maudline and the two puritans have no entry, though they speak; similarly, the Nurse has no entry at III. ii. 6, nor re-entry at III. ii. 110; and (though this by itself would not be significant) there are some twenty-odd missing exits in the play. Faults of this extent and kind make it unlikely that the text was revised for either playhouse or printing.[1]

The MS. behind the 1630 edition, then, was probably a fair copy of Middleton's foul papers, censored but otherwise unrevised for production or printing. The most probable source for such copy in 1630 would be Middleton's son, Edward,[2] who was enough in-

[1] George (*Critical Edition*, intro.) and W. T. Jewkes (*Act Division in Elizabethan and Jacobean Plays* (1958), pp. 317–18) come to much the same conclusion, though Jewkes thinks that the copy may also have been foul papers and George suggests that a fair copy may have been made earlier for private circulation. The addition of a list of *dramatis personae* is not proof of the latter, however, since such lists occur even in playhouse texts. Alan Brissenden (*New Mermaid* ed., 1968, p. xxv) thinks it 'a carefully prepared manuscript', not close to the prompt-book except in one place, but with 'few of the contractions and punctuations peculiar to Middleton's own hand'.

[2] Jewkes (*Act Division*, p. 317) argues that the title-page's circumstantial

volved in his father's dramatic activities to be summoned before the Privy Council in 1624 to answer for *A Game at Chesse*. The family seems to have been left in financial difficulties by Middleton's death in 1627,[1] and perhaps in this lies the explanation of the play's release so many years after its first performance.

2. THE PLAY

Date

It is almost certain that *A Chaste Maid in Cheapside* was first performed between March and August of 1613, when Middleton was thirty-three years old.[2] The combination of Lady Elizabeth's Men and the Swan Theatre on the 1630 title-page narrows the focus considerably.[3] Lady Elizabeth's Men were formed and licensed in April 1611, and moved into the Swan only after signing an agreement with Philip Henslowe on 29 August the same year. By the autumn of 1614 they had moved to Henslowe's new theatre, the Hope, where they acted *Bartholomew Fair* on 31 October 1614. They never returned to the Swan. The precise date when they vacated it is uncertain, but it was probably in December 1613. John Taylor's complaint on behalf of the watermen in January 1613/14 says that only the King's Men were on the Bankside at that time;[4] it was contracted that the Hope should be completed by

---

detail about performance shows that the copy came from a company, not a private source. The company mentioned had disappeared fifteen years earlier, however.

[1] Middleton's widow had to petition the city for charity on 7 Feb. 1628. She died the same year. See Barker, p. 24.

[2] For a summary of Middleton's life, see N. W. Bawcutt, ed. *C.* (1959), pp. xviii–xxi, to which may be added S. Schoenbaum, 'A New Middleton Record', *M.L.R.*, LV (1960), 82–4, about his debts in 1610–11, and some new data about his time at Oxford in David F. George, *A Critical Study of Thomas Middleton's Borrowings and of his Imitations of other Authors in his Prose, Poetry, and Dramatic Works* (Ph.D. thesis, University of London, 1966), chap. I.

[3] See Chambers, II. 257–80; J. T. Murray, *English Dramatic Companies, 1558–1642* (1910), I. 243 ff.; C. W. Wallace, 'The Swan Theatre and the Earl of Pembroke's Servants', *Englische Studien*, XLIII (1910–11), 391; Brinsley Nicholson, 'Notes on the Dates of *C.M. in C.*, etc.', *N. & Q.*, 4th ser., vol. XI (1873), 317; R. C. Bald, 'The Chronology of Middleton's Plays', *M.L.R.*, XXXII (1937), 39–40.

[4] See *infra*, p. xxxiii.

30 November 1613; and a letter of Robert Daborne to Henslowe on 9 December 1613 implies that the Company was then ready to move in; so, if Taylor is correct, by the beginning of 1613 they must have vacated the Swan but not yet have opened at the Hope (which also was on Bankside).[1]

Fleay seems to assume that March 1613 must be a *terminus ad quem* for the play because at that time Lady Elizabeth's Men amalgamated with the Queen's Revels, and he speculates that the combined company may then have acted at Whitefriars before moving to the Hope.[2] There is no evidence of the combined company's being at Whitefriars this early, however, and it seems more logical to reverse Fleay's argument and regard March 1613 rather as the *terminus a quo*.

As William Gaskill found in his recent revival, *A Chaste Maid* is remarkable for the number of its female rôles.[3] Even if some of these were acted as grotesques by men (as in Gaskill's production), the number would still be too large for an ordinary adult company. Only the addition of Queen's Revels boys could have enabled Lady Elizabeth's Company to fill all the parts.[4] Moreover, the play is much closer to the 'citizen comedies' which Middleton had already written for the Revels than to the romantic comedies and tragi-

[1] See W. W. Greg, ed., *The Henslowe Papers* (1907), p. 20, l. 20, and p. 79, n. 4. Another Daborne letter of 5 June 1613 mentions a decision being made about the company going to Oxford or 'coming over' (*ibid.*, p. 72), perhaps referring to an earlier projected move from the Swan to Henslowe's 'private house', the Whitefriars Theatre, to whose company Daborne belonged.

[2] Fleay, *Biographical Chronicle of the English Drama* (1891), II. 96, and *Chronicle History of the English Stage* (1890), 203–4. Fleay also identifies *C.M. in C.* with *The Proud Maid*, a tragedy which Lady Elizabeth's Men acted at Court on 25 Feb. 1612/13 (*Chronicle*, p. 186), a mistake which led E. K. Chambers to date *C.M. in C.* 1611 (Chambers, II. 257, III. 441)—though, as Bald objects, our 'play is not a tragedy, and there is no proud maid in it'.

[3] There are eighteen female rôles and in III. ii most of them are on stage together, so little doubling would be possible. The balanced funeral processions in V. iv suggest a company about equally divided between men and 'women' players. See Appendix V, p. 150.

[4] The insistence on Sir Oliver's 'shortness' (see note to III. iii. 96) and Tim's claim to be 'homunculus' (see note to IV. i. 111–14) also suggest non-adult actors. Chambers (II. 251) says that 'The Lady Elizabeth's Men, as constituted in 1613, were very much the Queen's Revels over again.'

comedies which he was later to write for the adult companies; and he seems to have had no connection with this Lady Elizabeth's Company before or after *A Chaste Maid*.[1]

The evidence from theatrical history is supported by internal references, of which the most important is the emphasis on Lent. Regulations forbidding the sale of meat in Lent had been progressively tightened up since 1608, but they were made extra strict for 1613 because a bad harvest in 1612 had left the cattle without winter feed, and consequently there were fears of a dearth.[2] A notable feature of this strictness was that not even the few butchers normally allowed to sell meat to invalids and pregnant women were granted a licence, and the Privy Council (to the Lord Mayor's annoyance) went to the length of appointing its own 'messengers' to spy out abuses. This is clearly reflected in the play. When Allwit jeers at the promoters 'My wife lies in—a foutra for promoters' (II. ii. 94), they reply 'That shall not serve your turn'; and the Country Wench's excuse for leaving them with her basket presumes that her 'mistress' would have to have had a special licence even if she were sick (II. ii. 139–40). This total prohibition was in force only during the Lent of 1613.[3]

One of the difficulties involved in satirizing the 1613 strictness, however, was that the prohibition was known to have originated from James I himself,[4] and Lady Elizabeth's Men depended on royal patronage: their sponsor was James's eldest daughter and they played frequently at court—had been there twice during Shrovetide 1612/13, in fact.[5] This probably explains Touch-

[1] This is not quite certain, as *N.W.N.H.* (1612 ?) may also have been for Lady Elizabeth's; *C.* (1622) and *S.G.* (1623), however, were for a quite different 'Lady Elizabeth's' group (Bentley, I. 183).

[2] For Stow's comment, see Appendix III.

[3] See W. H. and H. C. Overall, *Analytical Index to the Remembrancia of London* (1878), III. 398–400. The key entries are reproduced in Appendix III.

[4] See *Calendar of State Papers Domestic*, 5 Feb. 1612/13, and Privy Council letter to the Lord Mayor, 9 Feb. 1612/13, in *The Remembrancia of London*, III, no. 72.

[5] W. Power (*N. & Q.*, CII, pp. 528–9) suggests that Middleton too was anxious to ingratiate himself with James at this period; if so, *C.M. in C.* was singularly ill-timed. For a discussion of Middleton's later relations with James, see Rhodes Dunlap's article on *Peace*, in *Studies in English Renaissance Drama*, ed. J. W. Bennett *et al.* (1959), 82–95.

wood Senior's uncharacteristic highmindedness at II. i. 112–14:

> There has been more religious wholesome laws
> In the half circle of a year erected
> For common good, than memory ever knew of...

The literary effect of this will be discussed later (it is not Touchwood Senior's only inconsistency), but it seems likely that the speech was an afterthought designed to offset the satire on Lent.[1] It has the air of an interpolation and may possibly have been added when the play was censored.

Now, if we take 'half circle of a year' specifically, it suggests late June as a *terminus ad quem*, and this is borne out by other dates within the play—though it is risky, of course, to assume too close a correspondence between references in the fictitious action and the actual writing (or production) of the play. The time-scheme of *A Chaste Maid* stretches from before Lent (see note to I. i. 148), through the fasting season (it is not yet 'Mid-Lent Sunday' at II. ii. 169), to the 'resurrections' of Moll and Touchwood Junior which must take place at Easter if Lady Kix is to have time to find herself pregnant after her 'physicking' at the end of III. iii.[2] Sir Oliver's celebratory bonfire before his door (V. iii. 6–7), however, like Tim's chatter about 'watching in armour' (IV. iv. 41), seems to refer to London celebrations which were normally connected with the Feasts of St Peter the Apostle (28 June) and John the Baptist (23 June).[3] They may, therefore, reflect the time of production rather than time within the play. Certainly, the references to 'Barthol'mew-eve last' (II. i. 163) and 'last Lammas' (III. ii. 92) suggest that the play was put on before August.

The 1613 date is also supported by other contemporary refer-

[1] Fleay's suggestion that 'religious wholesome laws' refers to 'the statutes of 1610' is rightly dismissed by Bald (*loc. cit.*): 'what he is referring to I am at a loss to know'; and George's discussion of recusancy proclamations is irrelevant to the topic of the speech.

[2] Wilbur Dunkel's one-week time-scheme is too cramped (*The Dramatic Technique of Thomas Middleton in His Comedies of London Life* (Chicago, 1925), pp. 44–7).

[3] See Stow, pp. 93–5, 231. The practices apparently derived from pagan celebrations of the summer solstice. Frazer (*Golden Bough*, abridged ed., 1924, pp. 614 ff.) also refers to *Easter Eve* fire festivals (in the Catholic countries of Europe only, however).

ences. Minor details, discussed in the commentary, are a notorious case of a young man whipped by his mother (see note to III. ii. 131), a lawsuit about Rider's Dictionary (see note to IV. i. 89), the opening of a new waterworks, and a new patent for waterworks driven by windmills (see note to I. ii. 28).[1] More important is the way that Mrs Allwit's elaborate lying in (I. ii. 31 ff.) reflects contemporary awe at the extravagance of the Countess of Salisbury's recent childbed, as reported by John Chamberlain, 4 February 1612/13:

> About this day sevenit the Countess of Salisburie was brought abed of a daughter, and lies in very richly, for the hangings of her chamber, beeing white satin, embroidered with gold (or silver) perle is valued at foureteen thousand pounds.[2]

Allwit's comment that 'A lady lies not in like her' (I. ii. 31) is made precise by one of the gossips: 'See . . . and she lies not in like a countess' (III. ii. 89); the baby is called 'little countess' (II. ii. 25); and at V. i. 162 Allwit gloats 'for furniture, we may lodge a countess.'

Another obviously contemporary reference is the play's propaganda in favour of watermen. Touchwood Senior's story about the rescue from Blackfriars (IV. iii. 1–12) will probably date the play exactly if the event to which it refers can ever be traced, and the speeches given to the watermen seem designed to exploit a popular sympathy rather than further the plot.[3] There are two possible reasons why the Swan company may have wanted to please watermen at this time. They could be flattering the waterman Jacob Meade, who was Henslowe's new partner in the contract drawn up when the companies amalgamated in March;[4] or, more probably, they could be soothing the watermen's resentment at the decrease in their vital theatre business, which finally resulted in a water-

[1] Note also that Touchwood Senior talks of seven country girls he made lie in 'last progress' (II. i. 62) and the Country Wench then accuses him of ruining her 'poor cousin in Derbyshire' (l. 75). If 'progress' is meant literally, this could be a reference to King James's progress of July 1612, on which, contrary to his normal custom, he went as far north as Belvoir, Newark (Notts.), Rufford, and Nottingham.

[2] John Chamberlain, *Letters*, ed. N. E. McClure (1939), I. 415.

[3] Were actual watermen brought on stage, perhaps?

[4] See *Henslowe Papers*, p. 19.

men's petition to the Privy Council in January 1613/14.[1] The author of this petition, John Taylor the water poet, seems to have had some connection with Lady Elizabeth's Men: one of the witnesses to the company's original bond with Henslowe in 1611 was a 'John Taylor' who Murray conjectures was the poet, and he certainly wrote verses praising them in 1614.[2] The Swan was farther from London Bridge than the other Bankside theatres and therefore more reliant on water traffic, and it may be that knowledge of its imminent closure can be read in Maudline's 'She plays the swan / And sings herself to death' (v. ii. 45–6).[3]

Traces of another contemporary trade quarrel can be seen in the squabble between the grocer's wife and the apothecary's wife at II. iv. 5–10. The Company of the Apothecaries was incorporated with that of the Grocers in 1608 under the title of the Grocers' Company, but relations between them had grown fierce enough by 29 May 1614 for the Privy Council to ask Lord Chief Justice Coke and Sir Thomas Lake to make a special inquiry,[4] with the result that the companies were parted again in 1615. Middleton plays on the ambiguous nature of the combined company to reinforce his food–lust theme, Sir Oliver buying aphrodisiacs to induce pregnancy and Sir Walter comfits to celebrate it and 'restoratives' to provoke lust again.

Allwit has the slightly puzzling remark that Mrs Allwit's restoratives are sufficient

> . . . to set up a young pothecary,
> And richly stock the foreman of a drug-shop.
> (I. ii. 35–6)

The second line may be no more than an expansion of the first—'enable the foreman of a drug-shop to set up for himself with a rich stock'. But it is just possibly a reference to Dr Simon Forman, the

[1] See John Taylor, 'The True Cause of the *Watermen's* Suit concerning *Players*', *Works* (1889), pp. 333–8.

[2] See Murray, *English Dramatic Companies*, I, 244, n., and 249.

[3] The same image is certainly used about the theatre in Goodman, *Holland's Leaguer* (1632), sig. F2, which could have been influenced by the printing of *C.M. in C.* in 1630.

[4] *Remembrancia*, III, no. 148. Middleton's stepfather, Thomas Harvey, was a member of the Grocers' Company, and it was the Grocers who first gave Middleton his chance with city pageants later in 1613.

most notorious dealer in love philtres in London, who died spectacularly in a boat on the Thames in 1611, having foretold his own sudden death several days before. Forman may have been in the news again in 1613 because of the scandalous Essex divorce case. The full story of Lady Essex's dealings with Forman and Mrs Turner, their poisoning of Sir Thomas Overbury and drugging of Essex, did not emerge till 1614, but already

> By early 1613 it was common talk at court that the young Essexes wanted a divorce. It was also becoming common talk that the royal favourite Carr was in love with the Countess. Some said that she was his mistress.[1]

By 26 February there was already an investigation into Lady Essex's dealings with another charlatan, Mary Woods, who accused Lady Essex of trying to poison her husband, and on 16 May the Commission for hearing the divorce was set up.[2] The Essexes publicly accused each other of sexual incapacity, both insisted on their own sexual normality and fitness to remarry, intimate physical details and sensational charges of drugging were bandied about, scandal and prurient gossip were rife about Lady Essex.[3] All London was by the ears. If we concede that a probable date for *A Chaste Maid* is June 1613, then it seems inconceivable that the Kix situation, with its public quarrelling about impotency, talk of drugs and divorce, implication of the lady's scandalous past at court (III. iii. 51–4), and good offices of a third person who is really the lady's lover, could have failed to recall the current scandal. The very name 'Kix' resembles 'Essex'. Moreover, when the divorce finally went through and Carr married Lady Essex, Middleton wrote a *Masque of Cupid* for them which was performed at Merchant Taylors' Hall on 4 January 1613/14. So there is every reason to suppose he may have been interested in the divorce proceedings.[4] The connection with

[1] G. P. V. Akrigg, *Jacobean Pageant* (1962), p. 181.

[2] See *Calendar of State Papers, Domestic 1613*, 26 Feb., 29 April, 15 May, 16 May, 17 May.

[3] See *Cobbett's State Trials* (1809), II. 786 ff., especially the Archbishop of Canterbury's account of the rumours about Lady Essex which made him vote against the divorce, p. 818.

[4] Bullen considers that 'search me ... Like the forewoman of a female jury' in *C.* (Revels ed.), IV. i. 100–1, refers to the divorce trial, and R. C. Bald ('Chronology', p. 41) suggests that Sebastian's use of charms to

the play must remain conjectural, however, and already the problem of dating is encroaching on the related question of sources. The last two arguments for 1613 will, in fact, depend on source ascriptions.[1]

Sources

A Chaste Maid has no proper 'sources' in the sense of indisputable influences;[2] at most, it has analogues. And it is remarkable for the way it incorporates into a unique whole situations, characters, and themes which had been stock material of European drama for at least a century, and which Middleton himself had used before and would often use again.

The Kix–Touchwood Senior situation, for example, may have been influenced by the Essex divorce, as has been argued, but it also draws on the strong *novella* tradition of Italian, particularly Florentine, literature. As George shows, it seems specifically related to Machiavelli's famous comedy *Mandragola* (printed 1524) and its more farcical Venetian derivative *La Potione* by Andrea Calmo (1552).[3] *Mandragola* is about a couple who are childless after six years of marriage in spite of prayers and curative baths, the old husband loudly maintaining his virility and blaming his young wife; a gallant offers to cure the infertility with a miraculous infu-

prevent Antonio consummating his marriage in *Wit.* reflects the Forman–Mrs Turner scandal.

[1] H. N. Hillebrand identifies Yellowhammer with Robert Kayser, a Cheapside goldsmith who as manager of the Queen's Revels sued Middleton for breach of contract in 1609. Middleton claimed to have fulfilled their agreement with 'The Viper and her Brood', a play now lost (*M.L.N.*, XLII, 1927). If this identification were correct, it would point to a date before 1613. There is no suggestion of theatrical interests about Yellowhammer, however, and a goldsmith is an obvious enough emblem for the commercial world in general: Touchstone in *Eastward Ho!* (1605) provides the same symbolism, though to different effect.

[2] Karl Christ, *Quellenstudien zu den Dramen Thomas Middleton's* (1905) drew a complete blank. Suggestions since then, along with some new material, are presented in David F. George, *A Critical Study of Thomas Middleton's Borrowings and of his Imitations of other Authors in his Prose, Poetry and Dramatic Works* (Ph.D. thesis, University of London, 1966).

[3] See Marvin T. Herrick, *Italian Comedy in the Renaissance* (1960), p. 55. George discusses Middleton's wide reading in Italian after *N.W.N.H.* in *Middleton's Borrowings*, p. 299.

sion of 'mandrake' root; the wife reluctantly lets herself be persuaded that adultery is no worse than eating fish on Fridays; and, afterwards, the absurdly complaisant husband invites the seducer to perpetual board and lodging. There are differences, however, which make it hazardous to see *Mandragola* as a direct source. The wife lacks Lady Kix's dubious past (III. iii. 51–4) and readiness for seduction; she is actually loved by the seducer, who promises her marriage after the husband's death; and the plot is invented by a parasite for whom there is no equivalent in *A Chaste Maid* (the nearest is Davy, but he has no share in Touchwood Senior's scheme). Moreover, the plot is quite different: in *Mandragola* the wife, not the husband, drinks the potion; this supposedly entails the death of the first man to sleep with her afterwards; and the seducer in disguise lets himself be kidnapped by the husband for this purpose. Thus in Machiavelli the husband is a knowing cuckold, unlike Sir Oliver. And he also has a self-defeating pedant element which Middleton siphons off separately into Tim and the tutor.

Calmo's simplified version, *La Potione*, is in some ways closer to *A Chaste Maid*. The husband's recourse to aphrodisiacs is specifically mentioned; the mother and confessor who persuade the wife in *Mandragola* are omitted; and by limiting the wife to one short speech, the romantic relationship between her and the seducer is cut out. The plot is still manipulated by a parasite, however; the wife still drinks the potion; it still involves the 'death' of the first man to sleep with her afterwards; and the disguised seducer still lets himself be kidnapped for this purpose. Moreover, most of the play is written in difficult Italian dialects, which makes it all the less probable as Middleton's source.[1]

Another element for which an Italian source has been put forward is the situation of Allwit, the prosperous wittol.[2] There are no close parallels with the Modio texts suggested, however, and

[1] George (*Middleton's Borrowings*, p. 124) argues that Calmo's dialects may have influenced Middleton's mingling of English, Latin, and Welsh in *C.M. in C.* Long sections of Latin also occur in *Wit.* and *G. at C.*, however, and foreign languages are fairly common in Jacobean drama.

[2] See A. H. Gilbert, 'The Prosperous Wittol in Giovanni Battista Modio and Thomas Middleton', *S.P.*, XLI (1944), 235–7.

English analogues exist which are much closer. Middleton had himself used similar characters before: Purge in *The Family of Love* (1602 ?), the Captain in *The Phoenix* (1603 ?), Gallipot in *The Roaring Girl* (1610 ?), and, later, Knavesby in *Anything for a Quiet Life* (1621 ?) are all wittols or would-be wittols. Knavesby has a speech like Allwit's enumerating the advantages of wittoldry (Bullen, v. 320); and a similar eulogy can be found earlier in *The Second Maiden's Tragedy* (1611 ?), a play which Barker and Schoenbaum have also attributed to Middleton.[1] A more specific influence on this speech, however, has been traced to Thomas Campion's *Observations in the Art of English Poesie* (1602),[2] where the 8th epigram of chapter 6 runs:

> *Barnzy* stiffly vows that hees no Cuckold
> Yet the vulgar eu'rywhere salutes him,
> With strange signes of hornes, from eu'ry corner;
> Wheresoere he commes, a sundry Cucco
> Still frequents his eares; yet he's no Cuccold.
> But this *Barnzy* knowes that his *Matilda*,
> Skorning him, with *Haruy* playes the wanton.
> Knowes it ? nay deserues it, and by prayers
> Dayly begs of heau'n, that it for euer
> May stand firm for him; yet hees no Cuccold.
> And 'tis true, for *Haruy* keeps *Matilda*,
> Fosters *Barnzy*, and relieues his houshold,
> Buyes the Cradle, and begets the children,
> Payes the Nurces, eu'ry charge defraying,
> And thus truly playes *Matilda's* husband:
> So that *Barnzy* now becomes a cypher,
> And himself th'adulter of *Matilda*.
> Mock not him with hornes, the case is alterd;
> *Haruy* bears the wrong, *he* proues the Cuccold.[3]

[1] R. H. Barker, 'The Authorship of *S.M.T.* and *R.T.*', *Sh.A.B.*, XX (1945), 51–62, 121–33; Schoenbaum, *Middleton's Tragedies* (1955), 183–202; the speech is reprinted in Appendix IV, no. 1. If John B. Brooks is right in connecting the Captain in *P.* with Middleton's stepfather, Thomas Harvey (*N. & Q.*, CCVI (1961), 382–4), this might explain the playwright's fascination with the type.

[2] E. L. Buckingham, *P.M.L.A.*, XLIII (1928), 784–92; R. C. Bald, 'The Sources of Middleton's City Comedies', *J.E.G.P.*, XXXIII (1934), 373–87.

[3] G. G. Smith, *Elizabethan Critical Essays* (1937), II. 342–3; cf. also the 5th epigram in elegiac verse (*ibid.*, p. 346). Smith, following Bullen, thinks the epigram refers to Barnabe Barnes and Gabriel Harvey (*ibid.*, p. 456).

If this poem is indeed a source (and the ingenuities of the cuckold praying to heaven and himself being in the position of adulterer are close to details of *A Chaste Maid*), it may confirm the play's date as 1612/13. Although at III. ii. 67 and IV. i. 210 the liaison between Sir Walter and Mrs Allwit is said to have begun *seven* years ago (seven is a recurrent number in the play), earlier, at I. ii. 15 and II. iii. 7, it is said to have lasted *ten* years; and ten years from the date of Campion's book would bring us to 1612.

The woes of a husband during his wife's childbed and the self-congratulation of bachelors who are spared such troubles seem to have been part of contemporary folk-lore,[1] but a particular influence on the Allwit christening scenes may perhaps be found in chapter 3 of Thomas Dekker's (?) *The Batchelars Banquet* (1603): 'The humour of a woman lying in Child-bed'.[2] Although the wife in *The Batchelars Banquet* is having her first child whereas Mrs Allwit has reached her seventh, and the gossips in the pamphlet attack the husband for neglect, which they do not do in the play, there are still striking resemblances between them; and the likelihood of this being a direct source is strengthened by the existence of a similar scene in *Blurt, Master Constable* (1602) which derives independently from *The Batchelars Banquet*.[3] In III. iii. 20 ff. of that play, citizens' wives sit round on low stools at a courtezan's house, listening to a lecture on how to dominate their husbands—including the advice to demand luxuries in childbed; then they jostle for precedence in leaving the room, like the gossips in II. iv of *A Chaste Maid*.

Another possible influence which would strengthen the date of

[1] See, for example, 'The Batchelor's Feast, or the difference between a single life and a double ...', *Roxburghe Ballads*, ed. C. Hindley (1873), I. 61–2, of which the relevant verses are reprinted in Appendix IV, no. 3. Note especially the 'dildo' refrain which Allwit too uses, and compare the reference to candles, sugar-sops, and soap with the promoters' lament at II. ii. 161 ff.

[2] See Bullen, v. 56, n.; F. P. Wilson, ed., *The Batchelars Banquet* (1929), p. xxii. The book is a translation of a French satire, *Les XV joyes de mariage* (1450 ?), possibly by Antoine de la Salle. Wilson argues for Robert Tofte as the author of the English translation. See Appendix IV, no. 2, for quotations.

[3] See Marilyn C. Williamson, *N. & Q.*, CCII (1957), 519–21.

1613 is Francis Beaumont's *The Knight of the Burning Pestle* (acted by the Children of the Revels in 1607—the year Middleton joined them—but not printed till 1613). The Induction to this play (ll. 113–19) satirizes the apothecary-grocer quarrel which we have already seen in *A Chaste Maid*.[1] More important, however, are the relations between Rafe's mock heroics and Tim Yellowhammer's unexpected enthusiasm for watching in armour with 'Harry the Fifth's' sword (IV. iv. 42–7), and the close resemblance of the fake funeral scenes which conclude both plays.[2] Again it is dangerous to assume direct influence, however. Before *The Knight of the Burning Pestle* was written, Middleton had used a rather similar situation in *The Family of Love*, III. vii, where Gerardine is considered dead even by the heroine but emerges unexpectedly from a trunk with the comment that she has raised 'the dead corpse of her friend to life'.[3] In fact, it has been argued that the coffin scene in Beaumont was a deliberate parody of the earlier Middleton scene.[4] Moreover, surprise resurrections which resolve the plot, and supposed deaths which provoke an agreement to marriage, are stock situations of the time.[5]

The last scene for which anything resembling a source has been suggested is the scene in which the Country Wench dupes the Lent promoters (II. ii. 127 ff.). This is something like a scene in Robert Greene's *A Looking Glass for London and England* (1594), in which the clown hides food in his slops to avoid the Lenten searchers.[6] Such clown acts must have been common, however, and a much closer analogue, which also supports the 1613 date, can be seen in

[1] See *supra*, p. xxxiii.

[2] First remarked on by R. C. Bald, 'Sources', p. 387.

[3] A similar coffin device is used for a minor character in IV. iii of *Pur.* (1604).

[4] Baldwin Maxwell, '"Twenty Good-nights"—*K. of B.P.* and Middleton's *F. of L.*', *M.L.N.*, LXIII (1948), 233–7; W. J. Olive, '"Twenty Good-nights"—*K. of B.P.*, *F. of L.*, and *Rom.*', *S.P.*, XLVII (1950), 182–9.

[5] See R. S. Forsythe, *Shirley's Plays* (1914), pp. 74, 89–91, 296. Resurrection from coffins for marriage was a favourite Commedia dell' arte trick (see K. M. Lea, *Italian Popular Comedy* (1934), I. 182) and an Italian company visited London in 1602, just as Middleton was beginning his career (A. Nicoll, *The World of Harlequin* (1963), p. 169).

[6] *The Plays and Poems of Robert Greene*, ed. J. Churton Collins (1905), I. 209–12.

the anonymous pamphlet, *The severall Notorious & lewd Cousnages of John West and Alice West . . . who were Arraigned and Convicted for the same, at the Sessions House in the Old Bayly, the 14. of Ianuarie, this present yeare, 1613* (1613: STC 25262+), where Alice West is represented as saying:

> Neyther is my purpose to trouble you with any long discourse of practices in any other kinde, as to kneele downe to prayers in Pauls, & leave a handbasket carelessly by, with Capons legs hanging out, which when a cheater hath cunningly come behinde the Orisant & stolne away, when he hath ransackt for poultrie, he hath found a child to call him father. (sig. A4; on C2 she tells how she cozened a grocer in this way.)

Like the woes of marriage, however, this theme was probably also part of the folk-lore of the time. The most interesting parallel to the situation in *A Chaste Maid* can be found in another ballad of the Roxburghe collection: 'The Country Girl's Policie, Or, the Cockney outwitted' (*circa* 1750), where a Country Girl tricks two 'stock-jobbers' by concealing her baby in a basket containing geese, and they take the basket to a tavern, meet their wives, and quarrel over how to eat the spoil, while the Country Girl determines to pass still for a maid.[1] C. R. Baskervill also notes a jig 'Cheaters Cheated' in Thomas Jordan's *The Royal Arbor of Loyal Poesie* (1664) and another ballad 'Bite upon Bite: or the Miser outwitted by the Country Lass' (Douce, III. 4), both of which deal with the same sort of trick but in ways further removed from the *Chaste Maid* situation.[2] These are all too late to qualify as 'sources', of course, but Baskervill comments: 'It is not improbable that Jordan was imitating some form found in an earlier farce or ballad,' and notes that the same situation appears in Julien Tiersot, *Chansons Populaires receuillies dans les Alpes françaises* (1903), pp. 203–4, with a town deputy impounding a peasant girl's pannier.[3]

[1] See Appendix IV, no. 4. In *C.M. in C.* the meat is mutton, but there are also many references to Lenten geese in the play.

[2] C. R. Baskervill, *The Elizabethan Jig* (1929), pp. 316–21. See Appendix IV, no. 5, for a summary of the jig. Baskervill also lists some later 18th- and 19th-century analogues.

[3] *Ibid.*, p. 321, n. 3. I failed to find any analogue among the clown–baby *lazzi* of the Commedia dell' arte, though this seems a likely source for the joke.

This wide range of possible influences is typical of the play. Except possibly for *The Batchelars Banquet*, none of the analogues is precise enough to be considered a proper source, and what we are left with are dramatic clichés and proverbial jokes: the drunken scene, the comic disputation and false construe, the comic use of Welsh, the learned idiot with a foolish servant, the ambitious citizen's wife, the courtezan who poses as virgin and heiress, and, of course, the traditional triangle of poor hero, rich old rival, and heroine bullied by her parents. Other situations are commonplaces within Middleton's own canon: the whore turned 'honest' by marriage, the speech in favour of married sex, the doggerel marriage ceremony, the fool's objection to marrying a 'stranger', the concern about incest (I. ii. 111–13, V. i. 106–8), and the final feast which unexpectedly serves two purposes—all situations which Middleton had used more than once before *A Chaste Maid*. The final effect, then, is rather one of synthesis than of particular sources: a gathering together, an ordering, and a comment on many previous themes.

3. CRITICAL APPRECIATION

A Chaste Maid in Cheapside is the richest and most typical of Middleton's comedies. Coming at the midpoint of his career, it forms a kind of watershed, with plays on either side of it of quite different kinds. Before, from 1602 to 1613, he mostly wrote satiric 'city comedies' for the boy players of Paul's and the Chapel (later known as the Queen's Revels). After 1613, he concentrated on tragi-comedies and tragedies for the adult companies, and—interestingly for some aspects of our play—on city pageants.[1] *A Chaste Maid* includes all these elements: citizen intrigue for money and sex in a detailed London setting; tragi-comic pseudo-pathos over the supposed deaths of the lovers, plus an ironically non-miraculous 'resurrection' carefully concealed so as to surprise the audience, in the manner of Beaumont and Fletcher; passages of remorse and

[1] The two periods are not absolutely distinct: there were earlier, lost tragedies, and two collaborations with Dekker (*The Honest Whore*, Part I, and *The Roaring Girl*) for the adult Prince Henry's Men. Nevertheless, the division is broadly accurate. For the canon and chronology of Middleton's drama, see: Chambers, III. 437–44; Bentley, IV. 855–912; Barker, 155–209; R. C. Bald, 'Chronology'.

spiritual collapse from Sir Walter Whorehound which anticipate the authentic horror of *The Changeling* and *Women Beware Women*; and a reliance on the contemporary associations of certain London localities which gives them symbolic value not unlike the technique of the city pageants. Thus, in this one play, as Una Ellis-Fermor has noted, we get a 'microcosm of that immense range that characterizes Middleton's work'.[1]

Structure

The complex action which results from these influences is more tightly organized than may at first appear, though it is not without loose ends[2] and its structure is not classical. From that point of view, the Roman comedy triangle of Moll, Touchwood Junior, and Sir Walter would have to be considered central, with an ironic Terentian parallel plot in Tim and the Welsh Gentlewoman, Davy as vestigial 'parasite', and Susan the traditional 'clever servant'. The latter's crediting with the intrigue is so late and unexpected, however, that it almost seems parodic; the love intrigue itself is reduced to three attempts to elope, of which we see only the climaxes, not the planning; and so little does it dominate the action that it has even been dismissed as a 'neutral frame' on which to 'hang the more interesting comedy of fleshly passions and follies'.[3] The intriguer in effect is not Susan but Touchwood Senior, who works as much for himself as for his brother, and the major 'parasite' rôle is extended independently in Allwit, who has no effect on the main action at all, though he tries at one point to interfere. The Allwit and Kix 'sub'-plots are developed till they rival the lovers' plot in importance, and the scenes with the promoters, the gossips, the tutor (and, to a lesser extent, the watermen) are treated at a length out of all proportion to their function in the intrigue. The

[1] *The Jacobean Drama* (1958 ed.), p. 136.

[2] For instance: if Touchwood Junior knows that the Welsh woman is Sir Walter's 'mutton' (I. i. 135–6), why does he never tell? What significance has the letter that he gives Moll in scene one? Making the promoters swear to 'keep' the Country Wench's basket scarcely motivates their taking responsibility for her bastard; etc.

[3] Madeleine Doran, *Endeavors of Art* (1954), pp. 150, 291. See also M. C. Bradbrook, *The Growth and Structure of Elizabethan Comedy* (1955), p. 162.

result is a non-classical confederation of plots and episodes which must be analysed in terms of parallelism and thematic consistency if we hope to find its unity.

The four main actions of *A Chaste Maid* are: the Moll and Touchwood Junior intrigue; the Allwits and Sir Walter; the Kixes and Touchwood Senior; and, slightly less important, the Welsh Gentlewoman and Tim.[1] Besides familial, neighbourly, and co-religionist links,[2] these four actions are causally interdependent. They overlap in the person of Sir Walter, who is Touchwood Junior's rival, Allwit's cuckolder, the keeper of the Welsh Gentlewoman who marries her off to Tim, and the heir of the Kixes disinherited by Touchwood Senior's potency. The latter seduces Lady Kix to help his brother as well as himself (III. iii. 1–2, 20–2); Allwit tries to disrupt Sir Walter's engagement to Moll to safeguard the affair with Mrs Allwit; the duel with Touchwood Junior first alienates Sir Walter from the Allwits, then gives them an excuse to turn him out when they learn of Lady Kix's pregnancy; and this same pregnancy, plus their discovery of the Welshwoman's real character, finally reconciles Moll's parents to her marriage with Touchwood Junior.

Moreover, the personages of these various plots are brought together in two ironically balanced ensemble scenes, and the parallelism between the debased christening in Act III and the joyous funeral of Act V reveals another main structural device of the play. All four intrigues are sex triangles with two men and one woman, with the Touchwood Junior–Moll plot paralleling the Tim–Welsh Gentlewoman plot, and the Allwit situation ironically balancing the Kixes'. Moll and Tim, for example, are treated very much alike by their vulgar mother, Maudline Yellowhammer. She is concerned about the social climbing education of both, music, dancing, and gesture for Moll paralleling logic and Latin verse for Tim; and her sentimental incomprehension of Tim's grammar lesson (IV. i. 59) foreshadows her later reaction to Moll's song. She takes a vicarious

[1] I am much indebted here to Richard Levin's 'The Four Plots of *C.M. in C.*', *R.E.S.*, XVL (1965), 14–24, though I depart from Professor Levin's analysis in detail and interpret the play as a whole quite differently.

[2] The Yellowhammers and the Allwits are puritans, as are probably the Kixes: see *infra*, p. li.

sexual pleasure in both children's wooing, talking to Sir Walter of her daughter's 'trembling thighs' and preparing the Welsh Gentlewoman for Tim's kiss, reminiscing to one child about the dancing master who 'miss'd me not a night' and to the other of 'an honest gentleman that knew me / When I was a maid'. Both children run off-stage from her sexual bullying and are thereupon accused by her of bashfulness; she locks Tim *in* with his suitor and Moll *away* from hers; and her cruelty in dragging Moll publicly by the hair as an example to the neighbours' daughters is foreshadowed by her threat to have Tim publicly whipped. These parallels are set off by no less balanced contrasts: in one plot a wit marries a chaste maid, in the other a fool is married by a whore; the maid's dowry of £2,000 is balanced by the whore's 2,000 non-existent 'runts'; the Welsh Gentlewoman is really the 'strumpet' which Moll is twice unjustly called (III. i. 21, IV. iv. 29); each girl has a song, one bawdy, the other pathetic; and in one plot Sir Walter fails by losing a girl but in the other triumphs by getting rid of a girl. Similarly, the Allwits' and the Kixes' are balanced plots of middle-aged adultery, the Allwits' moving from the birth of Mrs Allwit's seventh 'bastard', an established situation which is then destroyed, the other ending with Lady Kix's first adulterous pregnancy and indications that the situation will continue with Touchwood Senior established at the Kixes' as Sir Walter once was at the Allwits'. In fact, Sir Oliver's final elation (V. iii. 12–13) echoes the actual phrasing of Allwit's opening praise of wittoldry (I. ii. 11 ff.), and Lady Kix's original barrenness is paralleled by Sir Walter bequeathing to Mrs Allwit 'All barrenness of joy, a drouth of virtue, / And dearth of all repentance' (V. i. 103–4). Touchwood Senior, who has potency but no money, complements Kix, who has money but no children, so that Sir Walter, the adulterous father, is ironically disinherited by an adulterine child.

The parallelism here raises certain problems, however. Though we are expected to assess Sir Walter and Touchwood Senior differently, their careers are curiously alike. They are old acquaintances (II. ii. 45) and each has been in town seven years: Sir Walter's Welsh mistress is paralleled by Touchwood Senior's Country Wench; and Sir Walter's seven children by Mrs Allwit (contrasting with Lady Kix's seven years of fruitless marriage) are matched by the seven country girls whom Touchwood Senior made lie in 'last progress'. It is ironical, of course, that one seducer should supplant the other, but it undercuts any simple moral interpretation of the play. And, as if to emphasize this ambiguity, it is precisely these two seducers who are given the most 'moral' speeches in *A Chaste Maid*, with Sir Walter's 'legacy' to Mrs Allwit in Act v anticipated by Touchwood Senior's forecast about cursing the woman who has seduced one into lechery (II. i. 25–35).

Another difficulty with the four-plot analysis is that it leaves certain relationships unaccounted for. Touchwood Senior's account of true married housekeeping (II. i), for instance, is balanced against Allwit's immediately preceding praise of wittoldry (I. ii), each resigning his family duties for different but not unrelated reasons. Similarly, Moll's £2,000 dowry is also suggested for Mrs Allwit's latest child; one of her sons is writing Latin verse like Tim; the Welshwoman has red hair, which the puritans dread; and so on. Moreover, the four-plot analysis omits the fifth triangle of Touchwood Senior, his wife, and the Country Wench, and fails to account for the great emphasis put on the christening scene and the scene with the promoters. To understand these we have to dig deeper and analyse *A Chaste Maid* thematically, recognizing it as an impressive, if unpleasantly disturbing, work of poetry—interpreting 'poetry' widely to include ideas, actions, repeated words, and stage pictures, as well as imagery.

Setting

It has been noted that *A Chaste Maid* is remarkable for the density of its local references,[1] being set far more specifically in time and space than any other Middleton play, and assuming a quite detailed knowledge of contemporary London in its audience. The flight up-

[1] Bradbrook, *Growth*, p. 162. Middleton's first city pageants were produced just after *C.M. in C.* in Sept. and Oct. 1613, though he had collaborated in an entertainment by Dekker as early as 1603/4; his first city masque followed in Jan. 1613/14. After this he was in constant demand till 1626. He was appointed City Chronologer in 1620 and apparently gave satisfaction in this office too. See Barker, p. 14; R. C. Bald, 'Middleton's Civic Employments', *M.P.*, XXXI (1933), 65–78, and his edition of *H.E.* (1953).

river, for example, is carefully worked out in terms of Thames topography. Moll and Touchwood Senior apparently embark from Trig Stairs, which, according to Strype, were 'indifferently well supplied by watermen';[1] Touchwood Junior, therefore, has to look for a boat at Paul's Wharf, the next landing upstream; but Maudline, by going even higher to Puddle Wharf, is able to cut the fugitives off. Tim and the Tutor have meanwhile hurried to Trig Stairs and Yellowhammer is at 'the dock below [i.e., downstream from Puddle Wharf]', where the whole company eventually assembles. This latter may mean Paul's Wharf, to which we know Touchwood Junior was heading, but more accurately it should mean the Dung Wharf where the city's refuse was loaded on to barges for dispersal. This would explain Tim's reference to his 'silly' father and also tie in with the play's excretion references.[2]

Middleton here contrives to make his local colour serve both action and theme. As in his city pageants (which began in Paul's Churchyard and progressed down Cheapside), he uses associations and names allusively, converting topography to allegory like the authors of *Eastward Ho!* 'Trig', for example, besides a narrow defile, can also mean 'coxcomb', and is thus a suitable destination for Tim. Queenhithe, to which the promoters take their stolen meat, was actually where the fish for Lent was landed, and also plays on 'quean' a few lines earlier. The Lenten significance of the Thames is behind Maudline's seizure of a 'smelt' boat to catch 'gudgeons', both fish being also slang for 'fool'; and the fact that the 'common stairs' at Puddle Wharf was her destination seems linked to the play's sexual–urine connotations.[3] Bucklersbury (III. ii. 70), just south of Cheapside, where the confectioner's wife has her shop, is described by Stow as 'possessed of grocers and apothecaries', thus emblematizing the play's sweets–physic association; and the irony of the Allwits' future is lost unless we know that the Strand, besides being the most fashionable street in town, was also notorious for high-priced courtezans. The very title seems to have

[1] J. Stow and J. Strype, *Survey of London* (1754), I. 700b.

[2] See *infra*, pp. liv–lv.

[3] Similar connotations are exploited by the puppet play in *Bartholomew Fair* (1614) when Leander, a dyer's son from Puddle Wharf, falls in love with Hero at Trig Stairs.

been semi-proverbial, since the usual women 'chased' in Cheapside were the prostitutes whipped through it at a cart's tail;[1] and it also presents, of course, the paradox of a society which tries to make chastity a marketable commodity like everything else. Most interesting of all is the location of Allwit's house, which the promoters picket during Lent. Since it overlooks 'Pissing-Conduit' (III. ii. 174), it must be situated in the 'Stocks' meat market, where Cornhill meets Poultry at the east end of Cheapside. The play is thus built on a double paradox of topography: not only chastity in Cheapside but fasting in a meat market,[2] the thematic interplay between them being emblematized by their position at each end of the most famous street in town, 'the heart of the city of London' (I. i. 94, IV. i. 129). The centre of the play, therefore, is not a character or a plot but Cheapside itself[3] and what Yeats condemned as 'the emotions of cities'.

Themes and Imagery

The sickness of Jacobean city life is traced to its perversions of natural eroticism, with a consistency which strikingly anticipates the theories of Freud. There is a constant undertow of sexual *double entendre* in the play which gives it extraordinary thematic unity. Scarcely a phrase lacks its lewd implication. Most of the characters make dirty jokes deliberately, and even when they intend no wordplay, there is usually an ironic one there for the audience: the phallic symbolism of the standard with two drums which Allwit claims to see passing Pissing Conduit, for example, or Sir Walter's christening gift to his mistress of a great standing cup and two spoons, one of them gilt. The sexual reference is so absolutely pervasive that it

[1] See John Taylor, 'A chac'd unchaste woman', *Epigrammes* (1651).

[2] For a similar structure of double paradox, see: P. Ure, 'Patient Madman and Honest Whore: the Dekker–Middleton oxymoron', *E.S.E.A.* (1966), 18–40. The 'Goose-Bow' references (I. i. 80–3) and Moll's escape into a 'gutter' (IV. iv. 7) may have sprung to mind because there was also a Goose Lane behind St Mary's Le Beau immediately east of Goldsmiths' Row, and a Gutter Lane debouching north just opposite.

[3] *C.M. in C.* thus helped to pioneer the 'topographical comedy' so popular in the Caroline period: see R. H. Perkinson, *ELH*, III (1936), 270–90; T. Miles, *R.E.S.*, XVIII (1942), 428–40. It seems to have been influenced particularly by Chapman, Jonson, and Marston's *Eastward Ho!*

gradually ceases to be amusing and we feel like protesting with a character in one of Middleton's other plays:

> ... how many honest words have suffered corruption since Chaucer's day! a virgin would speak those words then that a very midwife would blush to hear now, ... And who is this 'long on, but such wags as you, that use your words like your wenches? you cannot let 'em pass honestly by you, but you must still have a flirt at 'em.[1]

This unease is intended, however. Middleton is criticizing the taste by ruthlessly indulging it, so that the sexual reference in *A Chaste Maid* modulates between exuberant vitality and a sense of degeneracy like that in the sexual tragedies of *The Changeling* and *Women Beware Women*.[2]

The play's most obvious perversion of sexuality is its link with competitive materialism.[3] Goldsmiths' Row was London's symbol of successful trade, one of the sights of the city, and this is stamped on the audience's awareness in scene one by the 'shop' set and the business with the gold chain and the ring. In Cheapside sexual relationships are reduced to terms of mercantile advantage: marriage is a business contract, fertility and chastity commodities (the latter 'worth £40', according to Sir Walter, the former costing Sir Oliver £400); maids are 'turned to gold';[4] and adultery is a 'busi-

[1] *N.W.N.H.*, II. i. 80–7.

[2] See Christopher Ricks, 'The Moral and Poetic Structure of *C.*', *E.C.*, X (1960), 290–306, and 'Wordplay in *W.B.W.*', *R.E.S.*, XII (1961), 238–50. *C.*'s finger-ring symbolism, for instance, is anticipated by Touchwood Junior's jokes in I. i and the marriage doggerel of III. i. 13–16. Touchwood Senior too has a 'fatal finger' in seduction (II. i. 59), his bastard lacks a 'nail or two', and the gossips are said to dip 'long fingers' thrice a day in urine (III. ii. 52–3).

[3] Freud's association of desire for money with eroticism (*Collected Papers*, ed. Riviere and Strachey, 1924–50, II. 45–50, 164–71) was anticipated by Plato, who equated the concupiscent instinct in the soul with the rôle of the money-loving man of business in society (*Republic*, IX. 580, trans. F. Cornford, 1948, p. 300). In *C.M. in C.* this association focuses in puns like those on 'gear' (II. i. 17) or 'mark' (II. i. 128–9). See also Quomodo's tendency to think of land in sexual terms in *M.T.*, II. iii. 91–3, IV. i. 117, and willingness to regard it as an acceptable substitute for a woman, I. i. 104–6, V. iii. 68–71.

[4] Sir Walter brings the Welshwoman to London to turn her 'bright trade' into gold (I. i. 100–2). Moll is locked away like gold (III. i. 40–3), though for Maudline she 'counterfeits' (IV. iv. 23). For Tim she is changed

ness' in which Touchwood Senior is paid by results (Sir Oliver having clinched his 'bargain' for £100 less than he expected). At its basest it becomes Allwit's pride in petty possessions (I. ii. 15 ff., V. i. 156–64), culminating Freudianly in a close-stool. The language is full of inflated numbers, with gold and commerce metaphors contaminating it throughout.[1] At the end these become sinister as Sir Walter, computing the 'dear account my soul stands charged with', finds he has 'exchanged' that soul for pleasure, while Touchwood Junior is said to have 'paid enough' for the 'dear' love which 'cost' no less than life; and they culminate in the Yellowhammers' attempt to revive Moll with promises of the very wealth which has destroyed her.

Such materialism is shown to foster class conflict. The struggle between the Jacobean gentry and the climbing middle classes,[2] described by R. H. Tawney and L. C. Knights, is clearly reflected in the relationship between Sir Walter and the Yellowhammers. The citizens' mixture of servility and truculence is beautifully caught in Maudline's desire to have Tim educated like a gentleman yet contempt for everything he learns and in Yellowhammer's refusal to have Moll called 'lady' though he boasts himself descended from a county family. On occasion Yellowhammer does not hesitate even to chide Sir Walter (III. i. 21–2), and there is a nice distinction of tone between the knight's bluster in this family and the airs which his economic, not his social, advantage allows him to adopt with the Allwits. This social competitiveness is also shown within the citizen class itself, as Maudline's opening distinction between a goldsmith's daughter and a plumber's (I. i. 21–3) is farcically developed in the gossips' jostle for precedence in II. 4; and it comes flashing out in one of those simple, profound insights

---

from gold to 'white money' (V. ii. 16–17) and, like Shylock, he weighs her loss against his father's plate (IV. ii. 1–5).

[1] See, for example, the jewel-set-in-gold image which runs through I. i. 102, 174, I. ii. 40, III. iii. 91–2, IV. iv. 24, climaxing in V. iv. 17. A detailed study of the play's imagery can be found in Ruby Chatterji, 'Theme, Imagery and Unity in *C.M. in C.*', *R.D.*, VIII (1965), 105–26.

[2] Middleton's interest in class warfare was perhaps a reflection of his own ambiguous social position: the son of a bricklayer, who styled himself 'gentleman'.

into human meanness for which Middleton has no equal, when the Yellowhammers' first reaction to the news of their daughter's death is 'All the whole street will hate us.'

This last example also shows a deeper level of corruption: the perversion of family relationships on which a wider society is built.[1] *A Chaste Maid* is built on four marriages which existed before the play began and two which are brought about during the course of the action. The very *dramatis personae* in the first edition are grouped according to marriage, instead of the more usual division into male and female categories,[2] and the separate entrance of men and women in v. iv, brought together visually by the lovers' funeral, seems to emblematize an action where all wedlocks are confirmed (albeit ironically) and only Whorehound is punished. Even more important than husband–wife relations, however, is the ambiguous relationship between parents and children in the play. There is a constant opposition between the irresponsibility of 'getting' and the responsibility of 'keeping'. All the babies in *A Chaste Maid* are adulterine (Mrs Allwit's, the Country Wench's, and Lady Kix's child to come; even the promoter's whore is pregnant, II. ii. 113), while the grown children are either neglected or exploited socially by their parents. At a more basic level, the opposition becomes a contradiction between money and fertility itself; as Touchwood Senior complains:

> Some only can get riches and no children,
> We only can get children and no riches! (II. i. 11–12)

But the play's attitude to fertility is not the unqualified approval assumed by Ian Scott Kilvert.[3] The lack of fertility is seen as comic;

[1] Chatterji, following S. Schoenbaum, '*C.M. in C.* and Middleton's City Comedy', *Studies in Renaissance Drama ... in Memory of Karl J. Holzknecht*, ed. J. W. Bennett *et al.* (1959), 292–3, finds this the central theme of the play, reflected in repeated 'house' references (I. ii. 15–17; II. i. 90–1, 168; III. iii. 59, 63; V. i. 8–9, 136, 142–3; V. iv. 49). Against these may be set a minor strain of 'stranger' references that looks forward to the key use of that word in *Women Beware Women* (I. i. 161; I. ii. 80; II. ii. 71; IV. i. 77–8, 81, 95, 138; V. i. 29).

[2] Noted by A. F. Marotti, *Middleton's Mature Drama: 1611–1623* (Ph.D. thesis, Johns Hopkins University, 1965), p. 79.

[3] Ian Scott Kilvert, 'Thomas Middleton's Work in Elizabethan Drama', *Nine*, II, no. 4 (1950), 315 ff.

but Sir Walter is as fertile as Touchwood Senior and is not approved of, while Touchwood Senior himself sees children wholly as a drawback; and there is no mention of procreation in the erotic celebration of the resurrection scene. Significantly, Middleton puts the idea that sex is only a way to get children into the mouth of one of his hypocritical puritans, the lecherous Mrs Underman (III. ii. 33–5). As a view of eroticism, it is revealed as another perversion, this time a religious one.

It is certainly significant that many of the characters in *A Chaste Maid* are puritans. The Yellowhammers' parson is said to consider Latin 'papistry' (I. i. 91), an opinion which Maudline seems to share (IV. i. 141), and Tim has been sent to puritan Cambridge, 'the wellspring of discipline / That waters all the brethren' (III. ii. 163–4). Maudline is also gossip to Mrs Allwit, whose child, one of the puritans tells us, was baptized 'After the pure manner of Amsterdam' (III. ii. 5); and, since Lady Kix is another gossip, it is possible that she is puritan too: 'Oliver' was certainly a name which Middleton later used for a puritan in *Hengist*. This puritanism is used to reflect both economic and sexual hypocrisy. R. H. Tawney has demonstrated how closely puritanism was involved with commercial individualism,[1] a connection which is parodied in Allwit's adaptation of the 23rd psalm to wittoldry (I. ii. 12–13) and his remark that Wat and Nick would kneel to Sir Walter if only they knew some prayers (I. ii. 108–9). It is chiefly its sexual hypocrisy, however, that Middleton is concerned with, and, on this level, puritanism is involved with the second main theme of the play,[2] the ambivalences of Lent.

In England by 1613 the Lenten prohibitions against meat-eating had become wholly economic in intention and were very unpopular, especially with the puritans who objected to them as a remnant of 'popery'.[3] In *The Family of Love*, for instance—Middleton's

[1] Tawney, *Religion and the Rise of Capitalism* (1928). See also L. C. Knights, *Drama and Society in the Age of Jonson* (1937).

[2] The Lenten business in *C.M. in C.* is purely thematic, with no effect on the four main plots. Martin Short's production at Cambridge cut all the Lenten references and action without any confusion of the intrigue. See *infra*, p. lxvii.

[3] See Bertil Johannsen, *Religion and Superstition in the Plays of Jonson*

earlier satire on the sectarians—Lipsalve says he has been converted from the 'notorious crime' of eating fish on Fridays (IV. i. 88) and Dryfat qualifies for a puritan conventicle by claiming 'I keep no holydays nor fasts, but eat most flesh o' Fridays' (III. iii. 72–3).[1] Inevitably, this obstinacy was attributed to gluttony rather than religious conviction, so that Plumporridge in *The Inner Temple Masque* (anticipating Zeal-of-the-land Busy) is made to declare:

> I was born an *Anabaptist*, a fell Foe
> To fish and Fridays, Pig's my absolute sweetheart.
> (ll. 53–4)

And, playing on the relationship of appetites and the ambiguity of 'flesh', gluttony was immediately identified with lust. 'Kind Kit of Kingston', for instance, calls Lent

> . . . that selected time of the yere, when no man is suffered to be a mutton-monger, without a speciall priviledge from those in authoritie: and no man is licensed to enjoy a flesh-bit, but those who are so weake, that the very sight contents their appetite: yet every man desireth flesh, that is no whore-master.[2]

Chastity and fasting, located at either end of Cheapside, are thus identified, a relationship spelled clearly out in *The Family of Love*:

> Love is like fasting-days, but the body is like flesh-days, and 'tis our English gallants' fashion to prefer a morsel of flesh before all the fasting days in the whole year. (I. i. 43–6)[3]

The play's attitude to chastity–fasting is ambiguous, however: Touchwood Senior will praise it theoretically (II. i. 110 ff.) yet apparently ignore it in practice. And this ambiguity was inherent in the non-religious reasons for fasting themselves, which claimed that the restriction not only conserved meat but encouraged the

---

and Middleton (1950), p. 53. Lent was particularly hated by theatre people because it often closed the playhouses (cf. *M.W.M.M.*, I. i. 35): see G. E. Bentley, 'Lenten Performances in the Jacobean and Caroline Theatres', *Essays in Shakespeare . . . presented to Hardin Craig*, ed. R. Hosley (1963), pp. 351–9.

[1] See also *Y.F.G.*, I. i. 307–13, and *Pur.*, I. iii. 11–12.

[2] Kind Kit of Kingston, *Westward for Smelts* (1603 ?), in *Early English Poetry, etc.* (Percy Soc., 1848), XXII. 5.

[3] See also *M.W.M.M.*, IV. v. 57–60, and *W.B.W.*, IV. i. 31–3.

breeding of cattle.[1] John Taylor, for instance, describes Lent as a time when

> The Cow, the Sow, the Ewe may safely feed,
> And laugh, grunt, bleate, and fructifie and breed.[2]

This paradox of Lent as a period of self-denial which nonetheless encourages breeding is behind *A Chaste Maid*'s ambiguous attitude to 'carnal strictness' (II. ii. 72), which is seen both as the equivalent of chastity and as a cloak and provocative to lust.[3] Thus even for Touchwood Junior the chaste maid's presence can whet a 'stomach, which is too sharp-set already' (I. i. 140–1).[4]

The animals in the quotation from Taylor all occur in *A Chaste Maid*. The Welshwoman is called Sir Walter's 'ewe-mutton' brought up 'to find / A ram at London' (I. i. 135–6); Mrs Allwit 'grunts' and 'wallows' like a pregnant sow (I. ii. 6, 30); and the promoters' bawds are described as witch cows (II. ii. 66–8). These and other beast comparisons emphasize the animal side of Lent. A related thread of symbolism is the constant reference to food and drink, which are seen both as directly provocative and as metaphors for lust. There is a particular emphasis on sweetmeats (pointed by the otherwise unnecessary comfit-maker's man in II. iii), which the ambiguous nature of the Grocers' Company relates to the use of provocative drugs, these in turn modulating into poison references in the final scene. This image cluster focuses strikingly in the christening, where drunken puritans gorge phallic sweetmeats[5] and

[1] Cf. *Tudor Royal Proclamations*, ed. P. L. Hughes and J. F. Larkin (1964), I. 510: 'by the eating of fish and forbearing of flesh in [Lent], much flesh is bread [*sic*] and increased...'

[2] John Taylor, 'Jacke a Lent', *Works* (1869), p. 126.

[3] Cf. *M.W.M.M.*, IV. v. 57–8 (Bullen, III. 333): 'When there comes a restraint upon flesh we are almost greedy upon't:...'

[4] Cf. a verse which Middleton inserted into *W.S.P.*:

> The far-fet chastity of female sex
> Is nothing but allurement into lust (VI. 14),

and the fact that in *G. of L.*, while lamenting her fate, he untraditionally assigns Lucrece to hell. This ambivalence is perhaps also reflected in his alteration of the chaste maid's name from *Mary*, emblematizing chastity, to *Moll*, which *R.G.*, II. ii. 159–60, describes as a favourite name for whores.

[5] This scene has interesting parallels to the ritual of Attis (self-castrated father god) and Cybele (great mother) which culminated in the licence of the Roman spring feast of 'Hilaria' and, according to Frazer (*Golden Bough* (1907), Part IV, Book II, pp. 219 ff.), influenced the Christian Easter.

the wives of the grocer and apothecary jostle for precedence; but it also seeps into the language of the play more widely. Sir Walter, for example, 'too sweet' to part with, is made to 'stick by' Allwit's 'ribs' (IV. i. 237); in turn, he finds Allwit 'stuck here at my heart' (V. i. 144); as Tim, marrying a whore 'before breakfast', takes her too 'Next his heart' (V. iv. 63–4)—a periphrasis for 'fasting'. Yet the symbolism is not confined to the bad characters: Touchwood Senior speaks of the 'feast of marriage' and gorges on aphrodisiacs before 'physicking' Lady Kix, while his brother 'peaks o' famine' for a girl whose presence whets his 'stomach'. Once again the moral division is blurred. The imagery cuts right across the sympathetic–unsympathetic distinction of characters.

As we would expect in a Lent play, *meat* is the food most emphasized, the traditional double significance of 'flesh'. This starts in the opening lines with Mrs Yellowhammer describing husbands as 'a piece of flesh' necessary to complete Moll's 'salad' of 'green-sickness' (a play on the idea of fasting dispensations for the sick), and it continues through word-plays on 'geese' and 'mutton' to Allwit's direct comparison of wittoldry to the selling of meat (IV. i. 216–17) and Touchwood Senior's worry about how his mistress will dispose of their bastard ('this half yard of flesh', II. i. 84) in the strict time of Lent. Metaphor then becomes incarnate in the scene where the promoters are tricked into confiscating the baby (symbolically concealed beneath a 'loin of mutton') in the misapprehension that it is meat, only to discover it is an 'unlucky *breakfast*' (II. ii. 157).

This Swiftian equation of baby and meat is the most striking example of the play's pervasive emphasis on the physicality of man, a fleshly grossness which can describe Sir Oliver as 'brevity' or 'scarce the hinderquarter of a man' (III. iii. 81) and apostrophize Allwit's appetite with 'What cares colon here for Lent?' (II. ii. 79). In particular, there is a series of greasy images about human fat, sweat, tears, and milk, which culminates in references to defecation (e.g., V. i. 127, 163) and, especially, urination. Maudline threatens Moll with samphire, a plant which, according to John Gerard, provokes an appetite to meat and urination; Allwit bids the nurse wipe the baby he has been dandling; the gossips, their tongues incontinent with wine, talk of a nineteen-year-old girl who wets the bed, and are themselves accused of dipping fingers into urine; the puritan gossip ambiguously 'wets as she kisses'; and Allwit thinks the gossips have drunk so much that they need a 'looking-glass' (slang for 'chamber-pot'), distracts their attention to a procession passing 'Pissing Conduit', and suspiciously examines the wetness beneath their stools. The references are not just gratuitous filth, however; they embody an important double symbolism.

Water seems to have been particularly associated with Lent,[1] and it is given a sexual significance throughout *A Chaste Maid*. The emphasis on urine occurs in contexts which suggest sexual incontinence and embodies a criticism of eroticism pushed too far.[2] The very name Sir Walter is pronounced 'water' (V. iii. 14–15), so that Yellowhammer's remark that Moll 'catch'd her bane o' the water' has meanings beyond her mere dousing in the Thames. On the other hand, water is also the symbol of purification and renewal. As Levin notes,[3] Moll's half-drowning is a kind of 'death by water', the second of a magical triad of 'deaths' which purify the lovers for their Easter 'resurrection'. Hence, perhaps, the emphasis on the river scenes. A similar anthropological pattern is seen in the case of Sir Oliver Kix (whose name means 'dry stalk', though Oliver should mean 'fruitful'): his 'dry barrenness', 'drought and coldness', is cured by Touchwood Senior's miraculous 'water', which shakes down 'golden fruit' to save Lady Kix from 'dry ground'.

A similar ambivalence can be found in the recurrent fish references in the play, which culminate in Tim's comparison of his half-drowned sister to a mermaid:

> She hath brought her from the water like a mermaid;
> She's but half my sister now, as far as the flesh goes,
> The rest may be sold to fishwives. (IV. iv. 26–8)

Tim's meaning here is wholly lewd (see commentary), but the

[1] See Kind Kit of Kingston, *Westward for Smelts*, p. 6: 'this was Lent time, a time profitable onely for those that deale with liquid commodities . . .'

[2] A similar connection of lust and excretion can be found in *F. of L.*, where they are also associated with puritanism.

[3] 'Four Plots . . .', p. 20.

ambiguity of 'as far as the flesh goes' reminds us that fish was also a traditional symbol for spirituality, quite apart from its association with Lenten self-denial; so there may also be a purification image behind the lewdness. Such ambivalences spring naturally from the ambiguities of Lent itself, the season of crucifixion followed by resurrection, of dearth and spring renewal, when 'Lenten is come with love to toune'.[1]

Point of View

Middleton's moral standpoint in the play is thus hard to pin down. He seems to be both for and against lust, for and against its social and religious disciplining, and his solution of the plot is miraculous rather than moral, but with the 'miracle' qualified by irony and emphatically distanced from reality.

In *A Chaste Maid*'s world of hypocrisy and deceitful appearance, where all authorities are discredited—parents, promoters, puritans, parson, tutor, logic, and 'the laws of the university'—the most successful standard becomes 'wit', the shrewd yet ludicrous self-interest epitomized in Allwit.[2] The people who triumph at the end of the play do so not because they are good but because they are clever intriguers; it is 'wit' that the Country Wench calls on to deceive the promoters (II. ii. 128); and there is irony in Tim's reconciliation to his Welshwoman because of her 'wit' (V. iv. 111), since by that word he once meant merely 'learning' (IV. i. 120–3). Around this standard of 'wit' wind two further skeins of reference: 'blindness' references for characters who fail to realize their true advantage, and 'gaming' references for the characters trying to live by 'wit'.

From Maudline's opening accusation that Moll is 'dull-eyed', *A Chaste Maid* is full of sight–blindness references, and an ironically repeated pattern of 'watcher deceived' is built up. The promoters who 'watch hard for a living' complain of being tricked; Tim, who volunteered to watch his sister in full armour, finds at

[1] *Early English Lyrics*, ed. E. K. Chambers and F. Sidgwick (1947), no. 5.

[2] The facets of Allwit's character can be nicely summed up by a line from Shakespeare's *Merry Wives*, V. v. 123–4: 'See now how wit may be made a Jack-a-Lent when 'tis upon ill employment.'

the end 'there's such a mist' that he cannot find his bride's dowry (v. iv. 90); Yellowhammer's complacency about the posy 'Love that's wise / Blinds parents' eyes' recoils on his own head in III. i. Most subtle of all is Sir Walter, whose blindness takes the form of moral self-righteousness, a sense of conscience which merely misleads him further. Without deliberate hypocrisy, he can say he will avoid Touchwood Junior like 'the disease of lust' (III. i. 52), and, although its effect is merely to prompt him to greater deceit, he prides himself on having a more sensitive conscience than Allwit, whose 'eyes of shame' are blurred by the 'fat of ease' (II. ii. 36–7). This lends extraordinary irony to his repentance in v. i, a scene full of sight–blindness references. Reversing his former position, he now blames Allwit for seeing his damnation and not telling him of it; he repudiates his earlier fear of incest among his bastards (I. ii. 111–13) by shuffling it off on to Mrs Allwit (v. i. 106–8); and his recognition of responsibility takes the form of refusing to look at the children who stand between him and 'the sight of heaven', a cravenness which is paralleled by the Yellowhammers' determination to avoid their daughter's funeral. The ignobility of Sir Walter's collapse, his repentance for reasons which merely confirm his blindness, is as searingly worded as any passage in Middleton. The farcical surface of the play seems suddenly to buckle, exposing the authentic horror of *The Changeling* and *Women Beware Women* beneath. It reminds us that, although he is so contemptuous of puritans, Middleton's work is bracketed by works of distinctly puritan bias.[1] And, although the 'wit' level is then re-established by the humour of Allwit's effrontery, the energy of the resurrection, and the anticlimax of a mere imprisonment for debt, the realities of death and moral responsibility raised in this scene (and diluted sentimentally by Moll in the next) never disappear but remain like a shadow behind the gaiety of the conclusion.

Sir Walter's last line is 'Gamesters, farewell, I have nothing left to play' (v. i. 149), on which Allwit comments:

[1] i.e., *The Wisdom of Solomon Paraphrased* (1597), *The Ghost of Lucrece* (1600), and *The Marriage of the Old and New Testament* (1620). If the last of these is any indication of Middleton's own belief, he appears to see no escape from man's predestined sin except the paradox of God's unmerited mercy.

And let this stand in every gallant's chamber:
'There's no gamester like a politic sinner,
For whoe'er games, the box is sure a winner.'

(v. i. 166–8)

—seeming to associate the dicing 'box' (like the 'bank' in cards) with both the close-stool he was talking about immediately before and the coffin which is heralded by the first line of the following scene: 'she will die, she will die.' 'Gamester' is slang for 'whore-master', and Touchwood Senior's career ironically begins with the same renunciation which ends Sir Walter's: recognizing sex as 'that game / That ever pleas'd both genders' (II. i. 54–5), he fears he must 'give o'er the set, throw down the cards' because he 'ne'er play'd yet / Under a bastard'. Allwit, on the other hand, is himself a 'Jack', only 'one pip' above his own servants, and, as Sir Walter begins to domineer, he remarks that his 'game begins already' (I. ii. 73). Gaming imagery of this kind pervades the play,[1] and its ultimate deadliness emerges in the duel between Sir Walter and Touchwood Junior in IV. iv where no less than life is 'in play', with no 'dealing', till Sir Walter, 'of an even hand', refuses to 'play' longer.

It would be a serious distortion of the play, however, to under-estimate another aspect of the 'gaming' image: the sense of recreation or sport in the play, its ingenuity, gaiety, and the 'releasing' quality of its bawdry. Middleton never claimed more than entertainment for his comedies, and, despite its disturbing aspects, *A Chaste Maid* is mostly a successful farce, a world where 'meretrix' is acceptable as 'merry tricks' (v. iv. 104, 107–10).[2] This aspect would probably have been emphasized by the burlesque acting of the Queen's Revels boys,[3] and it is on this note that *A Chaste Maid* ends. The serious ambiguities of value in the play are resolved theatrically, not morally, by the trick of the resurrection scene; and the purely literary nature of the solution is emphasized by crediting

[1] See also: I. i. 184–5, 206; II. i. 37, 183; III. iii. 7; IV. i. 160, 176; V. i. 158; V. ii. 98–9.

[2] See the prefaces to *R.G.* and *F. of L.*, the prologue to *N.W.N.H.*, and the dedication of *Wit.* for Middleton's claim merely to amuse. His interest in the 'game' aspect of drama can be seen in *G. at C.* and the chess scene of *W.B.W.*

[3] See Anthony Caputi, *John Marston, Satirist* (1961), pp. 80–116, for a discussion of the parodic bent of the Boys' Companies.

it surprisingly to Susan and following it with the anticlimax of Tim's marriage, where the Welshwoman claims that marriage automatically makes her honest (an argument debunked earlier when Yellowhammer cynically claimed that marriage could redeem Sir Walter, IV. i. 240–1), and Tim as usual tries to order life by a mere juggling of words, 'Uxor non est meretrix' and the 'meretrix–merry tricks' pun.[1]

It is useless, therefore, to expect a single moral point of view in *A Chaste Maid*. What we have is a self-consistent play world, reflecting on but clearly distinguished from the real world. It modulates between several dramatic modes and relative moralities in a way which looks back to the guilt and gaiety of primitive Lent and forward to modern 'black comedy'. With the exception of Moll (and even her chastity is seen slightly askance), the characters are all morally ambivalent to a greater or lesser degree, and the mode of their presentation spans the comic range of romance, satiric realism, and a saturnalian inversion of all accepted standards which dips momentarily into horror. At the play's centre stands Allwit, a palindrome of disorder, simultaneously a 'wit' who successfully inverts the customary values and an ironic exposé of a wittol, combining in his single person the saturnalian comedy of outrageous release and the moral criticism of satire. The mixture of realism and exaggeration, exuberance and disgust, in this character is expanded in the key scenes of the promoters and the christening feast to create a mood of soiled saturnalia, farce stretched over moral discomfort, which is uniquely Middleton's own.[2]

4. PRODUCTIONS

A Chaste Maid in Cheapside has a remarkably slight stage history. Though Langbaine says it was 'very successful on the stage',[3] he seems to have based his opinion solely on the phrase 'as it was often

[1] Cf. the scholar in Wye Saltonstall, *Picturae Loquentes* (1631), C12^{v}–D: 'He studies so long words of Art, that all his learning at last is but an Art of words.'

[2] The closest critical term would seem to be *grotesque*, as defined by Arthur Clayborough, *The Grotesque in English Literature* (1966).

[3] Gerard Langbaine, *The Lives and Characters of the English Dramatic Poets* (1699), p. 98.

acted' of the 1630 title-page. Between the original production and the modern revivals of the last decade there is no record of any performance of the play. The closest it gets to revival is to be plagiarized, along with Massinger's *The City Madam*, in a slight Restoration piece called *The Life of Mother Shipton*, dated 1668–71 by Harbage and usually attributed to Thomas Thompson.[1]

This combination is ironic since Massinger appears to have disliked *A Chaste Maid*, at least if we take his commendatory verses to James Shirley's *The Grateful Servant* (1630) as referring to actual plays:

> Here are no forced expressions, no rack'd phrases, ...
> No obscene syllable, that only may compel
> A blush from a chaste maid; but all well
> Express'd and order'd, as wise men must say,
> It is a grateful poem, a good play.[2]

And probably it was this sort of objection which kept *A Chaste Maid* from the stage for nearly 350 years.

The Original Production

Happily the absence of records is compensated for by the interest of both the original production and the play's professional revival in 1966. *A Chaste Maid* has the distinction of being the only play that we know for certain was acted at the Swan, and the Swan in turn happens to be the only theatre of which we possess an eyewitness drawing and description.[3] Since all discussions of Eliza-

[1] See Montague Summers, *The Playhouse of Pepys* (1935), p. 354; A. Harbage and S. Schoenbaum, *Annals of English Drama* (1964), p. 168.

[2] James Shirley, *The Grateful Servant* (1630), sig. A4.

[3] Arend van Buschell's copy of Johannes de Witt's 1596 drawing and description, discovered by Karl T. Gaedertz in 1888. One of the best reproductions of the drawing is in *Sh.S.*, I (1948), plate 3, where a facsimile and transcript of the Latin commentary can also be found (plates 2 and 4; pp. 23–4). The Swan was built about 1595 and stood in the Manor of Paris Garden, on the south bank of the Thames almost directly opposite Blackfriars. Its exact location can be seen in John Norden's 1600 revision of his 1593 map and in a 1627 map of Paris Garden, reprinted as plates VII and IXB respectively in I. A. Shapiro, 'The Bankside Theatres: Early Engravings', *Sh.S.*, I (1948), 25–37. If Shapiro is correct in identifying it as the playhouse shown in two drawings made by Inigo Jones about 1637 (*ibid.*, plates XIVA and B), these must be the last trace of the Swan extant. It is mentioned in *R.G.* (*circa* 1610), V. i. 316, as the place where a knight's purse

bethan theatre structure—and hence of production methods—centre on this drawing, the evidence afforded by the original stage-directions of *A Chaste Maid* is of the utmost historical and theatrical importance. However, we must enter one caveat: if the MS. from which the play was printed was *not* revised for a prompt-book, as has been argued, then its stage-directions may not be based on the practices of the Swan so much as on Middleton's own previous experience in the private theatres; and this possibility is strengthened if it is agreed that he designed the play originally for the Queen's Revels and handed it over to Lady Elizabeth's Men only when the two companies amalgamated in March 1613.[1] It is possible, therefore, that the stage-directions of *A Chaste Maid* reflect private, not public, theatre practice.

De Witt's drawing seems to show that the Swan had no 'inner stage' and that its above-stage gallery was used for spectators and not as an acting area or 'upper stage'. Certain directions in *A Chaste Maid* bear directly on these questions. To take the latter point first: there are no directions in the play which mention an upper acting area and no scenes which seem to require one. At IV. ii. 7–8 Tim refers to his father waiting 'at the dock below', but this seems to refer to a dock downstream from the wharf where Maudline has gone, not to a stage location. Similarly, the watermen at IV. iii. 23 say 'We'll wait below' more in reference to their situation on the riverbank than to their placing on the stage. Either of these scenes might have been played in the gallery, but neither requires it and it is improbable that *both* were 'above' since they are contiguous scenes. The only other scene which need be considered is III. ii, where, as Chambers notes, Tim and his tutor are shown 'up' to the room where the gossips are congregated (ll. 101, 122). This scene is an ensemble scene, however, for which the gallery would scarcely have room; moreover, it begins with the direction '*A bed thrust out upon the stage, Allwit's wife in it*', which makes it almost certain to have been set on the main stage.

---

was stolen 'at the last new play'. A detailed description of the playhouse can be found in Richard Hosley, 'Reconstitution du théâtre du Swan', in *Le Lieu théâtrale à la Renaissance*, ed. J. Jacquot (1964), pp. 295–316.

[1] See *supra*, pp. xxix–xxx.

On the other hand, although there is no evidence of 'upper stage' action, the direction beginning v. iv calls for '*a sad song in the music-room*'; and, while all scholars agree that the music room was above the stage, there is disagreement about whether it was a separate balcony above the stage gallery and directly under the roof, or whether the stage gallery itself may not have functioned indifferently as the 'lords' room' (or 'rooms') for privileged spectators, as music room, and as an upper acting area.[1] The latter theory seems to be supported by De Witt's drawing, where the roof over the stage allows no space for a third-storey music room. The gallery in the drawing, moreover, is divided into six separate compartments, each about six feet wide; and Hosley argues persuasively that only the middle compartment (or compartments) need have been curtained to serve as music room or acting area, with spectators still in the compartments on either side, as in the view of the Red Bull theatre on the title-page of Kirkman's *The Wits* (1662).[2]

This is related to the question of when the music room was introduced into the public playhouse. Both J. C. Adams and W. J. Lawrence assume that some sort of music room was always a feature of the public theatres; Chambers and Hosley, on the other hand, remembering that inter-act music was a characteristic of the private theatres 'not received' in the Globe's piracy of *The Malcontent* in 1604, argue that the music room became part of the public theatres only when the custom of inter-act music was taken over too, and that the existing stage galleries were then adapted to this new purpose. Chambers ties this in neatly with another private theatre influence when he suggests that allowing spectators to sit on stools on the public stages (not 'received' in 1604 either) lessened the modish demand for seats in the 'lords' rooms', which thus became

[1] For the latter opinion, see Chambers, II. 542–3, n. 4; W. J. Lawrence, *The Physical Conditions of the Elizabethan Public Playhouse* (1927), pp. 81 ff.; Richard Hosley, 'The Gallery over the Stage in the Public Playhouses of Shakespeare's Time', *Sh.Q.*, X (1957), and 'Was there a Music-room in Shakespeare's Globe?', *Sh.S.*, XIII (1960); and Glynne Wickham, *Early English Stages, 1300–1660*, II, Part I (1963), p. 320.

[2] The frontispiece of the 1711 edition of *Wit at Several Weapons* (reprinted in Allardyce Nicoll, *The English Theatre*, 1936, facing p. 38) shows the gallery being used as a music room in this way, but its late date makes the drawing of dubious relevance to the Jacobean stage.

more readily available for musicians. The whole question becomes hopelessly involved, however, when we remember that Middleton's stage-direction may have been written with the Whitefriars private theatre, not the Swan at all, in mind.[1]

The question of the 'inner stage' is even more complicated. De Witt's drawing shows no central opening in the tire-house façade of the Swan, merely massive double-leaved doors at each side. Most, but not all, of the *Chaste Maid* evidence supports this picture. There is no action in the play which positively requires a 'study' or alcove behind the main playing area, and the fluidity with which several scenes move from 'domestic' to 'public' situations warns us against any rigid division into 'interior' and 'exterior' scenes. At I. ii. 10, for example, though Allwit bids Davy 'Go in', as though he himself were outside (or at least in an outer room of the house), Davy then comes back in company with Sir Walter Whorehound, who behaves as though he now *entered* the house for the first time; in II. ii Allwit moves from a 'domestic' scene with Sir Walter, the nurse, and the new baby to an encounter with the promoters on a 'street-corner'; and II. i switches from a 'domestic' scene with the Touchwood Seniors, through a 'public' scene in which he meets his ex-mistress and overhears the Kixes quarrelling, to another 'domestic' scene with the Kixes alone, Touchwood Senior having been rather obviously removed by his brother's request to procure a licence. None of these scenes offers any difficulty in staging, however, unless we try to pin them down to the precise kind of location suggested by the term 'inner stage'. In order to change properly, they need to be acted on a vaguely localized main stage. And the direction '*A bed thrust out upon the stage, Allwit's wife in it*' (III. ii. 0.1) is clear proof that Middleton was using the main stage for interior scenes in this way.

The direction '*at one door* ... *at the other door*' (V. iv. 0.1–5) implies that there were only two doors, again agreeing with De Witt's drawing; but there is another direction which suggests that

[1] See, for example, the interesting S.D. at V. iii. 49.1–2 in John Marston's *Antonio's Revenge* (ed. G. K. Hunter, 1965), a Paul's Boys' play of about 1600: '*While the measure is dancing*, Andrugio's *ghost is placed betwixt the music-houses*,' from which position he comments, 'Here will I sit, spectator of revenge...' (l. 53).

smoe scenes may have been what Chambers calls 'threshold scenes': scenes, that is, acted on the fluid main stage but beginning or ending before a definite locale. The first direction of the play is '*Enter Maudline and Moll, a shop being discovered*,' which suggests that this scene at least was localized. The order of the direction implies that the shop was in the nature of a background, not an acting area on an 'inner stage', but, since De Witt shows no centre alcove at all, there is still the problem of how such a 'discovery' could be made on the Swan stage. There have been several solutions put forward for this, in addition to Adams's contention that De Witt (or van Buschell) botched the whole drawing, or the present edition's caveat that Middleton may not have composed with the Swan specifically in mind. The Swan may have had a discovery alcove which was not in use when De Witt visited the theatre; improbably, there may have been curtains between the pillars supporting the stage roof; the 'shop' may have been a movable lath and canvas booth, not a permanent feature of the set; it may have been erected in one of the two large side doors; it may have consisted of curtains hanging from a removable penthouse jutting out from the tire-house wall, like the 'j wooden canopie' included in Henslowe's prop-list for the Admiral's Men (*Henslowe Papers*, ed. W. W. Greg, 1907, p. 116); or there may have been curtains right across the façade of the tire-house, hanging from the penthouse or 'jutty' of the stage gallery, which could be drawn back in the centre to create a shallow 'discovery' alcove.[1] The last theory seems to have most to recommend it. The De Witt drawing shows shading under the stage gallery which seems to indicate an overhang; we know that the

[1] These theories are put forward respectively by: R. Southern, 'On reconstructing an Elizabethan Stage', *Sh.S.*, XII (1959), 32; W. Archer, 'A 16th century Playhouse', *Universal Review*, I (1888), 285–6; G. F. Reynolds, *The Staging of Elizabethan Plays at the Red Bull* (1940), and C. Walter Hodges, *The Globe Restored* (1953); R. Hosley, 'The Discovery Space in Shakespeare's Globe', *Sh.S.*, XII (1959), 35–46; W. A. Armstrong, 'Actors and Theatres', *Sh.S.*, XVII (1964), 202–3 (with plates 27A and B), and Southern, 'On reconstructing ...', 34 (with plate IVB); and, finally, Lawrence, *Physical Conditions*..., p. 74, Hosley, 'Discovery Space', 43 (though in 'Reconstitution...', p. 311, he argues against an overhang), and Southern, 'Current Controversies about the Elizabethan Stage', *World Theatre*, XIII (1964), 76.

spectators' galleries of the Swan at this level 'juttied' out beyond the seats at ground level, so it seems logical that the tire-house gallery should do the same; we know that when Richard Vennar welched on the production of *England's Joy* in 1602, the enraged audience tore 'curtains' and 'hangings' at the Swan;[1] the title-page to *Messalina* (1640) seems to show the stage curtain depending from just such an overhang; and the effect would be very like the actual appearance of contemporary shops:

> From the front wall of the house there often projected, on the level of the first floor, a sloping tiled ledge, called the penthouse; on the ground beneath there stood a stall, which served as shop counter when the householder was engaged in retail trade.[2]

The effect of the first scene, then, with two doors and a discovery alcove, would be like the first scene of *Eastward Ho!* (Blackfriars, 1605) which Lady Elizabeth's Men acted at court in January 1614. This has the opening direction '*Enter Maister Touchstone, and Quicksilver at severall dores... At the middle dore, Enter Golding discovering a Gold-smith's shoppe, and walking short turns before it.*' The Swan probably had no middle door, but Yellowhammer may well have been 'discovered' working in the 'shop' before he 'enters' the main stage I. i. 23.[3]

The temptation is to imagine this 'shop' as always localizing the Yellowhammer scenes, with one of the doors associated with the Allwits, perhaps, and the other with the Kixes, like the three shops of Middleton and Dekker's *The Roaring Girl* (Fortune, *circa* 1610). The staging could probably be worked out in this way, but it would cramp the play's fluidity of movement. In fact, the shop is not really appropriate to any scene except the first. The only later scenes which certainly happen at the Yellowhammers' are IV. i, the scene of Tim's wooing and Allwit's attempt to disillusion Yellowhammer, and V. ii, the scene of Moll's 'demise'; but in neither of these is the shop mentioned or appropriate to the action. It is possible, therefore, that the shop was discovered at the beginning of *A Chaste*

[1] See John Chamberlain's letter, discussed by T. S. Graves, 'A Note on the Swan Theatre', *M.P.*, IX (1911–12), 431–4.

[2] J. A. Gotch, 'Elizabethan Architecture', *Shakespeare's England* (1926), II. 63. For a description of the Goldsmiths' Row fasçade, see note to I. i. 0.1.

[3] For an alternative suggestion, see note to I. i. 28.

Maid to establish the location of the whole play as Cheapside, rather than to identify exclusively Yellowhammer scenes, and that after the first scene it was not used again.[1]

An examination of the action and stage-directions of *A Chaste Maid*, then, tends to confirm De Witt's drawing of the Swan, though the conclusions can be only tentative. No 'upper stage' is required by the action of the play, though part of the stage gallery was probably adapted for a music room; nor is there any scene which requires an 'inner stage', the shop '*discovered*' at I. i. 0.1 serving for background, not acting area, and perhaps localizing the whole play rather than just the Yellowhammer scenes. The general impression is of fluidity; Middleton seems to think of place in terms of adaptable stage area rather than in terms of realistic locale. And it must be recognized that his stage-directions may reflect conditions at the Whitefriars private theatre and have no relation to De Witt's drawing at all.

Modern Revivals

Since 1955, when Schoenbaum's study of *Middleton's Tragedies* appeared, there has been a steady revival of interest in Middleton, including at least seven productions of *A Chaste Maid in Cheapside*. Six of these were for specialized audiences: (1) Leeds University Theatre Group, 29 November 1956 (reviewed *Manchester Guardian*, 30 November), a modernized version with rock and roll music; (2) Leverett House, Harvard University, directed by Alfred David as part of the 1956 Christmas celebrations (text in Harvard archives, HUD. 3519. 256), a heavily cut version with an all-male cast; (3) Embassy Theatre, Swiss Cottage, London, William Gaskill's first version of the play, for the Central School of Speech and Drama, 10 March 1961 (reviewed *The Times*, 11 March), heavily cut to leave room for improvisation and a clown 'framework' action; (4) University of Southampton, March 1962 (reviewed *Wessex*

[1] Another possibility is that it remained as background for the entire action, like one of the 'simultaneous' semi-symbolic mansions of the medieval stage (see Reynolds, *Staging . . . at the Red Bull*, for the survival of such 'incongruous' staging). There is certainly no direction to 'close' the shop, but this proves nothing because such directions are invariably omitted.

News, 22 March; see also *ibid.*, 27 February, for pictures of the cast), a conservative version with Jacobean dress and bare stage; (5) Jesus College, Cambridge University, directed by Martin Short as part of the May Week entertainments, 14 and 15 June 1964, an open-air version lasting one and a half hours, emphasizing the academic and Cambridge satire and omitting the Country Wench, the puritans, the promoters, and all references to Lent; (6) St Michael's College, University of Toronto, a conservative version based on the present text, directed by William Glassco, 2–4 February 1967 (reviewed *Toronto Telegram*, 3 February, *Toronto Globe and Mail*, 4 February).

And, if we except a condensed version of the play called *A Posy on the Ring*, which omitted the Allwit and Lenten scenes and was put on for only one performance on 16 September 1912 at a reconstructed 'Globe' theatre in the 'Shakespeare's England' exhibition at Earl's Court, the first professional revival for 350 years was William Gaskill's second version of *A Chaste Maid*, directed for the English Stage Company in their spring season at the Royal Court Theatre, London, opening 13 January 1966. This was a highly controversial production (see Appendix V) and characteristically critics were divided about the play, ranging from *The Bristol Evening Post* (14 January 1966): 'This filthy farce has laid [*sic*] undisturbed since its first performance 350 years ago, and no wonder,' to *The Times* (14 January 1966): 'This bawdy, realistic, and brilliantly directed comedy of Jacobean London is much the best thing that has appeared in the new Royal Court season... We could do with another Middleton.'

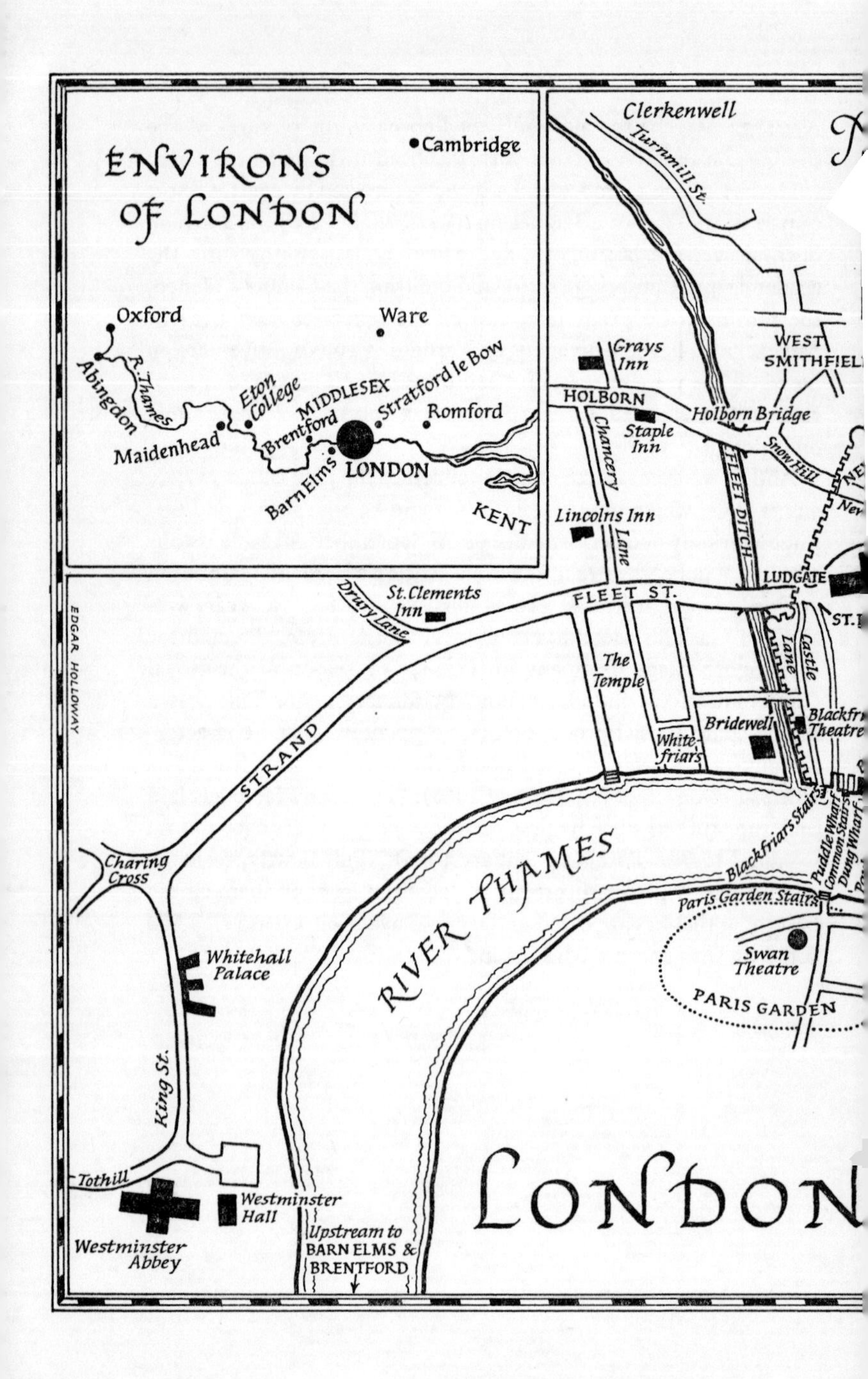
ENVIRONS OF LONDON
Cambridge
Oxford
Ware
Abingdon
R. Thames
Eton College
MIDDLESEX
Stratford le Bow
Romford
Maidenhead
Brentford
LONDON
Barn Elms
KENT
EDGAR HOLLOWAY
Clerkenwell
Turnmill St.
WEST SMITHFIELD
Grays Inn
HOLBORN
Staple Inn
Holborn Bridge
Chancery Lane
Snow Hill
FLEET DITCH
Lincolns Inn
LUDGATE
St. Clements Inn
Drury Lane
FLEET ST.
The Temple
Lane
Castle
Bridewell
Whitefriars
Blackfriars Theatre
STRAND
Blackfriars Stairs
Puddle Wharf
Common Stairs
Dung Wharf
Charing Cross
RIVER THAMES
Paris Garden Stairs
Whitehall Palace
Swan Theatre
PARIS GARDEN
King St.
Tothill
Westminster Hall
Westminster Abbey
Upstream to BARN ELMS & BRENTFORD
LONDON

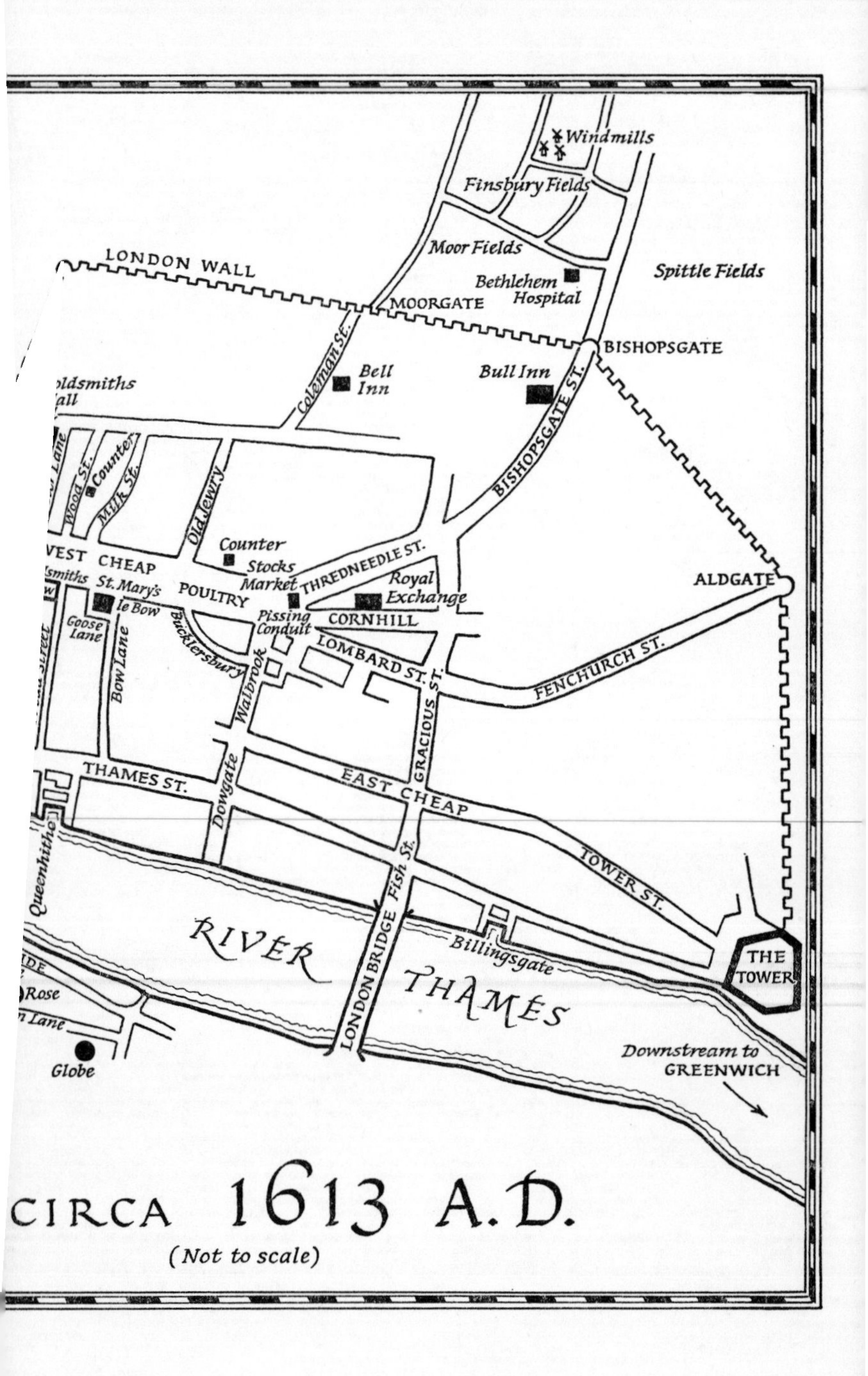

Windmills
Finsbury Fields
Moor Fields
Spittle Fields
LONDON WALL
Bethlehem Hospital
MOORGATE
BISHOPSGATE
Coleman St.
Bell Inn
Bull Inn
BISHOPSGATE ST.
Wood St.
Counter
Milk St.
Old Jewry
Counter
Stocks Market
THREDNEEDLE ST.
Royal Exchange
ALDGATE
CHEAP
St. Mary's le Bow
POULTRY
Pissing Conduit
CORNHILL
Goose Lane
Bow Lane
Bucklersbury
Walbrook
LOMBARD ST.
GRACIOUS ST.
FENCHURCH ST.
THAMES ST.
Dowgate
EAST CHEAP
Queenhithe
Fish St.
TOWER ST.
RIVER
LONDON BRIDGE
Billingsgate
THAMES
THE TOWER
Rose
Globe
Downstream to GREENWICH
CIRCA 1613 A.D.
(Not to scale)

A CHASTE MAID IN CHEAPSIDE

THE NAMES OF THE PRINCIPAL PERSONS

[as given in the first edition].

MR. YELLOWHAMMER, *a goldsmith.*
MAUDLINE, *his wife.*
TIM, *their son.*
MOLL, *their daughter.*
TUTOR, *to Tim.* 5
SIR WALTER WHOREHOUND, *a Suitor to* MOLL.
SIR OLIVER KIX, *and his* WIFE, *kin to* SIR WALTER.
MR. ALLWIT, *and his* WIFE, *whom* SIR WALTER *keeps.*
WELSH GENTLEWOMAN, SIR WALTER'*s whore.*

The Names of the Principal Persons. 0.1. Names] See R. Levin, 'Middleton's Way with Names in *C.M. in C.*', *N. & Q.*, new ser., XII (1965), 102–3, for a discussion of the names' connotations.

1. *Yellowhammer*] (1) describing his occupation of goldsmith; (2) a bird, contributing to the play's animal imagery; (3) 'slang for a gold coin' (*O.E.D.*, *sb.* 3): cf. *H.K.K.*, II. iii. 70; (4) slang for 'fool' (*O.E.D.*, *sb.* 2): cf. *B.M.C.*, III. i. 11; (5) associated with Shrove-Tuesday batter in *W.T.T.*, ll. 379–80. Cf. note to IV. i. 52.

2. *Maudline*] Middleton's own wife is variously called 'Magdalen' and 'Mary' in official documents. The name suits Mrs Yellowhammer's shady past and her trait of sentimentality. Note that the *personae* are grouped according to family, rather than the more usual division into male and female.

3. *Tim*] Cf. Sim, Quomodo's foolish son in *M.T.*, also a Cambridge graduate who spouts Latin tags. In *The Alchemist*, IV. vii. 46, Kastril calls Ananias 'A very tim' as a term of abuse.

4. *Moll*] The original name for this character may have been 'Mary' (see note to I. i. 115.1), emblematizing chastity. 'Moll', on the other hand, is described as a favourite name for whores in *R.G.*, II. ii. 159–60, and is the wanton daughter's name in *Pur.* See Intro., p. liii, n.4, and II. ii. 65.

6–11. *Whorehound*] Sir Walter's function as plot link is shown by his recurrence in the dramatis personae descriptions.

7. *Oliver Kix*] 'Oliver' means fruitful. 'Kix' (or 'Kex') means a dry, hollow plant stalk; hence figuratively 'a dried-up, sapless person' (*O.E.D.*, *sb.* 4; cf. Tilley, K22); it was the name of a minor character in *T.C.O.O.* Self-contradictory names are used similarly in *M.W.M.M.*

8. *Allwit*] inversion of 'wittol'; cf. Marston, *The Malcontent*, ed. M. L. Wine (1964), IV. v. 96–7. See Intro., p. lvi, for a discussion of 'wit' in the play.

9. *Welsh Gentlewoman*] Middleton's habit of not naming characters emphasizes their type characteristics, the Welsh being traditionally asso-

WAT *and* NICK, *his bastards.* 10
DAVY DAHUMMA, *his man.*
TOUCHWOOD SENIOR, *and his* WIFE, *a decayed gentleman.*
TOUCHWOOD JUNIOR, *another suitor to* MOLL.
Two Promoters.
Servants. 15
Watermen.

11. *Dahumma*] *Q; Dahanna Dyce.*

---

ciated with dubious claims to gentility and comic lechery (cf. IV. i. 145–6).

11. *Dahumma*] i.e., *dewch yma*, 'come hither' in Welsh (Bartley, p. 277).

12. *Touchwood*] tinder; especially that used to ignite the touchhole of a musket (cf. notes to II. i. 64, 69), with a sexual implication: cf. *M.D.B.W.*, III. i. 5, where a pregnant girl is called 'a piece of Touchwood'. In Touchwood Junior's case the name also implies 'an irascible or passionate person' (*O.E.D.*, *sb.* c).

decayed] fallen from prosperity.

14. *Promoters*] informers; at least two were required to swear to an infringement (cf. Hughes and Larkin, *Tudor Royal Proclamations*, I. 414). See note to II. i. 115.

16. *Watermen*] boatmen, plying for hire on the Thames.

[*DRAMATIS PERSONAE.*

YELLOWHAMMER, *a goldsmith.*
TIM YELLOWHAMMER, *his son, a graduate of Cambridge.*
Tutor, *to* TIM.
TOUCHWOOD JUNIOR, *a suitor to* MOLL YELLOWHAMMER.
TOUCHWOOD SENIOR, *his brother, a decayed gentleman.* 5
SIR WALTER WHOREHOUND, *another suitor to* MOLL YELLOWHAMMER.
SIR OLIVER KIX, *kinsman to* SIR WALTER.
ALLWIT, *a wittol whose wife is mistress to* SIR WALTER.
WAT *and* NICK, *sons of* SIR WALTER *and* MRS. ALLWIT. 10
DAVY DAHUMMA, *a poor relation of* SIR WALTER.

MAUDLINE, *wife to* YELLOWHAMMER.
MOLL, *daughter to* YELLOWHAMMER.
SUSAN, *maid to* YELLOWHAMMER.
LADY KIX, *wife to* SIR OLIVER. 15
MRS ALLWIT, *wife to* ALLWIT *and mistress of* SIR WALTER.
WELSH GENTLEWOMAN, *ex-mistress of* SIR WALTER.
MRS TOUCHWOOD, *wife to* TOUCHWOOD SENIOR.
Country Wench, *ex-mistress of* TOUCHWOOD SENIOR.

Two Promoters. 20
Nine Servants: *two to* ALLWIT, *one to a* Comfit-maker, *four to* KIX, *two to* SIR WALTER.
Two Watermen.
Parson.
Maid *to* KIX. 25
Porter.
Gentleman.
Dry Nurse *to* MRS ALLWIT'*s baby.*
Wet Nurse *to* MRS ALLWIT'*s baby.*

Dramatis Personae. 19. *Country Wench*] apparently from Derbyshire (II. i. 75): cf. the Northern Wench who is Lethe's mistress in *M.T.*

Midwife. 30
Two Men, *with meat in baskets.*
Two Puritan Women.
Five Gossips.]

A Chaste Maid in Cheapside

Act I

[I. i]

Enter MAUDLINE *and* MOLL, *a shop being discovered.*

Maudl. Have you play'd over all your old lessons
O' the virginals ?

Moll. Yes.

Maudl. Yes ? You are a dull maid o' late, methinks;

Act I] *Dyce; Actus Primus Q.* 3. methinks;] *This ed.;* me thinkes *Q.*

Q is divided into Acts, but not scenes, which were first added by Dyce.

The Title is a paradox like *Honest Whore* or *White Devil*, but also carries the implication of 'chastity for sale'. It may have been semi-proverbial: cf. John Taylor, 'A chac'd unchaste woman', *Epigrammes* (1651), ending 'For she was chac'd by Whippers through Cheapside', Donald Lupton, *London and the Country Carbonadoed* (1632): '[In Cheapside] there are many virtuous and honest women, some truly so, others are so for want of opportunity' (*Life in Shakespeare's England*, ed. J. D. Wilson (1954), p. 122), Thomas Dekker, *The Owl's Almanac* (1618), p. 8: 'A fair wench is to be seen every morning in some shop in Cheapside: And in summer afternoons the selfsame fair opens her booth at one of the garden-houses about Bunhill.'

0.1. shop] This would set the scene in Goldsmiths' Row, on the south side of Cheapside, described by John Stow (pp. 308–9) as 'the most beautiful frame of fair houses and shops that be within the walls of London, or elsewhere in England ... four stories high, beautified towards the street with the Goldsmith's arms and the likeness of woodmen, in memory of [Thomas Wood, who built the row in 1491], riding on monstrous beasts, all which is cast in lead, richly painted over and gilt ...' Beast-, lead-, and gilt imagery is exploited within the play. There are contemporary drawings of Goldsmiths' Row in F. J. Furnivall, ed., *Harrison's England* (1878), Part III. See also the sketch of Cheapside in 1660 in Sir W. Besant, *London in the Time of the Stuarts* (1903), p. 241.

discovered] See Intro., pp. lxiv–lxv.

2. *virginals*] (1) square, legless spinet, to play which was a ladylike acquirement: cf. *M.T.*, II. iii. 82; (2) sexual quibble: cf. *B.M.C.*, III. iii. 87 (Partridge, p. 217).

You had need have somewhat to quicken
Your green sickness—do you weep?—a husband! 5
Had not such a piece of flesh been ordained,
What had us wives been good for?—to make salads,
Or else cry'd up and down for samphire.
To see the difference of these seasons!
When I was of your youth, I was lightsome 10
And quick two years before I was married.
You fit for a knight's bed!
Drowsy-brow'd, dull-eyed, drossy-spirited!
I hold my life you have forgot your dancing:
When was the dancer with you?

Moll. The last week.

Maudl. Last week! 15
When I was of your bord, he miss'd me not a night;

9. seasons!] *Dyce;* seasons, *Q.* 13. spirited] *Dyce;* sprited *Q.* 16. bord] *Q;* board *Dyce.*

5–7.] For a similar chain of ideas see *H.K.K.*, III. ii. 10–14.

5. *green sickness*] '*Chlorosis*—an anaemic sickness of young women (with consequent greenish complexion). The Elizabethan dramatists emblematized it as a sign of a girl's love-sickness, or of vague desire for a man' (Partridge, p. 123).

7. *to make*] intransitive, 'to prove, become', i.e., women without men are green salads without meat (picking up the 'green sickness' metaphor).

salads] Q's 'Sallets' may also play on the meaning 'ribaldry': cf. *Hamlet*, II. ii. 420, Webster, *Appius and Virginia*, III. ii. 79. Salads were associated with impropriety because they were highly seasoned.

8. *cry'd up and down*] i.e., shouted for sale up and down the street. Bullen cites the first of two songs printed after Thomas Heywood's *Rape of Lucrece*:

> I ha' rock-samphire. I ha' rock-samphire!
> Thus go the cries in Rome's fair town:
> First they go up street, and then they go down.

samphire] the plant *Crithmum maritimum*, whose properties, according to John Gerard (*Herbal*, 1636, p. 534), were to provoke urine and women's sickness, to open the stoppings of the entrails, and to stir up an appetite to meat: cf. 'salads', l. 7, and *Lr.*, IV. vi. 15. The name derives from 'herbe de Saint Pierre', so Q's 'Sampier' was probably a trisyllable, regularizing the metre.

11. *quick*] punning on the meaning 'pregnant'.

14. *dancing*] (1) another genteel accomplishment; (2) sexual intercourse: cf. *M.D.B.W.*, V. i. 90 f., *W.B.W.*, III. ii. 184, IV. ii. 124–5.

16. *bord*] (1) bore, calibre; (2) quality, condition.

I was kept at it; I took delight to learn,
And he to teach me; pretty brown gentleman,
He took pleasure in my company;
But you are dull, nothing comes nimbly from you: 20
You dance like a plumber's daughter and deserve
Two thousand pound in lead to your marriage,
And not in goldsmith's ware.

Enter YELLOWHAMMER.

Yell. Now, what's the din
Betwixt mother and daughter, ha?
Maudl. Faith, small;
Telling your daughter Mary of her errors. 25
Yell. Errors? Nay, the city cannot hold you, wife,
But you must needs fetch words from Westminster.—
I ha' done, i' faith!—
Has no attorney's clerk been here o' late
And chang'd his half-crown-piece his mother sent him, 30
Or rather cozen'd you with a gilded twopence,
To bring the word in fashion for her faults
Or cracks in duty and obedience?
Term 'em e'en so, sweet wife.

28. I] *Q;* Ay, *conj. Dyce.* 33. obedience?] *Dyce;* obedience, *Q.*
34. e'en] *This ed.;* eeue *Q;* even *Dyce.*

---

22. *to*] 'for': cf. IV. i. 85.
23. *goldsmith's ware*] i.e., gold.
25. *Mary*] Cf. I. i. 115.1.
27. *fetch ... Westminster*] i.e., affect gallicisms like those used in Westminster Hall, where the Courts of Common Law and Chancery were conducted in law-French: cf. I. i. 89.
28.] If Yellowhammer enters from outside (as his query about recent customers suggests), he could be bringing the legal papers for Tim's marriage. This would fit in with the reference to Westminster and the legal phraseology of l. 45, and would allow l. 28 to be interpreted 'I have completed arrangements', thus prompting Moll's query at l. 38.
30. *half-crown-piece*] Difficult or uncommon words were also referred to as 'half-crown words' (Farmer and Henley, III. 249).
31. *gilded twopence*] i.e., silver twopenny-piece, gilded to seem gold: the first of several references to counterfeiting.

As there is no woman made without a flaw, 35
Your purest lawns have frays and cambrics bracks.
Maudl. But 'tis a husband solders up all cracks.
Moll. What, is he come, sir?
Yell. Sir Walter's come:
He was met at Holborn bridge, and in his company
A proper fair young gentlewoman, which I guess 40
By her red hair and other rank descriptions
To be his landed niece brought out of Wales,
Which Tim our son, the Cambridge boy, must marry.
'Tis a match of Sir Walter's own making,
To bind us to him and our heirs for ever. 45
Maudl. We are honour'd, then, if this baggage would be humble
And kiss him with devotion when he enters.
I cannot get her for my life
To instruct her hand thus, before and after,—
Which a knight will look for,—before and after. 50
I have told her still, 'tis the waving of a woman
Does often move a man and prevails strongly.

---

36. *cambrics*] fine white linens.
bracks] flaws: cf. Lyly, *Euphues* (ed. Arber), p. 33: 'The finest velvet [hath] his bracke.'
37.] (1) mends all imperfections; (2) bawdy: cf. *N.W.N.H.*, I. i. 108–9, T. Nabbes, *Totenham-Court* (1638), p. 16, J. Brome, *City Beggar* (*Works*, 1873, I. 226).
39. *Holborn bridge*] carrying the main road from Wales across the Fleet ditch (Stow, p. 26), to enter the city through Newgate.
41. *rank*] (1) richly dressed, showing status; (2) 'lustful' (*O.E.D.*, 13): cf. III. ii. 202 and note to III. ii. 44; (3) 'covered with coarse growth of grass' (*O.E.D.*, 10)—linking 'red hair' and 'landed' (l. 42)?
49.] F. L. Lucas (*Works of John Webster*, I. 209) notes an Elizabethan 'digitary ogle', involving 'a sort of motion of the little finger backwards and forwards, not unlike carving'. Thus 'before and after' may mean 'backwards and forwards'. But it is more likely to mean an affected carriage of the hands in front of and behind the body (cf. *Eastward Ho!*, I. ii. 58), with (inevitably) a sexual innuendo.
51. *waving*] perhaps the 'carving' discussed above, or some other provocative gesture or carriage. The Courtezan in *T.C.O.O.*, V. ii. 171–4, renounces 'Waving of fans ... Wringing of fingers ... The wanton gait, th' alluring trip'.

But, sweet, ha' you sent to Cambridge? Has Tim word on 't?
Yell. Had word just the day after, when you sent him
The silver spoon to eat his broth in the hall 55
Amongst the gentlemen commoners.
Maudl. O, 'twas timely.

Enter Porter.

Yell. How now?
Port. A letter from a gentleman in Cambridge.
Yell. O, one of Hobson's porters: thou art welcome!—
I told thee, Maud, we should hear from Tim.
[*Reads*] *Amantissimis carissimisque ambobus parentibus* 60
patri et matri.
Maudl. What's the matter?
Yell. Nay, by my troth, I know not,
Ask not me: he's grown too verbal, this learning is
A great witch.
Maudl. Pray, let me see it; I was wont
To understand him.— 65
[*Construes*] *Amantissimis carissimis*: he has sent the carrier's man, he says; *ambobus parentibus*: for a pair of boots; *patri et matri*: pay the porter or it makes no matter.
Port. Yes, by my faith, mistress! There's no true construction in that; I have took a great deal of pains and come from the 70

66. *Amantissimis carissimis*] *Dyce; amantissimus charissimus Q.*

---

56. *gentlemen commoners*] wealthy undergraduates who paid for special privileges, including the prerogative of dining together at a separate table from the poorer students; hence to get into this group was a favourite mode of social climbing. The term is not exclusive to Oxford, as George claims (see *O.E.D.*).

58. *Hobson*] the famous Cambridge carrier, on whose death in January 1630 the student John Milton wrote two epitaphs (see *Wits Recreations*, 1817 ed., p. 249). His wagon is mentioned in *F.H.T.* (Bullen, VIII. 101).

60–1.] To my father and mother, both my most loving and beloved parents.

69. *no true construction*] i.e., you have misconstrued the Latin. Comic misconstruing was popular, especially in 'school' plays. Middleton has another example in *Wit.*, II. ii. 16–24.

70–1. *the Bell*] See John Taylor, *Carriers Cosmography* (1637): 'The Waggons or Coaches from Cambridge, doe come every Thursday and

Bell sweating. Let me come to 't, for I was a scholar forty
years ago. 'Tis thus, I warrant you.—
[*Construes*] *Matri*: it makes no matter; *ambobus parentibus*:
for a pair of boots; *patri*: pay the porter; *amantissimis*
carissimis: he's the carrier's man, and his name is Sims.— 75
And there he says true, forsooth; my name is Sims indeed.
I have not forgot all my learning! A money matter; I
thought I should hit on 't.

Yell. Go, thou art an old fox! [*Gives money*] There's a tester
for thee.

Port. If I see your worship at Goose Fair, I have 80
A dish of birds for you.

Yell. Why, dost dwell at Bow?

Port. All my lifetime, sir; I could ever say
Bo to a goose! Farewell to your worship. *Exit.*

Yell. A merry porter!

Maudl. How can he choose but be so,
Coming with Cambridge letters from our son Tim? 85

Yell. What's here? [*Reads*] *Maxime diligo*? Faith,

76. forsooth;] *This ed.;* forsooth *Q;* forsooth, *Dyce.* 82. sir;] *Dyce;* Sir *Q.* 86. *Maxime*] *George; maximus Q.*

Friday to the blacke Bull in *Bishopsgate* street,' but 'The Carriers of *Cambridge*, doe lodge at the Bell in *Coleman Street.*' (*Works not in 1630 Folio*, 1873, II, sigs. B1ᵛ, B2). Dyce notes that Hobson was more usually connected with the former of these inns.

79. *tester*] sixpence.

80–1. *Goose Fair . . . Bow*] A fair selling young (or green) geese was held in Whitsun week at Stratford-le-Bow, a suburb in Essex, north-east of London: see John Taylor, 'Taylor's Goose', *Works* (1630), p. 11:

> At *Bowe* the Thursday after Pentecost
> There is a faire of Greene Geese, ready rost,
> Where as a Goose is very dog cheape there,
> The Sauce is onely somewhat sharpe and deare.

Cf. II. ii. 77 for Taylor's reference to 'Sauce'. Herford and Simpson say the fair was held on Whit-Monday (Jonson, *Poetaster*, III. iv. 135, n.). 'Goose' was slang for 'fool' (Farmer and Henley, III. 181, no. 2) and for 'whore' (*ibid.*, no. 6); Middleton also plays on *bow*, 'pudendum', in *M.T.*, II. i. 111–16.

83. *Bo to a goose*] Tilley, B481.

86. Maxime diligo] I love most greatly. Possibly *maxima diligo*, 'I esteem (or choose) the greatest.' Tim's motto is ironic in either case.

I must to my learned counsel with this gear,
'Twill ne'er be discern'd else.

Maudl. Go to my cousin, then,
At Inns of Court.

Yell. Fie, they are all for French;
They speak no Latin.

Maudl. The parson then will do it. 90

Enter a Gentleman *with a chain.*

Yell. Nay, he disclaims it, calls Latin 'papistry';
He will not deal with it.—What is 't you lack, gentleman?

Gent. Pray, weigh this chain. [*Yellowhammer weighs chain.*]

Enter SIR WALTER WHOREHOUND, Welsh Gentlewoman, *and* DAVY DAHUMMA.

Sir Walt. Now, wench, thou art welcome
To the heart of the city of London.

Welsh G. *Dugat a whee.* 95

Sir Walt. You can thank me in English, if you list.

Welsh G. I can, sir, simply.

Sir Walt. 'Twill serve to pass, wench;
'Twas strange that I should lie with thee so often

90.1.] *So Q; after* with it, *l. 92 Dyce.* 93.2. *Dahumma*] *This ed.; Dahanna Q.* 93. *Sir Walt.*] *So this ed. passim; S. Walt. Q passim.* 95. *Welsh G.*] *So this ed. passim; W. Gent. Q passim.*

---

87. *gear*] business: cf. *T.C.O.O.*, IV. v. 129.

88. *discern'd*] 'made out' (*O.E.D.*, 5).

89. *French*] (1) Law French was used extensively by the students at Inns of Court: cf. Jonson, *The Alchemist* (Revels ed.), IV. iv. 61–2:

> It goes like law-French,
> And that, they say, is the courtliest language;

(2) possibly a play on *French*, 'pox' (cf. V. i. 106).

90.1.] Cf. 'every well-dressed gentleman wore a gold chain', *Shakespeare's England* (1926), II. 115.

94.] Cf. Stow, *Survey of London* (1633 ed.), p. 272a; Cheap ward is 'neerest to the heart of the city'.

95.] i.e., *Duw gyda chwi*, 'God with you', or *Duw gatwo chwi*, 'God keep you' (J. O. Bartley, p. 278). Nares (1888 ed., p. 260) suggests *Duw cadw chwi*, 'God bless or preserve you'.

98. *'Twas*] It would be: cf. l. 162.

To leave thee without English; that were unnatural.
I bring thee up to turn thee into gold, wench, 100
And make thy fortune shine like your bright trade;
A goldsmith's shop sets out a city maid.
Davy Dahumma, not a word!

Davy. Mum, mum, sir.

Sir Walt. Here you must pass for a pure virgin.

Davy. [*Aside*] Pure Welsh virgin! 105
She lost her maidenhead in Brecknockshire.

Sir Walt. I hear you mumble, Davy.

Davy. I have teeth, sir;
I need not mumble yet this forty years.

Sir Walt. [*Aside*] The knave bites plaguily!

Yell. [*To Gentleman*] What's your price, sir?

Gent. A hundred pound, sir.

Yell. A hundred marks the utmost; 110
'Tis not for me else.—What, Sir Walter Whorehound?

[*Exit* Gentleman.]

Moll. O death! *Exit.*

Maudl. Why, daughter! Faith, the baggage!
[*To Sir Walter*] A bashful girl, sir; these young things
are shamefac'd;
Besides, you have a presence, sweet Sir Walter,
Able to daunt a maid brought up i' the city: 115

Enter MOLL.

103. Dahumma] *This ed.; Dahanna Q.* Davy.] *So this ed. passim; Dau. Q throughout I. i.* 112. baggage!] *This ed.;* Baggage *Q;* baggage is *Dyce.* 115.1.] *So this ed.; Enter Mary. Q; Reenter Moll. at l. 117.1 Dyce.*

---

101. *your*] impersonal 'one's' (contrast 'thy' in the same line)? Thus 'bright trade' may refer to the trade of goldsmith rather than that of whore; but see Intro., p. xlviii, n.4.

105. *Pure*] (1) thoroughly; (2) 'a kept mistress' (Farmer and Henley, v. 327): cf. l. 174?; (3) with an ironic reflection on *pure*, 'chaste' (*O.E.D.*, III. 3).

106. *Brecknockshire*] a county in Wales, but with a sexual pun: cf. *F.Q.*, v. i. 183–4 (Bullen, IV. 265).

110. *marks*] A mark was 13s. 4d., two-thirds of £1: see II. i. 129.

115.1] Q has *Mary*: cf. I. i. 25. The irregularity argues an unrevised

A brave court-spirit makes our virgins quiver
And kiss with trembling thighs. Yet see, she comes, sir.

Sir Walt. [*To Moll*] Why, how now, pretty mistress? Now I have
Caught you. What, can you injure so your time
To stray thus from your faithful servant?

Yell. Pish! 120
Stop your words, good knight,—'twill make her blush else,—
Which sound too high for the daughters of the freedom.
'Honour' and 'faithful servant'! They are compliments
For the worthies of Whitehall or Greenwich;
E'en plain, sufficient, subsidy words serves us, sir. 125
And is this gentlewoman your worthy niece?

Sir Walt. You may be bold with her on these terms; 'tis she, sir,
Heir to some nineteen mountains.

Yell. Bless us all!
You overwhelm me, sir, with love and riches.

Sir Walt. And all as high as Paul's.

Davy. [*Aside*] Here's work, i' faith! 130

Sir Walt. How sayest thou, Davy?

Davy. Higher, sir, by far;
You cannot see the top of 'em.

122. sound] *conj. Dyce;* wound *Q;* are wound *Lamb, George.* 124. worthies] *Q;* worthy ladies *Lamb.* 125. serves] *Q;* serve *Lamb, Dyce.*

MS. Moll's voluntary re-entry is curious; in a similar situation Tim is brought back by the Nurse, III.ii.115.1.

122. *the freedom*] i.e., 'men licensed to practise trade' (*O.E.D.*, 13).

123. *Honour*] Actually this was Maudline's word, l. 46.

124. *Whitehall or Greenwich*] royal palaces.

125. *subsidy*] 'of substantial, bourgeois worth' (*O.E.D.*, *sb.*, 4 *attrib.*): cf. 'subsidy citizens', *M.T.*, III. iv. 98, 195.

serves] Middleton frequently uses single verbs with plural subjects.

128. *mountains*] an Elizabethan cliché about Wales (see Bartley, p. 68); cf. *N.W.N.H.*, IV. i. 249–50.

130. *as high as Paul's*] proverbial (see Archer Taylor, 'Proverbs and Proverbial Phrases in the Plays of Thomas Middleton', *S.F.Q.*, XXIII (1959), 86; T. H. Svartengren, *Intensifying Similes in English* (1918), 284). Perhaps because of the mountains cliché, St Paul's was supposed especially to interest Welshmen (see Bartley, p. 67).

Yell. What, man!
Maudline, salute this gentlewoman, our daughter
If things hit right.

Enter TOUCHWOOD JUNIOR.

Touch. Jun. [*Aside*] My knight, with a brace of footmen,
Is come, and brought up his ewe-mutton to find 135
A ram at London; I must hasten it,
Or else peak o' famine; her blood's mine,
And that's the surest. Well, knight, that choice spoil
Is only kept for me. [*He whispers to Moll from behind.*]
Moll. Sir?
Touch. Jun. Turn not to me
Till thou mayst lawfully; it but whets 140
My stomach, which is too sharp-set already.
Read that note carefully [*giving her a letter*];
Keep me from suspicion still, nor know my zeal
But in thy heart. Read, and send but thy liking
In three words; I'll be at hand to take it. 145
Yell. [*To Sir Walter*] O, Tim, sir, Tim:
A poor plain boy, an university man;

134. *Touch. Jun.*] *So Dyce passim; T.I. Q passim.* 137. peak] *conj. Dyce;* picke *Q.* 138. spoil] *Dyce;* spoy *Q.* 146. Tim, sir, Tim:] *conj. Dyce;* turne Sir, turne. *Q.*

135. *ewe-mutton*] glossed as 'elderly' strumpet by Farmer and Henley (II. 360), but in this case surely only 'experienced'? *O.E.D.* cites '1700. B. E., *Dict. Cant. Crew*: *Ewe*, or the *White Ewe*, a Top-woman among the Canting crew, very beautiful'. Cf. Jonson, *The Alchemist*, V. v. 125.
136. *hasten it*] get a move on.
137. *peak*] dwindle, grow meagre.
blood] i.e., hot blood, as affected by sexual passion (Partridge, p. 75): cf. Christopher Ricks, 'Moral and Poetic Structure of *C.*', *E.C.*, X (1960), 290–306. Touchwood means 'she desires me sexually'.
138. *that's the surest*] i.e., 'the best assurance that Moll will be mine', scarcely an idealizing comment! See Intro., p. liii, n.4.
141. *stomach*] sexual appetite.
144. *liking*] 'approval, consent' (*O.E.D.*, *sb*[1], 4b), but perhaps with a pun on 'lust, sexual desire' (*ibid.*, 2b).
146. *Tim, sir, Tim*] Q's 'turne Sir, turne' was probably influenced by the 'Turne' which began l. 139 in Q.

Proceeds next Lent to a bachelor of art:
He will be call'd Sir Yellowhammer then
Over all Cambridge, and that's half a knight. 150

Maudl. Please you, draw near
And taste the welcome of the city, sir.

Yell. Come, good Sir Walter, and your virtuous niece here.

Sir Walt. 'Tis manners to take kindness.

Yell. Lead 'em in, wife.

Sir Walt. Your company, sir?

Yell. I'll give 't you instantly. 155

[*Exeunt* MAUDLINE, SIR WALTER, DAVY, *and* Welsh Gentlewoman.]

Touch. Jun. [*Aside*] How strangely busy is the devil and riches!
Poor soul, kept in too hard, her mother's eye
Is cruel toward her, being kind to him.
'Twere a good mirth now to set him a-work
To make her wedding ring; I must about it: 160
Rather than the gain should fall to a stranger,
'Twas honesty in me to enrich my father.

Yell. [*Aside*] The girl is wondrous peevish, I fear nothing
But that she's taken with some other love,
Then all's quite dash'd: that must be narrowly look'd to, 165
We cannot be too wary in our children.
[*To Touchwood Junior*] What is 't you lack?

152. sir.] *Dyce;* Sir? *Q.* 155. sir?] *Dyce;* Sir. *Q.* 155.1–2.] *Dyce.*
157. eye] *Dyce;* Eye, *Q.* 158. being kind] *This ed.;* being *Q.*

---

148. *next Lent*] Since Tim is already a B.A. in III. ii. 120, 135, presumably I. i and I. ii occur before Lent begins. Touchwood Senior first mentions Lent at II. i. 107.

149. *Sir Yellowhammer*] 'Sir' was a rendering of the Latin *dominus* (see IV. i. 5, 9) when used with the surname only—hence '*half* a knight' (l. 150).

154. *take*] accept.

155.1–2.] Apparently Moll is urged by Maudline to leave too (hence Touchwood Junior's comment, ll. 157–8), but resists (hence Yellowhammer's, ll. 163–6). Perhaps she re-enters at l. 168?

158. *being kind*] Q has only 'being': probably an adjective balancing 'cruel' dropped out accidentally; it is also possible that the MS. read 'bēing' (i.e., 'beaming'), though this would leave the line metrically irregular.

162. *'Twas*] See note to I. i. 98.

Touch. Jun. [*Aside to Moll*] O, nothing now; all that I wish is present;—
[*To Yellowhammer*] I would have a wedding ring made for a gentlewoman
With all speed that may be.

Yell. Of what weight, sir? 170

Touch. Jun. Of some half ounce; stand fair and comely
With the spark of a diamond, sir; 'twere pity
To lose the least grace.

Yell. Pray, let's see it.
[*Takes stone from Touchwood Junior.*]
Indeed, sir, 'tis a pure one.

Touch. Jun. So is the mistress.

Yell. Have you the wideness of her finger, sir? 175

Touch. Jun. Yes, sure, I think I have her measure about me.
Good faith, 'tis down; I cannot show 't you,
I must pull too many things out to be certain.
Let me see: long, and slender, and neatly jointed;
Just such another gentlewoman that's your daughter, sir. 180

Yell. And, therefore, sir, no gentlewoman.

Touch. Jun. I protest
I never saw two maids handed more alike;

---

168. S.D.] *This ed.; Dyce puts Aside after* now. 172. diamond, sir;] *This ed.;* Diamond. Sir *Q;* diamond; sir, *Dyce.* 180. gentlewoman] *Q;* gentlewoman— *Dyce.* sir.] *Q;* sir? *Dyce.*

---

171. *stand*] i.e., 'I would have it stand', in parallel to 'made' (l. 169): see *O.E.D.*, *vb*, II. 4.

172. *spark*] a small stone: cf. *N.W.N.H.*, I. i. 226. The popular form of wedding ring was an enamelled hoop with small stones and a motto engraved inside: *Shakespeare's England*, II. 144; cf. ll. 190–1.

174. *pure*] excellent; but Touchwood's reply relates it to the meaning 'kept mistress' (see note to l. 105).

175. *finger*] a play on the meaning 'intimate caress' (Partridge, p. 112). The sexual symbolism of ring-and-finger is recurrent in Middleton, e.g., *F. of L.*, V. iii. 419–20, *Y.F.G.*, II. i. 260–1, *C.*, I. ii. 27–31 (see Intro., p. xlviii, n.2).

176. *measure*] size; with a bawdy innuendo.

177. *down*] 'deep in my pocket': but with a play on 'detumescent'.

180.] i.e., another gentlewoman just such as your daughter is (see Abbott, para. 108).

I'll ne'er seek farther, if you'll give me leave, sir.
Yell. If you dare venture by her finger, sir.
Touch. Jun. Ay, and I'll 'bide all loss, sir.
Yell. Say you so, sir? 185
Let's see hither, girl.
Touch. Jun. Shall I make bold
With your finger, gentlewoman?
Moll. Your pleasure, sir.
Touch. Jun. That fits her to a hair, sir. [*Trying ring on Moll's finger*]
Yell. What's your posy now, sir?
Touch. Jun. Mass, that's true: posy? I' faith, e'en thus, sir:
'Love that's wise, 190
Blinds parents' eyes.'
Yell. How, how! If I may speak without offence, sir,
I hold my life—
Touch. Jun. What, sir?
Yell. Go to; you'll pardon me?
Touch. Jun. Pardon you? Ay, sir.
Yell. Will you, i' faith?
Touch. Jun. Yes, faith, I will.
Yell. You'll steal away some man's daughter: am I near you? 195
Do you turn aside? You gentlemen are mad wags!
I wonder things can be so warily carried,
And parents blinded so; but they're served right
That have two eyes and wear so dull a sight.
Touch. Jun. [*Aside*] Thy doom take hold of thee.
Yell. Tomorrow noon
Shall show your ring well done.

186. Let's see hither] *Q;* Let us see.—Hither *Dyce.* 193. life—] *Dyce;* life *Q.* 199. wear so dull a sight] *This ed.;* were so dull a sight *Q;* were so dull a' sight *Dyce.*

---

185. *'bide*] stand; i.e., 'if I'm wrong, I'll still pay'.

188. *hair*] (1) nicety; (2) 'female pubes' (Farmer and Henley, III. 246).

195. *am I near you?*] 'do I guess your intention (or your secret)?', but irony in the 'near' since Yellowhammer himself is the man in question.

199. *wear*] Q's 'were' spelling also occurs at IV. iv. 3 (sig. $H3^v$ in Q).

Touch. Jun. Being so, 'tis soon. 201
Thanks,—[*To Moll*] and your leave, sweet gentlewoman.
Moll. Sir, you are welcome. *Exit* [TOUCHWOOD JUNIOR].
[*Aside*] O, were I made of wishes, I went with thee.
Yell. Come now, we'll see how the rules go within. 205
Moll. [*Aside*] That robs my joy; there I lose all I win. *Exeunt.*

[I. ii]

Enter DAVY *and* ALLWIT *severally.*

Davy. [*Aside*] Honesty wash my eyes! I have spy'd a wittol.
Allw. What, Davy Dahumma? Welcome from North Wales,
i' faith;
And is Sir Walter come?
Davy. New come to town, sir.
Allw. In to the maids, sweet Davy, and give order
His chamber be made ready instantly. 5
My wife's as great as she can wallow, Davy, and longs
For nothing but pickled cucumbers and his coming;
And now she shall ha 't, boy.
Davy. She's sure of them, sir.
Allw. Thy very sight will hold my wife in pleasure
Till the knight come himself. Go in, in, in, Davy. *Exit* [DAVY].
The founder's come to town: I am like a man 11

206. S.D.] *Dyce; Exit. Q.*

I. ii. 2. *Allw.*] *So this ed. passim; All. Q passim.* Dahumma] *This ed.; Dahanna Q.*

---

205. *rules*] revels; the medial *v* being vocalized (see Kökeritz, p. 189, n. 4, p. 325). George thinks it might be glossed 'agreements', from *rule*, 'regulation'.

I. ii. I. *wash my eyes*] Cf. Jonson, *Tale of a Tub*, II. ii. 136: 'Where were your eyes then? out at washing?', *Volpone*, III. iv. 12: 'you ha' not wash'd your eies, yet?'

wittol] (1) accommodating cuckold; (2) a transposition of the name 'Allwit'.

6. *wallow*] 'go with a rolling or floundering gait' (*O.E.D.*, *vb*[1], 2c, cites W.M., *Man in the Moone* (1609), E2: 'Now he [Gluttony] approacheth wallowing like a woman with childe').

Finding a table furnish'd to his hand,
As mine is still to me, prays for the founder,—
'Bless the right worshipful the good founder's life.'
I thank him, 'has maintain'd my house this ten years, 15
Not only keeps my wife, but a keeps me
And all my family: I am at his table;
He gets me all my children, and pays the nurse
Monthly or weekly; puts me to nothing,
Rent, nor church-duties, not so much as the scavenger: 20
The happiest state that ever man was born to!
I walk out in a morning; come to breakfast,
Find excellent cheer; a good fire in winter;
Look in my coal-house about midsummer eve,
That's full, five or six chaldron new laid up; 25
Look in my backyard, I shall find a steeple
Made up with Kentish faggots, which o'erlooks
The water-house and the windmills: I say nothing,

12.] echoing Psalm xxiii, verse 5 (*Authorized Version*, 1611): 'Thou preparest a table before me . . .', the blasphemy being carried further in 'prays' (l. 13) and 'Bless' (l. 14): cf. Campion, 8th epigram, ll. 8–10 (Intro., p. xxxvii): 'by prayers / Dayly begs of heau'n, that it for euer / May stand firm for him'.

15. *ten years*] Cf. also II. iii. 7; but III. ii. 67 and IV. i. 210 say 'seven years'. See Intro., p. xxxviii.

16. *a*] he; frequent in Middleton.

18.] Cf. Campion, 8th epigram, ll. 13–14 (Intro., p. xxxvii): 'begets the children, / Payes the Nurces, eu'ry charge defraying'.

20. *church-duties . . . scavenger*] Church dues could be paid with money or parish work. The scavengers' job was to oversee repairs of the pavement, the cleansing of the streets, and the repair of chimneys and furnaces against the danger of fire (see F. P. Wilson, *Plague in Shakespeare's London*, 1927, pp. 26–8). Sir Walter has paid the church dues in cash, relieving Allwit of the alternative parish work.

25. *chaldron*] cauldron, a dry measure of 32 bushels.

27. *Kentish faggots*] 'Kent supplied a good part of the firewood of London' (Sugden): cf. John Taylor, 'Taylor's Feast' (*Works not in 1630 Folio*, III. 96): 'good Kentish faggots'.

o'erlooks] stands higher than.

28. *water-house and the windmills*] The water-house is probably goldsmith Hugh Middleton's recently completed reservoir for the New River in Islington (see plates XLIII, XLIV, in A. M. Hind, *Wencelaus Hollar and his View of London*, 1922); Thomas Middleton wrote an oration for its formal

But smile and pin the door. When she lies in,
As now she's even upon the point of grunting, 30
A lady lies not in like her; there's her embossings,
Embroid'rings, spanglings, and I know not what,
As if she lay with all the gaudy-shops
In Gresham's Burse about her; then her restoratives,
Able to set up a young pothecary, 35
And richly stock the foreman of a drug-shop;
Her sugar by whole loaves, her wines by runlets.
I see these things, but like a happy man
I pay for none at all; yet fools think 's mine;
I have the name, and in his gold I shine; 40
And where some merchants would in soul kiss hell

39. 's] *Q;* it *Lamb.*

---

opening at Michaelmas (29 Sept.), 1613 (see Bullen, VII. 227 ff.). In which case, the windmills are probably those on Windmill Hill in Finsbury Fields: cf. *F.Q.*, IV. i. 159–60: 'I have heard 'em roar from the six windmills to Islington'; *F.H.T.* (Bullen, VII. 96–7). Alternatively, it may refer to the force pump at Broken *W*harf on the Thames, erected by Bevis Bulmer in 1594–5, 'to convey *Thames* water into men's houses of West *Cheap*, about Pauls' (Stow, p. 18). In the views of Visscher (1616), Morden and Lea (1682), and Kips' 'Nouveau Théâtre de la Grande Bretagne' (1724), this is shown with a windmill on top, though it has no windmill in Merian's view of 1628 or Hollar's of 1647 (see Hugh Phillips, *The Thames about 1750*, 1951, p. 69, fig. 60; p. 205). Water-houses with windmills may have been of interest in 1613 because patents were taken out on 21 Sept. 1612 for a newly designed engine of this kind, which was later to be demonstrated to the public (see *Calendar of State Papers, Domestic*, LXIX. 133; LXX, 21 Sept. 1612; LXXI, 31 Dec. 1612).

29. *pin*] bolt.

31.] See Intro., p. xxxii.

embossings] embossed ornaments.

33. *gaudy-shops*] shops for finery.

34. *Gresham's Burse*] 'A place for merchants to assemble' (Stow, p. 173), built by Sir Thomas Gresham in 1566 and named 'The Royal Exchange' by Queen Elizabeth on a visit in 1570 (see Part II of Heywood's *If You Know not Me*, 1606). The south side of the Burse was a covered walk, called the Pawn, with stalls specializing in clothes, trinkets, etc.: cf. *B.B.* (Bullen, VIII. 28) and *M.C.* (*ibid.*, 118).

36. *foreman*] See Intro., pp. xxxiii–xxxiv: cf. *H.K.K.*, II. iii. 64–6.

37. *runlets*] A runlet is a cask of varying capacities up to 18½ gallons.

39. '*s*] abbreviation for 'it is'.

To buy a paradise for their wives, and dye
Their conscience in the bloods of prodigal heirs
To deck their night-piece, yet all this being done,
Eaten with jealousy to the inmost bone,— 45
As what affliction nature more constrains
Than feed the wife plump for another's veins?—
These torments stand I freed of; I am as clear
From jealousy of a wife as from the charge:
O, two miraculous blessings! 'Tis the knight 50
Hath took that labour all out of my hands:
I may sit still and play; he's jealous for me,
Watches her steps, sets spies; I live at ease,
He has both the cost and torment: when the strings
Of his heart frets, I feed, laugh, or sing: 55
[*Sings*] *La dildo, dildo la dildo, la dildo dildo de dildo.*

Enter two Servants.

1 Ser. What, has he got a singing in his head now?
2 Ser. Now 's out of work, he falls to making dildoes.
Allw. Now, sirs, Sir Walter's come.
1 Ser. Is our master come?
Allw. Your master! What am I?
1 Ser. Do not you know, sir? 60

54. strings] *Q;* string *Dyce.* 57, 59, 60, 61, 63. *1 Ser.*] *This ed.;* 1 *Q.*
58. *2 Ser.*] *This ed.;* 2 *Q.*

---

44. *night-piece*] 'bed-fellow' (Farmer and Henley, v. 41); possibly with a reference to 'night-triumph', a night pageant 'adorned and beautified with many lights' (*T. of I.*, Bullen, VII. 391).

46. *nature more constrains*] more violates nature (*O.E.D.*, 'constrain', 5b); 'nature' is the object.

47.] Cf. *M.D.B.W.*, II. iii. 108: 'Much like your man that labours to get treasure, / To keep his wife high, for another's pleasure.'

54–5. *strings . . . frets*] playing with a musical metaphor. The intervening 'heart' makes the verb singular, though grammatically it should be plural (see Abbott, § 35).

56. dildo] (1) a nonsense refrain common in ballads: cf. Appendix IV, no. 3; (2) an 'artificial penis' (Farmer and Henley, II. 286).

60–3.] Cf. the logic-chopping of Tim and the Tutor. *Ergo*, 'therefore'; *Negatur argumentum*, 'the argument is denied': cf. III. ii. 125, IV. i. 1.

Allw. Pray, am not I your master?
1 Ser. O, you are but
Our mistress's husband.
Allw. *Ergo*, knave, your master.

Enter SIR WALTER *and* DAVY.

1 Ser. *Negatur argumentum.*—Here comes Sir Walter.
[*Aside to 2 Servant*] Now a stands bare as well as we; make the most of him,
He's but one pip above a serving man, 65
And so much his horns make him.
Sir Walt. How dost, Jack?
Allw. Proud of your worship's health, sir.
Sir Walt. How does your wife?
Allw. E'en after your own making, sir; she's a tumbler, o' faith;
The nose and belly meets.
Sir Walt. They'll part in time again.
Allw. At the good hour they will, and please your worship. 70
Sir Walt. [*To Servant*] Here, sirrah, pull off my boots.—
[*To Allwit*] Put on, put on, Jack.
Allw. I thank your kind worship, sir.
Sir Walt. Slippers! [*Servant brings slippers.*] Heart,
You are sleepy!
Allw. [*Aside*] The game begins already.

62.1.] *So this ed.; after* Husband. *Q; at l. 63.1 Dyce; after* make him. *l. 66 George.* 65. pip] *This ed.;* peepe *Q.* 71. Put on, put on] *Dyce;* Put on, but on *Q.*

---

65. *pip*] the mark on playing cards or dice: cf. *F.H.T.* (Bullen, VIII. 84, 86); hence, 'degree'. Cf. the army insignia of rank known as 'pips'.

68. *after your own making*] 'according to your own fashioning', with perhaps an innuendo in *making*, 'mating'.

tumbler] (1) acrobat: cf. l. 69; (2) copulator: cf. *tumble*, 'copulate' (Partridge, p. 210), e.g., *O.L.*, II. ii. 43, *W.B.W.*, IV. ii. 106, *S.G.*, II. ii. 173–4.

69. *nose and belly meets*] a common description of pregnancy; Mrs Fisher cites T. Jordan, *Walks of Islington and Hogsdon* (1657), B1:

A maid servant I dare swear she is not,
For her nose and belly do almost meet.

71. *Put on*] i.e., put on your hat. The Jacobeans wore hats indoors; Allwit is standing bareheaded to show respect.

Sir Walt. Pish! Put on, Jack.
Allw. [*Aside*] Now I must do it, or he'll be
As angry now, as if I had put it on 75
At first bidding. 'Tis but observing—[*Puts on hat.*]
'Tis but observing a man's humour once,
And he may ha' him by the nose all his life.
Sir Walt. [*To Servant*] What entertainment has lain open here?
No strangers in my absence?
1 Ser. Sure, sir, not any. 80
Allw. [*Aside*] His jealousy begins. Am not I happy now
That can laugh inward whilst his marrow melts?
Sir Walt. How do you satisfy me?
1 Ser. Good sir, be patient.
Sir Walt. For two months' absence I'll be satisfied.
1 Ser. No living creature enter'd—
Sir Walt. Enter'd? Come, swear! 85
1 Ser. You will not hear me out, sir.
Sir Walt. Yes, I'll hear 't out, sir.
1 Ser. Sir, he can tell, himself.
Sir Walt. Heart, he can tell!
Do you think I'll trust him?—as a usurer
With forfeited lordships. Him? O monstrous injury!
Believe him? Can the devil speak ill of darkness? 90
[*To Allwit*] What can you say, sir?
Allw. Of my soul and conscience, sir,
She's a wife as honest of her body to me,
As any lord's proud lady can be.
Sir Walt. Yet, by your leave, I heard you were once off'ring
To go to bed to her.
Allw. No, I protest, sir! 95

85. enter'd—] *Dyce;* entred. *Q.* 93. lady] *Q;* lady e'er *Dyce.*

78. *by the nose*] at his mercy.
86. *out . . . out*] a word play: the first means 'to a finish', the second 'the whole story' (as in 'the truth will out').
87. *he*] i.e., Allwit.
89. *forfeited lordships*] i.e., property (*O.E.D.*, 2) which is forfeit to the usurer by non-repayment of a loan.

Sir Walt. Heart, if you do, you shall take all. I'll marry!
Allw. O, I beseech you, sir.
Sir Walt. [*Aside*] That wakes the slave,
And keeps his flesh in awe.
Allw. [*Aside*] I'll stop that gap
Where'er I find it open. I have poisoned
His hopes in marriage already— 100
Some old rich widows and some landed virgins,

Enter two Children [WAT *and* NICK].

And I'll fall to work still before I'll lose him,
He's yet too sweet to part from.
Wat. [*To Allwit*] God-den, father.
Allw. Ha, villain, peace!
Nick. God-den, father.
Allw. Peace, bastard!
[*Aside*] Should he hear 'em! [*Aloud*] These are two foolish children, 105
They do not know the gentleman that sits there.
Sir Walt. O, Wat! How dost, Nick? Go to school, ply your books, boys, ha?
Allw. [*Aside to boys*] Where's your legs, whoresons? [*Aside*] They should kneel indeed,
If they could say their prayers.
Sir Walt. [*Aside*] Let me see, stay;
How shall I dispose of these two brats now 110
When I am married? For they must not mingle
Amongst my children that I get in wedlock;
'Twill make foul work, that, and raise many storms.
I'll bind Wat prentice to a goldsmith,—
My father Yellowhammer, as fit as can be! 115

97. sir.] *This ed.;* Sir, *Q;* sir! *Dyce.* 100. already—] *This ed.;* already, *Q;* already with *Dyce.* 101.1.] *So Q; after* part from. *l. 103 Dyce.* 103. *Wat.*] *So Dyce;* 1 *Boy. Q.* 104. *Nick.*] *So Dyce;* 2 *Boy. Q.* 108. *Aside to boys*] *Wall.* *Aside*] *This ed.* 109. S.D.] *So Wall; Dyce puts only ll. 110–17 as aside.*

---

108. *legs*] bows.

Nick with some vintner; good, goldsmith and vintner;
There will be wine in bowls, i' faith.

Enter ALLWIT'*s* Wife.

Mrs Allw. Sweet knight,
Welcome! I have all my longings now in town;
Now, welcome the good hour. [*Embraces him.*] 119
Sir Walt. How cheers my mistress ?
Mrs Allw. Made lightsome e'en by him
That made me heavy.
Sir Walt. Methinks she shows gallantly,
Like a moon at full, sir.
Allw. True, and if she bear
A male child, there's the man in the moon, sir.
Sir Walt. 'Tis but the boy in the moon yet, goodman calf.
Allw. There was a man, the boy had never been there else. 125
Sir Walt. It shall be yours, sir.
Allw. No, by my troth, I'll swear
It's none of mine. Let him that got it
Keep it! [*Aside*] Thus do I rid myself of fear,
Lie soft, sleep hard, drink wine, and eat good cheer. [*Exeunt.*]

117. *Mrs Allw.*] *So this ed. passim; Wife. Q passim.* 129. S.D.] *Dyce.*

---

121. *heavy*] (1) sad; (2) pregnant.
124. *calf*] blockhead; perhaps with a play on *mooncalf*, 'false pregnancy'.
127–8. *Let ... it !*] Cf. Tilley, B43.

Act II

[II. i]

Enter TOUCHWOOD SENIOR *and his* Wife.

Mrs Touch. 'Twill be so tedious, sir, to live from you,
But that necessity must be obeyed.
Touch. Sen. I would it might not, wife. The tediousness
Will be the most part mine, that understand
The blessings I have in thee; so to part, 5
That drives the torment to a knowing heart.
But as thou say'st, we must give way to need,
And live awhile asunder; our desires
Are both too fruitful for our barren fortunes.
How adverse runs the destiny of some creatures: 10
Some only can get riches and no children,
We only can get children and no riches!
Then 'tis the prudent'st part to check our wills
And, till our state rise, make our bloods lie still.
Life, every year a child, and some years two; 15
Besides drinkings abroad, that's never reckon'd;

Act II] *Dyce; Actus Secundus. Q.* 1. *Mrs Touch.*] *So this ed. passim; Wife. Q passim.* 3. *Touch. Sen.*] *So this ed. passim; T.S. Q passim.* 13. prudent'st] *Dyce;* prudents *Q.* wills] *Q;* will *Dyce.*

5. *blessings*] (1) felicities, favours; (2) children: cf. II. i. 131, III. ii. 33; (3) therefore also a hint of the ironic euphemism for 'curses' (*O.E.D.*, 6)?

6. *knowing*] i.e., that understands the blessings that I have in thee (ll. 4–5).

11–12.] Cf. *M.T.*, Induction, 25–6, IV. i. 35–6, *W.B.W.*, I. i. 96–100.

13. *wills*] 'passionate sexual desires' (Partridge, p. 221).

14. *bloods*] See l. 51 and note to I. i. 137.

15. *Life*] abbreviation of 'By God's life'.

16. *drinkings*] euphemism for 'copulations'.

abroad] away from home.

This gear will not hold out.
Mrs Touch. Sir, for a time
I'll take the courtesy of my uncle's house,
If you be pleas'd to like on 't, till prosperity
Look with a friendly eye upon our states. 20
Touch. Sen. Honest wife, I thank thee; I ne'er knew
The perfect treasure thou brought'st with thee more
Than at this instant minute. A man's happy
When he's at poorest that has match'd his soul
As rightly as his body. Had I married 25
A sensual fool now, as 'tis hard to 'scape it
'Mongst gentlewomen of our time, she would ha' hang'd
About my neck, and never left her hold
Till she had kiss'd me into wanton businesses,
Which at the waking of my better judgment 30
I should have curs'd most bitterly,
And laid a thicker vengeance on my act
Than misery of the birth—which were enough
If it were born to greatness, whereas mine
Is sure of beggary, though it were got in wine. 35
Fullness of joy showeth the goodness in thee;
Thou art a matchless wife: farewell, my joy.
Mrs Touch. I shall not want your sight?
Touch. Sen. I'll see thee often,
Talk in mirth, and play at kisses with thee,
Anything, wench, but what may beget beggars; 40
There I give o'er the set, throw down the cards,

---

17. *gear*] (1) business, doings; (2) 'genitals' (*O.E.D.*, 5b): cf. *F.H.T.* (Bullen, VIII. 91).

32. *thicker vengeance*] i.e., the curse mentioned in l. 31; not infanticide, as George suggests.

33–5. *misery . . . beggary*] i.e., the birth itself is misery enough even if the child has good prospects in life, and the misery is compounded when the child has beggarly prospects.

37. *matchless*] (1) peerless; (2) without a husband? Cf. V. i. 158, V. ii. 98.

38. *want*] lack.

41. *give o'er*] abandon.

set] match, contest; 'a game at dice or cards' (*O.E.D.*, 25).

And dare not take them up.

Mrs Touch. Your will be mine, sir. *Exit.*

Touch. Sen. This does not only make her honesty perfect,
But her discretion, and approves her judgment.
Had her desires been wanton, they'd been blameless 45
In being lawful ever, but of all creatures
I hold that wife a most unmatched treasure
That can unto her fortunes fix her pleasure
And not unto her blood: this is like wedlock;
The feast of marriage is not lust but love 50
And care of the estate; when I please blood,
Merely I sing and suck out others'; then
'Tis many a wise man's fault, but of all men
I am the most unfortunate in that game
That ever pleas'd both genders: I ne'er play'd yet 55
Under a bastard: the poor wenches curse me
To the pit where'er I come; they were ne'er served so,
But us'd to have more words than one to a bargain.
I have such a fatal finger in such business
I must forth with 't, chiefly for country wenches, 60
For every harvest I shall hinder hay-making:

45. desires] *Dyce;* desire *Q.* 52. Merely] *This ed.;* Meerely *Q;* Merrily *Dyce.* others'; then] *This ed.;* others, then *Q;* others' then; *Dyce;* others then, *George.*

44. *approves*] attests, confirms.

50–1. *The feast . . . estate*] For similar arguments see *N.W.N.H.*, v. i. 7–12, *W.B.W.*, I. iii. 22–35, 41–9, III. i. 169–70.

52.] Lust is frequently emblematized as a flesh-fly in Middleton; 'sing' may be a misprint for 'sting' (cf. *R.G.*, III. ii. 31), 'st' being a ligature in Middleton's handwriting, but cf. also *sing*, 'have sexual intercourse with' (Partridge, p. 187).

56. *Under a bastard*] George notes that the image is one of having a bad hand and being left with a card which scores heavily against the player. At best, Touchstone Senior is left with a bastard to dispose of; at worst, with a legitimate child for whom he has to provide.

57. *pit . . . come . . . serv'd*] bawdy quibbles (see Partridge).

58.] i.e., used to have a say in the matter (of whether they became pregnant or not). Proverbial: cf. Tilley, W827: 'two words to a bargain', *Wid.*, v. i. 313.

61–2.] i.e., the 'harvest' of his pregnancies prevents wenches from hay-

Enter a [Country] Wench *with a child.*

I had no less than seven lay in last progress
Within three weeks of one another's time.

C. Wench. O, snap-hance, have I found you?

Touch. Sen. How snap-hance?

C. Wench. [*Showing him the child*] Do you see your workmanship?
Nay, turn not from it, 65
Nor offer to escape; for if you do,
I'll cry it through the streets and follow you.
Your name may well be called Touchwood,—
A pox on you!—you do but touch and take;
Thou hast undone me; I was a maid before, 70
I can bring a certificate for it
From both the churchwardens.

Touch. Sen. I'll have the parson's
Hand too, or I'll not yield to 't.

C. Wench. Thou shalt have more,
Thou villain! Nothing grieves me but Ellen,
My poor cousin in Derbyshire; thou hast crack'd 75

61.1.] *So Q; after l. 63 Dyce.* 64. *C. Wench.*] *So this ed. passim; Wench. Q passim.* 74. villain!] *Dyce;* villain, *Q.*

---

making in the real harvest. For the havoc created during Court Progresses, especially to the harvest, see *Calendar of State Papers, Venetian*, x. 267–8 (25 Aug. 1605).

62. *lay in*] be brought to bed with child, confined.

last progress] the last royal tour: see Intro., p. xxxii, n.1, and note to ll. 61–2.

64. *snap-hance*] (1) marauder; (2) flintlock, igniting 'touchwood' in the touchhole of a musket (for *touchhole*, 'pudend', see Partridge, *Dictionary of Slang*, p. 903). Cf. note on Touchwood, 'Names', l. 12.

69. *touch and take*] Cf. Tilley, T447; Levin, 'Middleton's Way with Names ...', cites *Lady Alimony* (1659), E2, where Madam Tinder is described: 'She's right *tinder*: no sooner touch than take'.

71. *certificate*] the certificate of good conduct required of all people moving out of their parish under the Statute 5 Eliz. c. 4. In the wench's case this would amount to a certificate of chastity. Mrs Fisher cites Lewis Matchin (?), *Every Woman in Her Humour* (1607), E4, and Newcastle, *The Triumphant Widow* (1677), p. 6:

Gervas. Is't possible a lusty widow live and die chast? ...
Pedlar. All the Parish Hands are to the Certificate to confirm it.

Cf. ll. 72–3.

Her marriage quite; she'll have a bout with thee.

Touch. Sen. Faith, when she will, I'll have a bout with her!

C. Wench. A law bout, sir, I mean.

Touch. Sen. True, lawyers use

Such bouts as other men do. And if that

Be all thy grief, I'll tender her a husband. 80

I keep of purpose two or three gulls in pickle

To eat such mutton with, and she shall choose one.

Do but in courtesy, faith, wench, excuse me

Of this half yard of flesh, in which, I think,

It wants a nail or two.

C. Wench. No, thou shalt find, villain, 85

It hath right shape and all the nails it should have.

Touch. Sen. Faith, I am poor. Do a charitable deed, wench;

I am a younger brother and have nothing.

C. Wench. Nothing! Thou hast too much, thou lying villain,

Unless thou wert more thankful.

Touch. Sen. I have no dwelling; 90

I brake up house but this morning. Pray thee, pity me;

I am a goodfellow, faith, have been too kind

To people of your gender; if I ha 't

Without my belly, none of your sex shall want it.

[*Aside*] That word has been of force to move a woman. 95

[*To her*] There's tricks enough to rid thy hand on 't, wench:

76–9. *bouts*] (1) law suits; (2) sexual encounters.

81. *in pickle*] (1) 'in reserve', like pickled vegetables; (2) 'poxed' (Farmer and Henley, v. 188)?

82. *mutton*] slang for whore; cf. I. i. 135, IV. i. 146.

85, 86. *nail*] (1) a cloth measure of 2¼ inches; (2) syphilitics' children sometimes lack nails, hence the Country Girl's indignant reply. 'Nail' is also American slang for venereal disease: see E. O'Neill, *The Iceman Cometh* (Random House, 1946), p. 236: 'I picked up a nail from some tart in Altoona'.

91. *brake up house*] (1) parted from my family; (2) with perhaps a play on 'dwelling', l. 90?

92. *goodfellow*] roisterer.

94. *Without my belly*] 'outside my belly', i.e., anything not actually eaten already; but with a sexual innuendo.

96–8.] Cf. *Wit.*, II. iii. 2–3: *Aberzanes*. ... Dost thou know the house? *Old Woman* [*with bastard*]. Nor matter for the house, I know the porch.

Some rich man's porch, tomorrow before day,
Or else anon i' the evening; twenty devices.
[*Giving money*] Here's all I have, i' faith, take purse and
all;
[*Aside*] And would I were rid of all the ware i' the shop so!
C. Wench. Where I find manly dealings, I am pitiful: 101
This shall not trouble you.
Touch. Sen. And I protest, wench,
The next I'll keep myself.
C. Wench. Soft, let it be got first!
[*Aside*] This is the fifth; if e'er I venture more,
Where I now go for a maid, may I ride for a whore. *Exit.* 105
Touch. Sen. What shift she'll make now with this piece of flesh
In this strict time of Lent, I cannot imagine;
Flesh dare not peep abroad now. I have known
This city now above this seven years,
But, I protest, in better state of government 110
I never knew it yet, nor ever heard of.
There has been more religious wholesome laws
In the half circle of a year erected
For common good, than memory ever knew of,

Enter SIR OLIVER KIX *and his* Lady.

Setting apart corruption of promoters, 115
And other poisonous officers that infect
And with a venomous breath taint every goodness.
Lady. O, that e'er I was begot, or bred, or born!

104. fifth] *Q;* first *conj. George.* 114.1.] *So Q; at l. 117 Dyce.*

---

98. *anon*] immediately.
100. *ware i' the shop*] Cf. Tilley, W68: 'When the Ware be gone shut up the shop', citing Webster, *The White Devil*, V. iv. 111. Ware usually has a bawdy implication in Middleton: cf. *F. of L.*, II. i. 22, V. i. 28–9, *R.G.*, II. i. 237, IV. ii. 140, *N.W.N.H.*, I. i. 209–10, etc.
104–5.] Cf. *M.T.*, I. i. 16–17: 'a virgin of five bastards'.
115. *Setting apart*] except for.
promoters] informers, spies. A satirical sketch of one is given in John Stephens, *Essays and Characters* (1615), vi. See note to *Names of the Principal Persons*, 14.

Sir Ol. Be content, sweet wife.
Touch. Sen. [*Aside*] What's here to do, now?
I hold my life she's in deep passion 120
For the imprisonment of veal and mutton
Now kept in garrets; weeps for some calf's head now.
Methinks her husband's head might serve with bacon.

Enter TOUCHWOOD JUNIOR.

Lady. Hist!
Sir Ol. Patience, sweet wife. [*They walk aside.*]
Touch. Jun. Brother, I have sought you strangely.
Touch. Sen. Why, what's the business?
Touch. Jun. With all speed thou canst
Procure a licence for me.
Touch. Sen. How, a licence? 126
Touch. Jun. Cud's foot, she's lost else! I shall miss her ever.
Touch. Sen. Nay, sure, thou shalt not miss so fair a mark
For thirteen shillings fourpence.
Touch. Jun. Thanks by hundreds!
[*Exeunt* TOUCHWOOD SENIOR *and* TOUCHWOOD JUNIOR.]

119. *Sir Ol.*] *So this ed. passim; S. Ol. Q passim.* 124. *Lady.*] *Q; Touch. Jun. Dyce subs.* 129.1.] *Dyce; Exit. Q.*

124. Lady.] Dyce and George change to *Touch. Jun.*, but 'Hist!' shows Lady Kix's wish not to be overheard by Touchwood Junior as he enters. Touchwood Senior, who was present before the Kixes, is not noticed by them.

127. *Cud's foot*] a corruption of the oath 'By God's foot'.

128. *mark*] (1) 'target', with a suggestion of 'pudend' (Partridge, p. 152); (2) a punning on the coin whose value is named at l. 129.

129.1.] There is an obscurity of plot here. If Touchwood Senior exits with his brother, as the contrivance of the request for a licence suggests, he cannot overhear the Kixes' quarrel about fertility. This means that the maid later announces his miraculous 'water' on her own initiative, not prompted by him; though she is not the 'Susan' praised for plotting in v. iv. Alternatively, Touchwood Senior might linger long enough to overhear the quarrel, yet exit in time to send in the maid (l. 167). A suitable cue for such a delayed exit might be Sir Oliver's repeated 'Sweet wife, have patience' (l. 134: cf. l. 124). See Appendix V, p. 148, for William Gaskill's solution to the problem.

Sir Ol. Nay, pray thee, cease; I'll be at more cost yet, 130
Thou know'st we are rich enough.
Lady. All but in blessings,
And there the beggar goes beyond us. O, O, O!
To be seven years a wife and not a child,
O, not a child!
Sir Ol. Sweet wife, have patience.
Lady. Can any woman have a greater cut? 135
Sir Ol. I know 'tis great, but what of that, wife?
I cannot do withal; there's things making,
By thine own doctor's advice, at pothecaries':
I spare for nothing, wife, no, if the price
Were forty marks a spoonfull, 140
I'd give a thousand pound to purchase fruitfulness:
'Tis but 'bating so many good works
In the erecting of bridewells and spittlehouses,
And so fetch it up again; for having none,
I mean to make good deeds my children. 145
Lady. Give me but those good deeds, and I'll find children.
Sir Ol. Hang thee, thou hast had too many!

136. wife] *Q;* sweet wife *Dyce.* 137. withal] *Dyce;* with all *Q.*

---

135. *cut*] (1) ill-fate, setback; (2) 'pudend' (cf. Kökeritz, p. 133, n. 1).

137. *cannot do withal*] (1) 'cannot help it' (*O.E.D.*, 'do' 54); (2) 'cannot copulate', playing on 'do' (Partridge, p. 103): cf. Shakespeare, *Mer.V.*, III. iv. 72, G. Chapman, *May Day*, I. i. 138, J. Day, *Isle of Gulls*, III. i (*Works*, ed. Bullen, VIII. 73).

142–5.] i.e., 'in order to make up the expenditure for fruitfulness [cf. l. 141], I would need only to reduce my charities—the building of bridewells and spittle-houses; for, having no children, I mean to be remembered for my good deeds.' The whole passage also has a sexual innuendo, however; see next note.

143. *bridewells and spittlehouses*] Bridewell was originally a palace given to the city by Edward VI as a workhouse for the poor but had degenerated to a house of correction for prostitutes; 'spittle' was originally a lazar-house but had come to mean a hospital for venereal diseases. The sexual implications are also evident in 'good works' (l. 142: cf. l. 146) and 'erecting' (l. 143).

144. *fetch ... again*] (1) make up the expense (of fruitfulness, l. 141); (2) regain sexual potency; the common denominator being 'to recruit one's strength after illness' (Farmer and Henley, II. 386).

Lady. Thou liest, brevity!

Sir Ol. O, horrible! Dar'st thou call me 'brevity'?
Dar'st thou be so short with me?

Lady. Thou deservest worse.
Think but upon the goodly lands and livings 150
That's kept back through want on 't.

Sir Ol. Talk not on 't, pray thee;
Thou'lt make me play the woman and weep too.

Lady. 'Tis our dry barrenness puffs up Sir Walter;
None gets by your not-getting but that knight;
He's made by th' means, and fats his fortunes shortly 155
In a great dowry with a goldsmith's daughter.

Sir Ol. They may be all deceived; be but you patient, wife.

Lady. I have suff'red a long time.

Sir Ol. Suffer thy heart out,
A pox suffer thee!

Lady. Nay, thee, thou desertless slave!

Sir Ol. Come, come, I ha' done; you'll to the gossiping 160
Of Mistress Allwit's child?

Lady. Yes, to my much joy!
Everyone gets before me; there's my sister
Was married but at Barthol'mew-eve last,
And she can have two children at a birth:
O, one of them, one of them, would ha' serv'd my turn. 165

Sir Ol. Sorrow consume thee, thou art still crossing me,
And know'st my nature—

161. Mistress] *This ed.;* Mr *Q;* Master *Dyce.* 167. nature—] *This ed.;* nature. *Q.*

---

147. *brevity*] (1) stingy; (2) sexually inadequate: cf. III. iii. 112, 114–15. See also Intro., p. xxix, n.4.

149. *short*] (1) rude, curt; (2) punning on 'brevity', l. 147.

150–1.] i.e., certain property will come to a child of the Kixes (cf. ll. 186–8), which otherwise will go to Sir Walter. He has borrowed money on his expectations (cf. ll. 154–5, V. iv. 68–70).

152. *play the woman*] behave like a woman.

155. *by th' means*] i.e., by thy (Sir Oliver's) infertility.

160. *gossiping*] christening feast.

163. *Barthol'mew-eve*] 23 Aug. Since it is not yet 'Mid-Lent Sunday' (II. ii. 169), the twins were doubtless conceived before marriage.

Enter a Maid.

Maid. O, mistress!—
[*Aside*] Weeping or railing, that's our house harmony!
Lady. What say'st, Jug?
Maid. The sweetest news!
Lady. What is 't, wench?
Maid. Throw down your doctor's drugs, they're all 170
But heretics; I bring certain remedy
That has been taught and prov'd and never fail'd.
Sir Ol. O that, that, that, or nothing!
Maid. There's a gentleman,
I haply have his name too, that has got
Nine children by one water that he useth: 175
It never misses; they come so fast upon him,
He was fain to give it over.
Lady. His name, sweet Jug?
Maid. One Master Touchwood, a fine gentleman,
But run behindhand much with getting children.
Sir Ol. Is 't possible?
Maid. Why sir, he'll undertake, 180
Using that water, within fifteen year,
For all your wealth, to make you a poor man,
You shall so swarm with children.
Sir Ol. I'll venture that, i' faith.
Lady. That shall you, husband.
Maid. But I must tell you first,
He's very dear.
Sir Ol. No matter; what serves wealth for? 185

172. prov'd] *This ed.;* proued *Q.*

169, 177. *Jug*] a familiar substitute for 'Joan', applied as a common noun to maid-servants (*O.E.D.*).

174. *haply*] by chance; or possibly a contraction of 'happily'.

175. *water*] (1) medicine; (2) semen; the double entendre is frequent in Middleton: cf. *F. of L.*, v. i. 9–10, *F.Q.*, II. ii. 139, *R.G.*, IV. ii. 78, *C.* (Revels ed.), IV. iii. 185–6, etc. The analogy is an obvious one but may derive specifically from Aristotle, *De Generatione Animalium* (735a–735b). Fertility recipes are common in the herbals of the time.

Lady. True, sweet husband.
Sir Ol. There's land to come. Put case his water
Stands me in some five hundred pound a pint,
'Twill fetch a thousand, and a kersten soul.
Lady. And that's worth all, sweet husband.
Sir Ol. I'll about it. *Exeunt*.

[II. ii]

Enter ALLWIT.

Allw. I'll go bid gossips presently myself.
That's all the work I'll do; nor need I stir,
But that it is my pleasure to walk forth
And air myself a little: I am tied
To nothing in this business; what I do 5
Is merely recreation, not constraint.
Here's running to and fro—nurse upon nurse,
Three charwomen, besides maids and neighbours' children!
Fie, what a trouble have I rid my hands on;
It makes me sweat to think on 't.

Enter SIR WALTER WHOREHOUND.

Sir Walt. How now, Jack? 10
Allw. I am going to bid gossips for your worship's child, sir;
A goodly girl, i' faith! give you joy on her!
She looks as if she had two thousand pound
To her portion, and run away with a tailor;

186. *Sir Ol.*] *George; not in Q.* 189. *Lady*] *This ed.; not in Q.* And . . . it.] *This ed.;* I'le . . . it. / And . . . Husband. *Q;* And . . . husband: I'll about it. *Dyce;* I'll . . . it. / [*Lady Kix*.] And . . . husband. *George.* *Exeunt*.] *Dyce; Exit. Q.*

187. *Stands me in*] costs me: cf. III. iii. 89.
188. *kersten*] 'christened' (*O.E.D.*), though see note to III. ii. 2.

II. ii. 1. *bid*] summon.
gossips] strictly 'godparents', but extending to mean friends invited to the christening.
presently] immediately.
14. *run . . . tailor*] i.e., because her clothes are so fine.

A fine, plump, black-ey'd slut: under correction, sir, 15
I take delight to see her.—Nurse!

Enter Dry Nurse.

Dry Nur. Do you call, sir?
Allw. I call not you, I call the wet nurse hither. *Exit* [Dry Nurse].
Give me the wet nurse!—

Enter Wet Nurse [*with child*].

Ay, 'tis thou; come hither, come hither!
Let's see her once again; I cannot choose
But buss her thrice an hour.
Wet Nur. You may be proud on 't, sir; 20
'Tis the best piece of work that e'er you did.
Allw. Think'st thou so, nurse? What sayest to Wat and Nick?
Wet Nur. They're pretty children both, but here's a wench
Will be a knocker.
Allw. [*Dandling child.*] Pup!—Say'st thou me so?—Pup,
little countess!— 25
Faith, sir, I thank your worship for this girl
Ten thousand times and upward.
Sir Walt. I am glad
I have her for you, sir.
Allw. Here, take her in, nurse;
Wipe her, and give her spoon-meat.

16.1. *Enter* Dry Nurse.] *Dyce subs.; after* portion *l. 14 Q.* *Dry Nur.*] *This ed.; Nurse Q.* 17. *Exit* Dry Nurse.] *So Dyce; Exit. after l. 16 Q.* 18.1.] *So Dyce; at l. 17.1 Q.* 20, 23, 29. *Wet Nur.*] *This ed.; Nurse Q.*

16.1. *Dry Nurse*] There are three nurses: a dry nurse (the 'midwife' of II. iv. 0.1?) and a wet nurse for the baby, and a nurse for Mrs Allwit. See Allwit's complaint, l. 7, and *The Batchelars Banquet* (Appendix IV, p. 142).

20. *buss*] kiss.

24. *knocker*] (1) 'of striking physical appearance' (*O.E.D.*, 1c); (2) 'notable copulator' (Partridge, *Dictionary of Slang*, p. 462).

25. *Pup*] a favourite all-purpose exclamation with Middleton; cf. *M.W.M.M.*, II. vii. 95, *T.C.O.O.*, V. ii. 1, etc.

countess] Cf. Intro., p. xxxii, and III. ii. 89. A bawdy pun?

29. *give her spoon-meat*] i.e., wean her; spoon-meat being soft food taken with a spoon by invalids or infants.

Wet Nur. Wipe your mouth, sir.

Exit [with child].

Allw. And now about these gossips.

Sir Walt. Get but two; 30

I'll stand for one myself.

Allw. To your own child, sir?

Sir Walt. The better policy, it prevents suspicion;

'Tis good to play with rumour at all weapons.

Allw. Troth, I commend your care, sir; 'tis a thing

That I should ne'er have thought on.

Sir Walt. [*Aside*] The more slave! 35

When man turns base, out goes his soul's pure flame,

The fat of ease o'erthrows the eyes of shame.

Allw. I am studying who to get for godmother

Suitable to your worship. Now I ha' thought on 't.

Sir Walt. I'll ease you of that care, and please myself in 't.— 40

[*Aside*] My love, the goldsmith's daughter; if I send,

Her father will command her.—Davy Dahumma!

Enter DAVY.

Allw. I'll fit your worship then with a male partner.

Sir Walt. What is he?

Allw. A kind, proper gentleman,

Brother to Master Touchwood.

Sir Walt. I know Touchwood: 45

Has he a brother living?

Allw. A neat bachelor.

Sir Walt. Now we know him, we'll make shift with him:

37. o'erthrows] *Q;* o'ergrows *conj. Dyce.*

---

29. *Wipe your mouth*] i.e., 'you speak like a fool or slobberer', though *O.E.D.* gives only 'exonerate yourself'.

31.] Besides its obvious hypocrisy, this may be a reference to the puritan insistence on standing godparent to one's own child: cf. F. L. Lucas's note to Webster, *The Devil's Law Case*, IV. ii. 250–3:

> . . . thus are many [cuckolds] serv'd,
> That take care to get Gossips for those children,
> To which they might be Godfathers themselves,
> And yet be no arch-Puritans neither.

Despatch, the time draws near.—Come hither, Davy.
Exit [*with* DAVY].

Allw. In troth, I pity him, he ne'er stands still;
Poor knight, what pains he takes: sends this way one, 50
That way another; has not an hour's leisure:
I would not have thy toil for all thy pleasure.

Enter two Promoters.

[*Aside*] Ha, how now? What are these that stand so close
At the street-corner, pricking up their ears
And snuffing up their noses, like rich men's dogs 55
When the first course goes in? By the mass, promoters!
'Tis so, I hold my life; and planted there
To arrest the dead corpse of poor calves and sheep,
Like ravenous creditors, that will not suffer
The bodies of their poor departed debtors 60
To go to th' grave, but e'en in death to vex
And stay the corpse with bills of Middlesex.
This Lent will fat the whoresons up with sweetbreads,
And lard their whores with lamb-stones; what their golls
Can clutch goes presently to their Molls and Dolls: 65
The bawds will be so fat with what they earn,
Their chins will hang like udders by Easter-eve

56. *By the mass*] 'asseverations like *by the mass* and *Birlady* survived the Reformation and still came naturally to Protestant lips' (F. P. Wilson, intro. to *The Batchelars Banquet*, 1929, p. xix).

58, 62. *corpse*] The original 'corps' was a plural form (cf. *F. of L.*, II. iv. 39), but 'corpses' would break the metre.

62. *bills of Middlesex*] a dubious method of extending the jurisdiction of the King's Bench, by arresting the defendant to answer a fictitious trespass in Middlesex (where juries were notoriously ruthless: cf. *T.C.O.O.*, IV. v. 178–80) and *also* to answer whatever the real charge was in the King's Bench. If the defendant was not actually in Middlesex, the bill could then be extended to cover all other areas by a writ of *latitat* (see *Shakespeare's England*, 1916, I. 391). Allwit pushes the device to its grotesque conclusion.

63–4. *sweetbreads ... lamb-stones*] the pancreas and testicles of a lamb, regarded as aphrodisiac; there is a suitor called 'Lambstone' in *N.W.N.H.*

64. *golls*] canting slang for hands.

67. *chins*] A double chin was considered the distinguishing mark of a

And, being strok'd, will give the milk of witches.
How did the mongrels hear my wife lies in?
Well, I may baffle 'em gallantly. [*To them*] By your favour, gentlemen, 70
I am a stranger both unto the city
And to her carnal strictness.

1 Prom. Good; your will, sir?

Allw. Pray, tell me where one dwells that kills this Lent?

1 Prom. How, kills? [*Aside to his fellow*] Come hither, Dick; a bird, a bird!

2 Prom. [*To Allwit*] What is 't that you would have?

Allw. Faith, any flesh;
But I long especially for veal and green-sauce. 76

1 Prom. [*Aside*] Green-goose, you shall be sauc'd.

Allw. I have half a scornful stomach,
No fish will be admitted.

1 Prom. Not this Lent, sir?

Allw. Lent? What cares colon here for Lent?

1 Prom. You say well, sir:
Good reason that the colon of a gentleman, 80
As you were lately pleas'd to term your worship's, sir,

81. worship's] *Dyce;* worship *Q.*

---

bawd: cf. J. Taylor, 'A Bawd', *Works* (1630), p. 98, *B.B.* (Bullen, VIII. 12): 'Her fat-sagg chin hanging down like a cow's udder'.

68. *milk of witches*] See G. B. Harrison, *The Elizabethan Journals* (1938), I. 224–6, for an account of a witch accused of having a familiar spirit in the form of a chicken which sucked on her chin.

70. *baffle*] publicly disgrace; cf. III. i. 56.

76. *for veal and green-sauce*] metaphorically 'to get what one deserves', hence 'to be cheated': Allwit uses the provocative connotation deliberately, and the promoters rise to it: see next note. Green-sauce was an antidote to raw or over-young meat (for recipes see Herford and Simpson's note to Jonson, *The Gypsies Metamorphosed*, l. 1083): cf. the proverb 'sweet meat will have sour sauce', Cotgrave, *Veau*: '*Il luy a fait manger des poids verds au veau.* He hath cheated him . . . so that he cannot perceive it.'

77. *Green-goose . . . sauc'd*] Cf. note to I. i. 80–1. 'Green-goose', literally 'gosling', here means 'fool'; 'sauc'd' means 'made to pay dearly' (*O.E.D.*, *vb*, 4, citing Shakespeare, *Wiv.*, IV. iii. 9).

79. *colon*] often used jocularly for appetite, hunger: cf. *M.D.B.W.*, III. ii.

Should be fulfill'd with answerable food,
To sharpen blood, delight health, and tickle nature.
Were you directed hither to this street, sir?

Allw. That I was, ay, marry.

2 Prom. And the butcher, belike, 85
Should kill and sell close in some upper room?

Allw. Some apple-loft, as I take it, or a coal-house;
I know not which, i' faith.

2 Prom. Either will serve:
This butcher shall kiss Newgate, 'less he turn up
The bottom of the pocket of his apron. 90
You go to seek him?

Allw. Where you shall not find him:
I'll buy, walk by your noses with my flesh,
Sheep-biting mongrels, hand-basket freebooters!
My wife lies in—a foutra for promoters. *Exit.*

1 Prom. That shall not serve your turn.—What a rogue's this! 95
How cunningly he came over us.

Enter a Man *with meat in a basket.*

88–90. Either . . . apron.] *So Q; marked Aside Dyce.*

104, Jonson, *Staple of News*, V. v. 45, Massinger, *The Picture* (ed. 1839, p. 219).

82. *fulfill'd*] satisfied. *answerable*] suitable.

86–7.] Cf. J. Taylor, 'Iacke-a-Lent', *Works* (1630), p. 116: 'Some [butchers] of the inferior sort doe scout into Stables, Priuies, Sellers, Sir *Francis Drake's* Ship at Detford, my Lord Mayor's Barge, & diuers secret and unsuspected places, & there they make priuate shambles . . . to the abuse of *Lent*, the deceiuing of the Informers, & the great griefe of euery zealous Fishmonger.'

86. *close*] clandestinely.

89. *kiss Newgate*] go to prison: cf. Tilley, C416: 'to kiss the Clink'. Newgate was the chief London prison. In the pamphlet *Bartholomew Fair* (1641) the phrase 'though they kisse Newgate for it' recurs like a refrain.

89–90. *turn up . . . pocket*] i.e., pays a bribe.

93. *hand-basket freebooters*] i.e., pirates who ransack handbaskets.

94. *My wife lies in*] Cf. J. Taylor, 'Iacke-a-Lent', *Works* (1889), p. 130: '[none allowed meat in Lent] except such as are sicke, and women with childe (for all which there is a lawfull toleration)': cf. ll. 136–7. See Intro., p. xxx.

foutra] obscene oath (French 'foutre').

2 Prom. Hush 't, stand close!

Man. I have 'scap'd well thus far; they say the knaves
Are wondrous hot and busy.

1 Prom. By your leave, sir,
We must see what you have under your cloak there.

Man. Have! I have nothing.

1 Prom. No? Do you tell us that? 100
What makes this lump stick out then? We must see, sir.

Man. What will you see, sir? A pair of sheets and two
Of my wife's foul smocks going to the washers?

2 Prom. O, we love that sight well! You cannot please us better.
[*Takes meat out of basket.*]
What, do you gull us? Call you these shirts and smocks? 105

Man. Now, a pox choke you!
You have cozen'd me and five of my wife's kindred
Of a good dinner; we must make it up now
With herrings and milk-pottage. *Exit.*

1 Prom. 'Tis all veal.

2 Prom. All veal? Pox, the worse luck! I promis'd faithfully 110
To send this morning a fat quarter of lamb
To a kind gentlewoman in Turnbull Street
That longs; and how I'm cross'd!

1 Prom. Let's share this, and see what hap comes next then.

Enter another [Man] *with a basket.*

2 Prom. Agreed. Stand close again: another booty. 115
What's he?

1 Prom. Sir, by your favour.

2 Man. Meaning me, sir?

97–8.] *So Q; marked Aside Wall.* 113. how] *Q;* now *conj. Wall.* 114.1.] *So Q; at l. 115.1 Dyce.* 116, 118. *2 Man.*] *This ed.; Man Q; Second Man. Wall.*

112. *Turnbull Street*] a corruption of Turnmill street, a noted haunt of prostitutes near Clerkenwell Green; called 'Townbull street' in *N.W.N.H.*, II. i. 239. See Sugden, p. 533.

113. *longs*] i.e., with the appetite of pregnancy.
cross'd] thwarted.

1 Prom. Good Master Oliver? Cry thee mercy, i' faith!
What hast thou there?

2 Man. A rack of mutton, sir,
And half a lamb; you know my mistress's diet.

1 Prom. Go, go, we see thee not; away, keep close!— 120
[*To 2 Promoter*] Heart, let him pass! Thou'lt never have the wit
To know our benefactors. [*Exit 2* Man.]

2 Prom. I have forgot him.

1 Prom. 'Tis Master Beggarland's man, the wealthy merchant
That is in fee with us.

2 Prom. Now I have a feeling of him.

1 Prom. You know he purchas'd the whole Lent together, 125
Gave us ten groats a-piece on Ash Wednesday.

2 Prom. True, true.

Enter a [Country] Wench *with a basket and a child in it under a loin of mutton.*

1 Prom. A wench!

2 Prom. Why, then, stand close indeed.

C. Wench. [*Aside*] Women had need of wit, if they'll shift here,
And she that hath wit may shift anywhere.

1 Prom. Look, look! Poor fool, she has left the rump uncover'd too, 130
More to betray her. This is like a murd'rer

122. *Exit 2* Man.] *So Wall; Exit Man. after l. 123 Dyce.* 127.1–2.] *So Q; after* indeed *Dyce.*

118. *rack*] neck, considered a delicacy suitable for invalids: cf. *Y.F.G.*, I. i. 325.

124. *in fee*] 'in league', having paid them a bribe (*O.E.D.*, *sb.*², 5b).

126. *Ash Wednesday*] the first day of Lent, on 21 February in 1613.

127.1. basket] A handbasket was particularly associated with prostitutes: cf. Marston, *The Malcontent*, ed. M. L. Wine (1964), v. vi. 97–9, Chapman, *Monsieur D'Olive*, I. i. 343–4: 'a prettie well pac'd chambermaid ... if she grow full or fulsome, give her but sixpence to buy her a handbasket, and send her the way of all flesh'.

128, 129. *shift*] (1) 'to make a living, succeed' (*O.E.D.*, *vb*, 5); (2) 'to live by fraud' (*O.E.D.*, *vb*, 6); (3) 'to palm off something on someone' (*O.E.D.*, *vb*, 12d); (4) 'to shift a chemise' (Partridge, 186–7)?

That will outface the deed with a bloody band.
2 Prom. What time of the year is 't, sister?
C. Wench. O, sweet gentlemen,
I am a poor servant, let me go.
1 Prom. You shall, wench,
But this must stay with us.
C. Wench. O, you undo me, sir! 135
'Tis for a wealthy gentlewoman that takes physic, sir;
The doctor does allow my mistress mutton.
O, as you tender the dear life of a gentlewoman!
I'll bring my master to you; he shall show you
A true authority from the higher powers, 140
And I'll run every foot.
2 Prom. Well, leave your basket then,
And run and spare not.
C. Wench. Will you swear then to me
To keep it till I come?
1 Prom. Now by this light I will.
C. Wench. What say you, gentleman?
2 Prom. What a strange wench 'tis!
Would we might perish else.
C. Wench. Nay, then I run sir. 145
[*Leaves the basket and*] *exit*.
1 Prom. And ne'er return I hope.
2 Prom. A politic baggage!
She makes us swear to keep it: I prithee
Look what market she hath made.
1 Prom. *Imprimis*, sir,
A good fat loin of mutton. What comes next

145.1. *Leaves . . . and*] *Dyce*.

132. *band*] possibly collar but more probably cuff: cf. *M.W.M.M.*, III. ii. 109: 'How comes your band bloody, sir?' and *C.* (Revels ed.), V. iii. 95.

136.] See note to l. 94.

146. *politic*] crafty: cf. III. i. 20, V. i. 167.

148. *market*] purchase.

Imprimis] word introducing the first of a number of items: cf. V. i. 96.

Under this cloth? Now for a quarter of lamb. 150

2 Prom. Now for a shoulder of mutton.

1 Prom. Done!

2 Prom. Why, done, sir!

1 Prom. By the mass, I feel I have lost;

'Tis of more weight, i' faith.

2 Prom. Some loin of veal?

1 Prom. No, faith, here's a lamb's head, I feel that plainly;

Why, I'll yet win my wager. [*Takes out child.*]

2 Prom. Ha?

1 Prom. 'Swounds, what's here?

2 Prom. A child!

1 Prom. A pox of all dissembling cunning whores! 156

2 Prom. Here's an unlucky breakfast!

1 Prom. What shall 's do?

2 Prom. The quean made us swear to keep it too.

1 Prom. We might leave it else.

2 Prom. Villainous strange!

Life, had she none to gull but poor promoters 160

That watch hard for a living?

1 Prom. Half our gettings

Must run in sugar-sops and nurses' wages now,

Besides many a pound of soap and tallow;

We have need to get loins of mutton still,

To save suet to change for candles. 165

2 Prom. Nothing mads me but this was a lamb's head with you;

You felt it! She has made calves' heads of us.

1 Prom. Prithee, no more on 't. There's time to get it up;

151. Now] *Wall;* Not *Q;* Not, *Dyce;* No, *Ellis.* 155. I'll] *Dyce; not in Q.*
S.D.] *So this ed.; Taking out a child. at l. 154.1 Dyce.*

---

158. *quean*] whore.

161. *watch*] stay up late.

162. *sugar-sops*] steeped slices of bread, sweetened and perhaps spiced.

165. *candles*] necessary because the baby will require attention at night: cf. Appendix IV, no. 3. The cheaper candles were of 'tallow' (l. 163), made from 'suet' or animal fat.

168. *get it up*] make up the requisite money.

It is not come to Mid-Lent Sunday yet.

2 Prom. I am so angry, I'll watch no more today. 170

1 Prom. Faith, nor I neither.

2 Prom. Why then, I'll make a motion.

1 Prom. Well, what is 't?

2 Prom. Let's e'en go to the Checker

At Queenhive, and roast the loin of mutton

Till young flood; then send the child to Brainford. [*Exeunt.*]

[II. iii]

Enter ALLWIT *in one of Sir Walter's suits and* DAVY *trussing him.*

Allw. 'Tis a busy day at our house, Davy.

Davy. Always the kurs'ning-day, sir.

Allw. Truss, truss me, Davy.

Davy. [*Aside*] No matter and you were hang'd, sir.

Allw. How does

This suit fit me, Davy?

Davy. Excellent neatly;

---

169. *Mid-Lent Sunday*] the 4th Sunday in Lent, 17 March in 1613.

172. *the Checker*] an inn with the sign of a chessboard; with perhaps a pun on *check*, 'set back', or on the short form of *exchequer*. It is not in Stow's or Taylor's lists of Elizabethan inns, though Stow does mention one a little further east on Dowgate (p. 208).

173. *Queenhive*] a frequent spelling of Queenhithe, a large quay just west of Southwark Bridge where most of the Lenten fish was landed (see Johannsen, *Religion and Superstition in the Works of Jonson and Middleton*, p. 54). In Webster and Dekker's *Westward Ho!* (IV. i) Birdlime says he will go to Queenhithe for a waterman to carry him to Brainford (cf. l. 174).

174. *young flood*] i.e., when the tide begins to flow up river: cf. *R.G.*, II. i. 364–5, *N.W.N.H.*, II. ii. 81.

Brainford] the common rendering of Brentford, a suburb up the Thames on the north bank opposite Kew: cf. V. iv. 87. Children were frequently put out to nurse there: cf. *M.T.*, II. iii. 184–6.

II. iii. 0.2. trussing] i.e., tying the 'points' or tagged laces which fastened the breeches to the doublet. In l. 3 Davy plays on a secondary meaning, 'to hang someone' (*O.E.D.*, 4).

2. *kurs'ning*] metathesized form of 'christening'.

3. *No matter and*] it would not matter if.

My master's things were ever fit for you, sir, 5
E'en to a hair, you know.

Allw. Thou hast hit it right, Davy,
We ever jump'd in one this ten years, Davy,
So well said.

Enter a Servant *with a box.*

What art thou?

Ser. Your comfit-maker's man, sir.

Allw. O, sweet youth, in to the nurse quick, quick,
'Tis time, i' faith; your mistress will be here? 10

Ser. She was setting forth, sir. [*Exit.*]

Enter two Puritans.

Allw. Here comes our gossips now;
O, I shall have such kissing work today!—
Sweet Mistress Underman, welcome, i' faith.

1 Pur. Give you joy of your fine girl, sir:
Grant that her education may be pure 15
And become one of the faithful.

Allw. Thanks to your
Sisterly wishes, Mistress Underman.

2 Pur. Are any of the brethren's wives yet come?

Allw. There are some wives within, and some at home.

1 Pur. Verily, thanks, sir. *Exeunt* [Puritans].

Allw. Verily, you are an ass, forsooth: 20
I must fit all these times, or there's no music.

8.1.] *So Dyce; at l. 7.1 Q.* 11.1. *Enter two* Puritans.] *So Q; at l. 12.1 Dyce.* 17. Mistress] *Dyce;* Mr *Q.* 20. S.D.] *Dyce; Exit Q.*

6. *to a hair*] See note to I. i. 188; also punning on 'heir'?

7. *jump'd in one*] 'agreed perfectly', but with a sexual entendre: cf. Anon., *The Welsh Embassadour* (ed. 1920), p. 63, l. 2017: 'dow and I jump into one hole'. It seems to be hinted that Allwit may be 'cuckolding' Sir Walter: cf. I. ii. 94–5, IV. i. 224–5, V. i. 156.

8. *comfit*] a sweetmeat made of fruit and preserved sugar.

16. *become*] suit.

21. *fit . . . times*] (1) 'harmonize with all these tunes', i.e., conform with the conversational habits of the visitors; (2) possibly the image is from

Enter two Gossips.

Here comes a friendly and familiar pair:
Now I like these wenches well.

1 Goss. How dost, sirrah?

Allw. Faith, well, I thank you, neighbour, and how dost thou?

2 Goss. Want nothing but such getting, sir, as thine. 25

Allw. My gettings, wench? They are poor.

1 Goss. Fie, that thou'lt say so!
Th' hast as fine children as a man can get.

Davy. [*Aside*] Ay, as a man can get, and that's my master.

Allw. They are pretty foolish things, put to making
In minutes; I ne'er stand long about 'em. 30
Will you walk in, wenches? [*Exeunt* Gossips.]

Enter TOUCHWOOD JUNIOR *and* MOLL.

Touch. Jun. The happiest meeting that our souls could wish for!
Here's the ring ready; I am beholding
Unto your father's haste, 'has kept his hour.

Moll. He never kept it better.

Enter SIR WALTER WHOREHOUND.

Touch. Jun. Back, be silent. 35

Sir Walt. Mistress and partner, I will put you both
Into one cup. [*Drinks their health.*]

Davy. [*Aside*] Into one cup! Most proper:
A fitting compliment for a goldsmith's daughter.

Allw. Yes, sir, that's he must be your worship's partner
In this day's business, Master Touchwood's brother. 40

Sir Walt. I embrace your acquaintance, sir.

Touch. Jun. It vows your service, sir.

Sir Walt. It's near high time. Come, Master Allwit.

21.1.] *So Q; at l. 22.1 Dyce.*

---

fencing: cf. G. Silver, *Paradoxes of Defence* (1599), p. 27: 'The names and numbers of times appertaining vnto fight both true and false'.

37. *Into one cup*] i.e., he pledges both in the one drink.

42. *high time*] (1) the appropriate time; (2) possibly 'noon' (*O.E.D.*,

Allw. Ready, sir.
Sir Walt. Will 't please you walk?
Touch. Jun. Sir, I obey your time. *Exeunt.*

[II. iv]

Enter Midwife *with the child*, [MAUDLINE, *the two* Puritans,] *and the* [*five*] Gossips *to the kurs'ning*. [*Exit* Midwife *with the child*.]

1 Goss. [*Offering precedence*] Good Mistress Yellowhammer.
Maudl. In faith, I will not.
1 Goss. Indeed, it shall be yours.
Maudl. I have sworn, i' faith.
1 Goss. I'll stand still then.
Maudl. So will you let the child
Go without company, and make me forsworn.
1 Goss. You are such another creature.
[*Exeunt* 1 Gossip *and* MAUDLINE.]
2 Goss. Before me? 5
I pray come down a little.
3 Goss. Not a whit;
I hope I know my place.
2 Goss. Your place? Great wonder, sure!
Are you any better than a comfit-maker's wife?

43. S.D.] *Dyce; Exit Q.*

'high' 11, citing G. Pooley, *Phil. Trans.* (1693), XVII. 673: 'the High time of the Day, or Twelve a Clock').

43. *obey your time*] Cf. note to l. 21.

II. iv. 5. *You . . . creature*] proverbial 'tu quoque' retort: cf. Tilley, A250, *Wid.*, I. ii. 69.

Before me?] The 2nd Gossip is an apothecary's wife: cf. Tilley, A277: 'As proud as an apothecary'. See Intro., p. xxxiii, for the quarrel between apothecaries and grocers.

6. *come down*] 'be socially humbler' (*O.E.D.*, *vb*, 56e): the 2nd Gossip objects because the 3rd Gossip is taking precedence of her by exiting first.

8. *comfit-maker's wife*] presumably the confectioner's wife whose arrival is heralded at II. iii. 10. Most probably her shop would be in Bucklersbury, just south of Cheapside, which Stow says was 'possessed of grocers and apothecaries' (see note to III. ii. 70).

3 Goss. And that's as good at all times as a pothecary's.

2 Goss. Ye lie! Yet I forbear you too. [*Exeunt* 2 *and* 3 Gossips.]

1 Pur. Come, sweet sister; 10

We go in unity, and show the fruits of peace,

Like children of the spirit.

2 Pur. I love lowliness. [*Exeunt* Puritans.]

4 Goss. True, so say I: though they strive more,

There comes as proud behind as goes before.

5 Goss. Every inch, i' faith. *Exeunt.* 15

15. S.D.] *Dyce; Exit Q.*

14.] proverbial: cf. Tilley, C536. The meaning of *proud* as 'sexually excited' is suggested by the next line, but see Intro., p. xxix, n.4, for an alternative interpretation.

Act III

[III. i]

Enter TOUCHWOOD JUNIOR *and a* Parson.

Touch. Jun. O sir, if ever you felt the force of love,
Pity it in me!

Par. Yes, though I ne'er was married, sir,
I have felt the force of love from good men's daughters,
And some that will be maids yet three years hence.
Have you got a licence?

Touch. Jun. Here, 'tis ready, sir. 5

Par. That's well.

Touch. Jun. The ring and all things perfect.
She'll steal hither.

Par. She shall be welcome, sir;
I'll not be long a-clapping you together.

Enter MOLL *and* TOUCHWOOD SENIOR.

Touch. Jun. O, here she's come, sir.

Par. What's he?

Touch. Jun. My honest brother.

Touch. Sen. Quick, make haste, sirs!

Moll. You must despatch with all
The speed you can, for I shall be miss'd straight; 11
I made hard shift for this small time I have.

Par. Then I'll not linger.

Act III] *Dyce; Actus Tertius. Q.*

3–4.] Cf. the innuendo at II. i. 72–3.

13–17.] The Parson continues this doggerel at V. iv. 34 exactly where he left off. There is a similar doggerel marriage ceremony in *T.C.O.O.*, IV. i. 1–8, and a serious verse betrothal in *S.G.*, IV. i. 65 ff.

Place that ring upon her finger:
This the finger plays the part, 15
Whose master-vein shoots from the heart.
[*Touchwood Junior puts ring on Moll's finger.*]
Now join hands—

Enter YELLOWHAMMER *and* SIR WALTER.

Yell. Which I will sever,
And so ne'er again meet never!
Moll. O, we are betray'd.
Touch. Jun. Hard fate!
Sir Walt. I am struck with wonder!
Yell. Was this the politic fetch, thou mystical baggage, 20
Thou disobedient strumpet! [*To Sir Walter*] And were you
So wise to send for her to such an end?
Sir Walt. Now I disclaim the end; you'll make me mad.
Yell. [*To Touchwood Junior*] And what are you, sir?
Touch. Jun. And you cannot see
With those two glasses, put on a pair more. 25
Yell. I dream'd of anger still!—Here, take your ring, sir.
[*Takes ring off Moll's finger.*]
Ha, this? Life, 'tis the same! Abominable!
Did not I sell this ring?
Touch. Jun. I think you did;
You received money for 't.
Yell. Heart, hark you, knight;
Here's no inconscionable villainy! 30
Set me a-work to make the wedding-ring,

16.1.] *So Dyce at l. 14.1.* 17. hands—] *Dyce;* Hands. *Q.* 18. ne'er] *Q;* near *conj. George.* 21. were] *Q;* were't *conj. George.* you] *Dyce subs.; not in Q.* 22. end?] *Dyce;* end, *Q.*

15–16.] The third finger of the left hand was popularly supposed to be connected directly with the 'master-vein' to the heart: see W. Jones, *Finger-Ring Lore* (1877), pp. 291–2.

20. *politic fetch*] cunning trick.

mystical] secret, unavowed, concealed: cf. *S.M.T.*, II. ii. 993: 'Confess, thou mystical panderess!'

And come with an intent to steal my daughter:
Did ever runaway match it?

Sir Walt. [*To Touchwood Senior*] 'This your brother, sir?

Touch. Sen. He can tell that as well as I.

Yell. The very posy mocks me to my face: 35
'Love that's wise,
Blinds parents' eyes'!
I thank your wisdom, sir, for blinding of us;
We have good hope to recover our sight shortly;
In the meantime I will lock up this baggage 40
As carefully as my gold: she shall see
As little sun, if a close room or so
Can keep her from the light on 't.

Moll. O, sweet father,
For love's sake, pity me!

Yell. Away!

Moll. [*To Touchwood Junior*] Farewell, sir,
All content bless thee, and take this for comfort: 45
Though violence keep me, thou canst lose me never,
I am ever thine although we part for ever.

Yell. Ay, we shall part you, minx. *Exit* [*with* MOLL].

Sir Walt. [*To Touchwood Junior*] Your acquaintance, sir,
Came very lately, yet it came too soon;
I must hereafter know you for no friend, 50
But one that I must shun like pestilence
Or the disease of lust.

Touch. Jun. Like enough, sir;
You ha' ta'en me at the worst time for words
That e'er ye pick'd out: faith, do not wrong me, sir.
Exit [*with* Parson].

Touch. Sen. Look after him, and spare not: there he walks 55

54. e'er] *Q;* ere *George.* pick'd] *Q;* pick't 'em *George.*

40–3. *In . . . on 't.*] Cf. the long complaint against usurers imprisoning gold in *F.H.T.* (Bullen, VIII. 104–8).

42. *close*] confined, shut up.

55. *Look after*] i.e., 'watch out for' (*O.E.D.*, *vb*, 12e, g); Touchwood Senior is warning Sir Walter.

That never yet received baffling: you're blest
More than e'er I knew; go, take your rest. *Exit.*
Sir Walt. I pardon you, you are both losers. *Exit.*

[III. ii]

A bed thrust out upon the stage, ALLWIT'*s Wife in it.*
Enter all the Gossips[, *the* Puritans, MAUDLINE,
LADY KIX, *and* Dry Nurse *with child*].

1 Goss. How is 't, woman? We have brought you home
A kersen soul.
Mrs Allw. Ay, I thank your pains.
1 Pur. And, verily, well kursen'd, i' the right way,
Without idolatry or superstition,
After the pure manner of Amsterdam. 5
Mrs Allw. Sit down, good neighbours.—Nurse!
Nur. At hand, forsooth.
Mrs Allw. Look they have all low stools.
Nur. They have, forsooth.
2 Goss. Bring the child hither, nurse.—How say you now, gossip,
Is 't not a chopping girl? So like the father.
3 Goss. As if it had been spit out of his mouth! 10
Ey'd, nos'd, and brow'd as like a girl can be,
Only indeed it has the mother's mouth.

III. ii. 3 (*and rest of scene*). *1 Pur.*] *This ed.; Pur. Q.* 6. *Nur.*] *So this ed. passim; Nurse. Q.* 11. like] *Q;* like as *Dyce.*

---

56. *baffling*] public disgrace (cf. II. ii. 70), a jousting term for the humiliation of an unworthy knight, which looks forward to the duel in IV. iv.
58.] Cf. Tilley, L458: 'Give losers leave to speak'; *T.C.O.O.*, IV. iv. 171.

III. ii. 0.1.] For staging see Intro., p. lxiii. Cf. T. Heywood, *The Silver Age*, III. i. 0.1, '*Enter Semele drawn out in her bed*', *A Woman Killed with Kindness* (Revels ed.), xvii. 38.1: '*Enter* ANNE *in her bed.*'
2. *kersen*] (1) christened; (2) play on 'cursed'?
5. *Amsterdam*] a notable centre of puritanism.
9. *chopping*] vigorous, strapping: cf. *N.W.N.H.*, I. i. 246.
10. *spit . . . mouth*] Cf. Tilley, M1246, *F. of L.*, III. ii. 17.

2 Goss. The mother's mouth up and down, up and down!
3 Goss. 'Tis a large child; she's but a little woman!
1 Pur. No, believe me, 15
A very spiny creature, but all heart;
Well mettled, like the faithful, to endure
Her tribulation here and raise up seed.
2 Goss. She had a sore labour on 't, I warrant you;
You can tell, neighbour.
3 Goss. O, she had great speed; 20
We were afraid once, but she made us all
Have joyful hearts again; 'tis a good soul, i' faith;
The midwife found her a most cheerful daughter.
1 Pur. 'Tis the spirit; the sisters are all like her.

Enter SIR WALTER *with two spoons and plate, and* ALLWIT.

2 Goss. O, here comes the chief gossip, neighbours. 25
[*Exit* Nurse *with child.*]
Sir Walt. The fatness of your wishes to you all, ladies.
3 Goss. O dear, sweet gentleman, what fine words he has:
'The fatness of our wishes'!
2 Goss. Calls us all 'ladies'!
4 Goss. I promise you, a fine gentleman and a courteous.
2 Goss. Methinks her husband shows like a clown to him. 30
3 Goss. I would not care what clown my husband were too,
So I had such fine children.
2 Goss. She's all fine children, gossip.
3 Goss. Ay, and see how fast they come.
1 Pur. Children are blessings,

---

13. *up and down*] (1) completely, entirely: cf. J. Day, *Law Tricks* (*Works*, ed. Bullen, II. 77): 'here's your own nose & thick kissing lip, up & downe'; (2) bawdy?

16. *spiny*] spare, lean: cf. *M.W.M.M.*, III. ii. 7.

17. *mettled*] (1) full of courage and spirit; (2) 'half-drunk' (*O.E.D.*, *a*, 2)? The First Puritan gets totally drunk later in the scene, so perhaps this aptitude is indicated early.

20. *she . . . speed*] i.e., she had good fortune.

26. *fatness*] 'the richest, best part' (*O.E.D.*, 4).

32. *She's*] She has.

If they be got with zeal by the brethren,
As I have five at home.

Sir Walt. [*To Mrs Allwit*] The worst is past, 35
I hope now, gossip.

Mrs Allw. So I hope too, good sir.

Allw. [*Aside*] Why, then, so hope I too for company;
I have nothing to do else.

Sir Walt. [*Giving cup and spoons*] A poor remembrance, lady,
To the love of the babe; I pray, accept of it.

Mrs Allw. O, you are at too much charge, sir!

2 Goss. Look, look! 40
What has he given her? What is 't, gossip?

3 Goss. Now, by my faith, a fair high standing-cup
And two great 'postle-spoons, one of them gilt.

1 Pur. Sure that was Judas then with the red beard.

2 Pur. I would not feed my daughter with that spoon 45
For all the world, for fear of colouring her hair;
Red hair the brethren like not, it consumes them much:
'Tis not the sisters' colour.

Enter Nurse *with comfits and wine.*

Allw. Well said, nurse;
About, about with them amongst the gossips!—

42–3. *standing-cup . . . 'postle-spoons*] a cup with a base or legs for standing; silver spoons with the figure of an apostle on the handle: the usual christening gifts at this time (see *Shakespeare's England*, 1932, II. 143); cf. note to l. 77. There is perhaps some sexual symbolism intended: cf. *T.C.O.O.*, II. i. 373–4: 'a good high standing cup will please a widow above all other pieces', *F. of L.*, I. iii. 147.

44.] Judas was traditionally represented as red-bearded (cf. Shakespeare, *AYL.*, III. iv. 7), and red hair was associated with lechery; cf. *F. of L.*, IV. iii. 116, V. i. 12–15, 74–80. See John Withals, *A Short Dictionarie in Latine and English* (1586), L7: 'Thou shalt knowe a lewde fellowe by his beard, eyther redde or yellowe', Kyd, *Spanish Tragedy*, 4th Addition, l. 137 (Revels ed., p. 132).

47–8. *Red . . . colour*] Cf. the puritan Mrs Glister's complaints in *F. of L.*, V. i. 12–15. Note that the Welsh Gentlewoman has red hair (I. i. 41).

47. *consumes*] i.e., 'eats them up' (with indignation, envy, etc.).

48. *Well said*] well done: cf. *H.E.*, Ent. vii, l. 9, Heywood, *Woman Killed with Kindness*, viii. 123 (Revels ed.).

[*Aside*] Now out comes all the tassell'd handkerchers, 50
They are spread abroad between their knees already;
Now in goes the long fingers that are wash'd
Some thrice a day in urine; my wife uses it.
Now we shall have such pocketing: see how
They lurch at the lower end!

1 Pur. Come hither, nurse. 55

Allw. [*Aside*] Again? She has taken twice already.

1 Pur. I had forgot a sister's child that's sick. [*Taking comfits*]

Allw. [*Aside*] A pox! It seems your purity loves sweet things well
That puts in thrice together. Had this been
All my cost now, I had been beggar'd; 60
These women have no consciences at sweetmeats,
Where'er they come; see and they have not cull'd out
All the long plums too, they have left nothing here
But short wriggle-tail comfits, not worth mouthing:
No mar'l I heard a citizen complain once 65

50–4. *tassell'd handkerchers . . . pocketing*] Cf. *Wit.*, I. ii. 216–17, 222, and *W.B.W.*, III. i. 267–8:

I'll step out and fetch two handkerchers
To pocket up some sweetmeats ...

Cf. J. Taylor, 'The Prayse of Cleane Linen', *Works* (1630), p. 168:

At Christening-banquets & at funerals,
At Weddings (Comfit-makers festivals)
A *Handkerchiefe* doth filch most manifold,
And shake & steale as much as it can hold.

In *R.G.*, V. i. 41, Jack Dapper swears by the tassels of his handkerchief.

52–3. *wash'd . . . urine*] i.e., as a cosmetic: cf. Jean Liebaut, *Trois Livres de l'Embellissement et Ornement du Corps Humain* (1582), p. 337: 'Lavez vos mains avec votre vrine ...', W. Warde, *Secretes of Alexis of Piedmont* (1580), I, fol. 26: dog's piss as a remedy for warts on the hand.

55. *lurch*] cheat (a term taken from bowling): cf. *B.B.* (Bullen, VIII. 41, 42).

lower end] i.e., the end of the room furthest from the host; but with a bawdy implication.

61–4.] Cf. *W.B.W.*, III. ii. 75–7, where the sexual innuendo is clearer because the woman referred to is an adulteress:

These women, when they come to sweet things once,
They forget all their friends, they grow so greedy,
Nay, oftentimes their husbands.

63. *plums*] i.e. sugar plums.

65. *mar'l*] marvel.

That his wife's belly only broke his back;
Mine had been all in fitters seven years since,
But for this worthy knight,
That with a prop upholds my wife and me,
And all my estate buried in Bucklersbury. 70

Mrs Allw. [*Pledges them*] Here, Mistress Yellowhammer and neighbours,
To you all that have taken pains with me,
All the good wives at once! [*Nurse takes round wine.*]

1 Pur. I'll answer for them.
They wish all health and strength, and that you may
Courageously go forward, to perform 75
The like and many such, like a true sister,
With motherly bearing. [*Drinks.*]

Allw. [*Aside*] Now the cups troll about
To wet the gossips' whistles. It pours down, i' faith;
They never think of payment.

1 Pur. Fill again, nurse. [*Drinks.*]

Allw. [*Aside*] Now, bless thee, two at once! I'll stay no longer; 80
It would kill me and if I paid for 't.—
[*To Sir Walter*] Will it please you to walk down and leave the women?

Sir Walt. With all my heart, Jack.

Allw. Troth, I cannot blame you.

Sir Walt. Sit you all merry, ladies.

---

66. *belly . . . broke his back*] (1) her greed made him overwork to remain solvent (cf. Tilley, B16); (2) her lust overtaxed his virility.

67. *fitters*] small pieces.

70. *Bucklersbury*] a street running south from Cheapside to Walbrook; cf. Stow, p. 233: 'This whole street called Buckles bury on both sides throughout is possessed of grocers and apothecaries towards the west end thereof.' See Intro., p. xlvi.

77. *troll*] pass, circulate; Mrs Fisher cites *Shipman's Gossip* (1666):

. . . gossips now
Eat more at Christenings, than bestow,
Formerly when they used to troul
Gilt bowls of sack, they gave the bowl;
Two spoons at least; an use ill kept;
'Tis now well if our own be left.

All Goss. Thank your worship, sir.
1 Pur. Thank your worship, sir. 85
Allw. [*Aside*] A pox twice tipple ye, you are last and lowest!
Exeunt [SIR WALTER *and* ALLWIT].
1 Pur. Bring hither that same cup, nurse; I would fain
Drive away this—hup!—antichristian grief. [*Drinks.*]
3 Goss. See, gossip, and she lies not in like a countess;
Would I had such a husband for my daughter! 90
4 Goss. Is not she toward marriage?
3 Goss. O no, sweet gossip!
4 Goss. Why, she's nineteen!
3 Goss. Ay, that she was last Lammas,
But she has a fault, gossip, a secret fault.
[*Nurse replenishes glass, then exit.*]
4 Goss. A fault? What is 't?
3 Goss. I'll tell you when I have drunk. [*Drinks.*]
4 Goss. [*Aside*] Wine can do that, I see, that friendship cannot. 95
3 Goss. And now I'll tell you, gossip: she's too free.
4 Goss. Too free?
3 Goss. O ay, she cannot lie dry in her bed.
4 Goss. What, and nineteen?
3 Goss. 'Tis as I tell you, gossip.

[*Enter* Nurse, *and whispers to Maudline.*]

Maudl. Speak with me, nurse? Who is 't?
Nur. A gentleman
From Cambridge; I think it be your son, forsooth. 100
Maudl. 'Tis my son Tim, i' faith; prithee, call him up
Among the women, 'twill embolden him well, [*Exit* Nurse.]
For he wants nothing but audacity.

86.1.] *Dyce; Exit Q.* 93.1.] *This ed.; Exit Nurse. after l. 96 Dyce.*

---

86. *tipple*] topple, tumble over.
last and lowest] a variation of the proverb 'Last but not least'.
89. *countess*] See Intro., p. xxxii, and note to II. ii. 25.
91. *toward marriage*] going to be married: cf. III. ii. 108, IV. i. 199.
92. *Lammas*] 1 Aug., the Christian harvest festival: see Intro., p. xxxi.

'Would the Welsh gentlewoman at home
Were here now.

Lady. Is your son come, forsooth? 105

Maudl. Yes, from the university, forsooth.

Lady. 'Tis great joy on ye.

Maudl. There's a great marriage
Towards for him.

Lady. A marriage?

Maudl. Yes, sure,
A huge heir in Wales at least to nineteen mountains,
Besides her goods and cattle.

Enter [Nurse *with*] TIM.

Tim. O, I'm betray'd! *Exit.* 110

Maudl. What, gone again?—Run after him, good nurse;
[*Exit* Nurse.]
He's so bashful, that's the spoil of youth:
In the university they're kept still to men,
And ne'er train'd up to women's company.

Lady. 'Tis a great spoil of youth, indeed. 115

Enter Nurse *and* TIM.

Nur. Your mother will have it so.

Maudl. Why son, why Tim!
What, must I rise and fetch you? For shame, son!

Tim. Mother, you do entreat like a freshwoman;
'Tis against the laws of the university
For any that has answer'd under bachelor 120
To thrust 'mongst married wives.

104–5. 'Would . . . now.] *So Q; marked Aside Dyce.* 120. answer'd] *This ed.;* answered *Q.*

---

110. *cattle*] Q 'Cattell': (1) *chattel*, 'wealth, goods'; (2) literally *cattle*, her two thousand runts: cf. IV. i. 86.

112, 115. *spoil*] 'ruination' (*O.E.D.*, *sb.*, 7).

113–14.] a commonplace: cf. *F. of L.*, II. iv. 28, *Y.F.G.*, II. i. 79–80.

118. *freshwoman*] by analogy with 'freshman', a first-year student at university.

120, 130. *answer'd under*] 'satisfied the requirements of' (*O.E.D.*, 10b).

Maudl. Come, we'll excuse you here.
Tim. Call up my tutor, mother, and I care not.
Maudl. What, is your tutor come? Have you brought him up?
Tim. I ha' not brought him up, he stands at door:
Negatur. There's logic to begin with you, mother. 125
Maudl. Run, call the gentleman, nurse; he's my son's tutor.
[*Exit* Nurse.]
[*To Tim*] Here, eat some plums.
Tim. Come I from Cambridge,
And offer me six plums!
Maudl. Why, how now, Tim?
Will not your old tricks yet be left?
Tim. Serv'd like a child,
When I have answer'd under bachelor! 130
Maudl. You'll never lin till I make your tutor whip you;
You know how I serv'd you once at the free-school
In Paul's church-yard?
Tim. O monstrous absurdity!
Ne'er was the like in Cambridge since my time;
Life, whip a bachelor! You'd be laugh'd at soundly; 135
Let not my tutor hear you! 'Twould be a jest
Through the whole university. No more words, mother.

Enter Tutor.

Maudl. Is this your tutor, Tim?
Tut. Yes, surely, lady;
I am the man that brought him in league

---

125. Negatur] It is denied: cf. note to I. ii. 60–3.

131.] Bullen notes that, according to Aubrey, John Milton was whipped at Cambridge by his tutor, William Chappell. Cf. also *The Letters of John Chamberlain*, ed. N. E. McClure (1939), I. 335: 'a sonne of the bishop of Bristowes his eldest, of 19 or 20 yeare killed himself, with a knife to avoyde the disgrace of breeching, which his mother or mother in law (I know not whether) wold needs have put him to for losing his monie at tennis' (12 Feb. 1612).

lin] cease, leave off.

132–3. *free-school / In Paul's church-yard*] founded by John Colet in 1512 (see Stow, p. 295, for details).

137.1.] Presumably the Nurse shows him in and then exits.

With logic and read the Dunces to him. 140

Tim. That did he, mother, but now I have 'em all
In my own pate, and can as well read 'em
To others.

Tut. That can he, mistress, for they flow
Naturally from him.

Maudl. I'm the more beholding
To your pains, sir.

Tut. *Non ideo sane.* 145

Maudl. True, he was an idiot indeed, when he
Went out of London, but now he's well mended.
Did you receive the two goose-pies I sent you?

Tut. And eat them heartily, thanks to your worship.

Maudl. [*To Gossips*] 'Tis my son Tim; I pray, bid him welcome,
gentlewomen. 150

Tim. 'Tim'? Hark you: 'Timotheus', mother, 'Timotheus'.

Maudl. How? Shall I deny your name? 'Timotheus', quoth he.
Faith, there's a name! 'Tis my son Tim, forsooth.

Lady. You're welcome, Master Tim. *Kiss*[*es Tim*].

Tim. [*Aside to Tutor*] O this is horrible,
She wets as she kisses! Your handkercher, sweet tutor, 155
To wipe them off as fast as they come on.

2 Goss. Welcome from Cambridge. *Kiss*[*es Tim*].

Tim. [*Aside to Tutor*] This is intolerable!
This woman has a villainous sweet breath,
Did she not stink of comfits. Help me, sweet tutor,

154. *Kisses Tim.*] *Dyce;* Kisse *Q.* *Aside to Tutor*] *This ed.;* O . . . kisses! *marked Aside Dyce.* 157. *Kisses Tim.*] *Dyce;* Kisse *Q.* *Aside to Tutor*] *This ed.;* This is . . . comfits. *marked Aside Dyce.*

---

140. *Dunces*] 'schoolmen', so called from John *Duns* Scotus; perhaps with a play on the abusive derivation, *dunce*, 'blockhead'.

144. *Naturally*] (1) spontaneously; (2) 'half-wittedly' (cf. *O.E.D. natural*, *a.*, 14a)?

145. Non ideo sane] disputant's tag: 'Not for that reason indeed'. Maudline thinks 'ideo' means 'idiot'.

151.] Cf. similar comedy when Simon is called Simonides in *H.K.K.*, III. iii. 130–3.

158–9. *sweet* . . . *comfits*] Actually 'kissing-comfits' were meant to sweeten the breath.

Or I shall rub my lips off.

Tut. I'll go kiss 160

The lower end the whilst.

Tim. Perhaps that's the sweeter,

And we shall despatch the sooner.

1 Pur. Let me come next.

Welcome from the wellspring of discipline

That waters all the brethren. *Reels and falls.*

Tim. Hoist, I beseech thee!

3 Goss. O bless the woman!—Mistress Underman! 165

1 Pur. 'Tis but the common affliction of the faithful;

We must embrace our falls.

Tim. [*Aside to Tutor*] I'm glad I 'scap'd it;

It was some rotten kiss, sure, it dropp'd down

Before it came at me.

Enter ALLWIT *and* DAVY.

Allw. [*Aside*] Here's a noise!

Not parted yet? Heyday, a looking glass! 170

They have drunk so hard in plate that some of them

Had need of other vessels. [*Aloud*] Yonder's

The bravest show!

All Goss. Where, where, sir?

Allw. Come along presently

By the Pissing-Conduit, with two brave drums

And a standard bearer.

165. Mistress] *Dyce;* Mr *Q.* 170. Heyday] *Ellis;* Hyda *Q;* hoida *Dyce.*

---

163. *wellspring of discipline*] Cambridge was notoriously puritan at this time.

164. *Hoist*] Lift (yourself) up; possibly 'Lift (her) up', addressed to the Tutor.

167. *We . . . falls*] a travesty of Calvin's doctrine that Man's fallen nature must be recognized and humbly accepted.

170. *looking glass*] 'chamber pot' (Farmer and Henley, IV. 233).

171. *in plate*] i.e., in the silver vessels brought out to adorn the christening: cf. IV. ii. 2.

174. *Pissing-Conduit*] See Stow, p. 164: 'the little conduit, called the pissing conduit, by the Stockes market...' It was close to the Royal

All Goss. O, brave!
Tim. Come, tutor! 175
Exit [*with* Tutor].
All Goss. [*To Mrs Allwit*] Farewell, sweet gossip. *Exeunt* [Gossips].
Mrs Allw. I thank you all for your pains.
1 Pur. Feed and grow strong.
[*Exeunt* MRS ALLWIT, MAUDLINE, LADY KIX, *and* Puritans.]
Allw. You had more need to sleep than eat;
Go, take a nap with some of the brethren, go,
And rise up a well-edify'd, boldify'd sister!
O, here's a day of toil well pass'd o'er, 180
Able to make a citizen hare-mad!
How hot they have made the rooms with their thick bums;
Dost not feel it, Davy?
Davy. Monstrous strong, sir.
Allw. What's here under the stools?
Davy. Nothing but wet, sir,
Some wine spilt here belike.
Allw. Is 't no worse, think'st thou?
Fair needlework stools cost nothing with them, Davy. 186

176. *Exeunt Gossips.*] *George; Exit Q; after* strong *l. 177 Dyce.* 177.1.] *This ed.; Exit Q; Exeunt Lady Kix, Maud., and all the Gossips. Dyce.*

Exchange, at the junction of Threadneedle Street and Cornhill. See Intro., p. xlvii. This area can be seen as background to the 'Winter' figure in Hollar's *Four Seasons* (see A. M. Hind, *Wencelaus Hollar and his Views of London*, 1922, plate VIII).

175. *standard bearer*] For the innuendo, cf. *M.D.B.W.*, IV. i. 185, where the clown asks to be made 'standard-bearer to the women's regiment', and the exploits of Shortyard, *M.T.*, II. i. 107–9.

177.1.] Presumably Mrs Allwit and her bed would also be taken off stage at this point; though she might merely draw the bed curtains, as in *Volpone*, III. ii.

178.] referring to the Anabaptist contention that any man and any woman could lie together if they were asleep (see Johannsen, *Religion and Superstition*, p. 158): cf. *Wid.*, I. ii. 176–7.

181. *hare-mad*] (1) mad as a hare: cf. Tilley, H148; (2) pun on *hair*, 'pudendum'?

182. *bums*] (1) bumbasts, padding; (2) posteriors.

186. *needlework stools*] i.e., stools with embroidered seats.

cost nothing with them] i.e., 'are not valued by them because they did not pay for them' (*O.E.D.*, 3).

Davy [*Aside*] Nor you neither, i' faith.
Allw. Look how they have laid them,
E'en as they lie themselves, with their heels up!
How they have shuffled up the rushes too, Davy,
With their short figging little shittle-cork-heels! 190
These women can let nothing stand as they find it.
But what's the secret thou'st about to tell me,
My honest Davy?
Davy. If you should disclose it, sir,—
Allw. Life, rip my belly up to the throat then, Davy.
Davy. My master's upon marriage. 195
Allw. Marriage, Davy? Send me to hanging rather!
Davy. [*Aside*] I have stung him.
Allw. When, where? What is she, Davy?
Davy. E'en the same was gossip, and gave the spoon.
Allw. I have no time to stay, nor scarce can speak,
I'll stop those wheels, or all the work will break. *Exit.* 200
Davy. I knew 'twould prick. Thus do I fashion still
All mine own ends by him and his rank toil:
'Tis my desire to keep him still from marriage;
Being his poor nearest kinsman, I may fare

190. shittle-cork-heels] Q^b; shittle-cokre-heels Q^a; shittle-cock heels *Dyce*. 193. sir,—] *Dyce*; Sir. *Q*.

---

189. *rushes*] Green rushes were strewn on floors instead of carpets.

190. *short*] Cf. Tilley, S397; 'shortheels' was slang for 'tart, whore' (Farmer and Henley, VI. 193).

figging] (1) *fidging*, 'fidgetting': cf. *B.B.* (Bullen, VIII. 23); (2) 'dressy' (Farmer and Henley, II. 393); (3) 'worthless', from *fig*, 'turd'?

shittle-cork heels] (1) 'shittle-cork' was the original form of 'shuttle-cock', which was also slang for whore: cf. *F.H.T.* (Bullen, VIII. 79); (2) fashionable cork heels were often associated with 'lightness' of behaviour: cf. *R.G.*, IV. ii. 83; J. Taylor, 'A Bawd', *Works not in 1630 Folio* (1873), III. 16: 'his wife wearing Corke-shooes, was somewhat light-heel'd.'

196. *hanging*] Cf. note to III. iii. 57.

199–200.] The 'speak ... break' rhyme was common, 'ea' being pronounced like the 'a' in modern 'bake'.

202. *him ... his*] i.e., Allwit.

rank] (1) excessive; (2) 'sweaty' (*O.E.D.*, *adj.* 12); (3) 'indecent, corrupt' (*ibid.*, 14).

203. *him*] i.e., Sir Walter.

The better at his death; there my hopes build, 205
Since my Lady Kix is dry and hath no child. *Exit.*

[III. iii]

Enter both the TOUCHWOODS.

Touch. Jun. Y' are in the happiest way to enrich yourself
And pleasure me, brother, as man's feet can tread in;
For though she be lock'd up, her vow is fix'd
Only to me; then time shall never grieve me,
For by that vow e'en absent I enjoy her, 5
Assuredly confirm'd that none else shall,
Which will make tedious years seem gameful to me.
In the mean space, lose you no time, sweet brother;
You have the means to strike at this knight's fortunes
And lay him level with his bankrout merit; 10
Get but his wife with child, perch at tree-top
And shake the golden fruit into her lap;
About it, before she weep herself to a dry ground

III. iii. 5. I] *Dyce subs.; not in Q.*

205–6.] For the 'build . . . child' rhyme, see Kökeritz, p. 218: cf. Shakespeare's 'child . . . spill'd', *Rom.*, III. i. 143–4.

206. *dry*] 'barren' (*O.E.D.*, II. 3), playing on 'Kix'; see note on *Names*, l. 7.

III. iii. 10. *him*] i.e., Sir Walter.

bankrout] bankrupt.

11. *his*] i.e., Sir Oliver's.

perch at tree-top] referring perhaps to the type of suburban 'bower' mentioned as a place for seduction in *Y.F.G.*, IV. viii. 180–1: 'You slave, that keeps fornication upon the tops of trees . . .'? (Cf. Chapman, *All Fools*, III. i. 296, *M. D'Olive*, I. i. 215; which Parrott traces to Ovid, Elegy II, xix.) The image is of a harvester shaking down fruit into the apron of his helper below: cf. *N.W.N.H.*, I. i. 157–8:

Let a man but shake the tree,
How soon they [women] 'll hold up their laps to receive comfort.

and *W.B.W.*, II. ii. 376–7, *S.G.*, III. ii. 44–7.

12. *golden fruit*] For sex as the apples of the Hesperides, cf. *C.* (Revels ed.), III. iii. 174–5.

13. *weep . . . ground*] Continuing the orchard conceit, Lady Kix is com-

And whine out all her goodness.
Touch. Sen. Prithee, cease;
I find a too much aptness in my blood 15
For such a business without provocation;
You might' well spar'd this banquet of eringoes,
Artichokes, potatoes, and your butter'd crab:
They were fitter kept for your own wedding dinner.
Touch. Jun. Nay, and you'll follow my suit and save my purse too,
Fortune dotes on me: he's in happy case 21
Finds such an honest friend i' the common-place.
Touch. Sen. Life, what makes thee so merry? Thou hast no cause
That I could hear of lately since thy crosses,
Unless there be news come with new additions. 25
Touch. Jun. Why, there thou hast it right: I look for her
This evening, brother.
Touch. Sen. How's that? Look for her?
Touch. Jun. I will deliver you of the wonder straight, brother:
By the firm secrecy and kind assistance
Of a good wench i' the house, who, made of pity, 30
Weighing the case her own, she's led through gutters,
Strange hidden ways, which none but love could find,
Or ha' the heart to venture; I expect her
Where you would little think.
Touch. Sen. I care not where,
So she be safe, and yours.
Touch. Jun. Hope tells me so; 35
But from your love and time my peace must grow. *Exit.*
Touch. Sen. You know the worst then, brother.—Now to my Kix,

---

pared to ground which must be planted immediately, before it becomes too 'dry' to support fertility. See Intro., p. lv.

17. *might'*] Q's apostrophe stands for the missing 'have'.

eringoes] sea-holly, considered an aphrodisiac.

18.] all delicacies which were considered sexually provocative.

22. *i' the common-place*] i.e., at need; literally 'in the Court of Common Pleas': cf. *M.W.M.M.*, I. i. 138–9: 'honesty is removed to the common-place'. Cf. Tilley, F687: 'Better a friend in court than a penny in purse'.

25. *additions*] wordplay with 'crosses' (l. 24), which means both 'set-backs, sorrows' and 'deletions'.

The barren he and she; they're i' the next room;
But to say which of their two humours hold them
Now at this instant, I cannot say truly. 40
Sir Ol. Thou liest, barrenness! *Kix to his Lady within.*
Touch. Sen. O, is 't that time of day? Give you joy of your tongue,
There's nothing else good in you: this their life
The whole day, from eyes open to eyes shut,
Kissing or scolding, and then must be made friends; 45
Then rail the second part of the first fit out,
And then be pleas'd again, no man knows which way:
Fall out like giants and fall in like children;
Their fruit can witness as much.

Enter SIR OLIVER KIX *and his* Lady.

Sir Ol. 'Tis thy fault.
Lady. Mine, drouth and coldness?
Sir Ol. Thine; 'tis thou art barren. 50
Lady. I barren? O life, that I durst but speak now
In mine own justice, in mine own right! I barren?
'Twas otherways with me when I was at court;
I was ne'er call'd so till I was married.
Sir Ol. I'll be divorc'd.
Lady. Be hang'd! I need not wish it. 55
That will come too soon to thee: I may say
'Marriage and hanging goes by destiny,'
For all the goodness I can find in 't yet.
Sir Ol. I'll give up house, and keep some fruitful whore,
Like an old bachelor, in a tradesman's chamber; 60
She and her children shall have all.

---

46. *fit*] (1) 'struggle' (*O.E.D.*, *sb.*[2], 1); (2) 'a part of a poem or song' (*O.E.D.*, *sb.*[1]) ? (3) paroxysm or seizure.

48. *Fall out . . . fall in*] quarrel . . . make up; but with a sexual meaning in 'fall in': cf. *T.C.O.O.*, I. i. 130–1: "tis as natural for old folks to fall out, as for young to fall in', Shakespeare, *Tr. and Cr.*, III. i. 112: 'Falling in after falling out may make them three'.

57.] Tilley, M682: 'marriage is destiny', and W232: 'wedding and hanging go by destiny': cf. III. ii. 196.

Lady. Where be they?
Touch. Sen. Pray, cease;
When there are friendlier courses took for you
To get and multiply within your house
At your own proper costs; in spite of censure,
Methinks an honest peace might be establish'd. 65
Sir Ol. What, with her? Never.
Touch. Sen. Sweet sir,—
Sir Ol. You work all in vain.
Lady. Then he doth all like thee.
Touch. Sen. Let me entreat, sir,—
Sir Ol. Singleness confound her! I took her with one smock.
Lady. But, indeed, you came not so single when
You came from shipboard. 70
Sir Ol. [*Aside*] Heart, she bit sore there!—[*To Touchwood Senior*]
Prithee, make 's friends.
Touch. Sen. [*Aside*] Is 't come to that? The peal begins to cease.
Sir Ol. [*To Lady Kix*] I'll sell all at an outcry!
Lady. Do thy worst, slave!—
[*To Touchwood Senior*] Good sweet sir, bring us into love again.
Touch. Sen. [*Aside*] Some would think this impossible to compass.— 75
[*To them*] Pray, let this storm fly over.
Sir Ol. Good sir, pardon me;
I'm master of this house, which I'll sell presently;

64. costs;] *This ed.;* costs, *Q.* 66. sir,—] *Dyce;* Sir. *Q.* 67. sir,—] *Dyce;* Sir. *Q.*

---

64. *proper*] personal, private.
in spite of censure] i.e., in spite of your mutual recrimination.
68. *Singleness*] i.e., divorce (cf. l. 55).
69. *single*] 'unaccompanied', with the implication that he was lousy, picked up in 'bit sore' of l. 71; with a playing on the sense 'marked by scantiness and simplicity of clothing' (*O.E.D.*, *a*, 9).
73. *outcry*] auction. At one point in his legal struggles with Middleton's mother, her second husband had to 'suffer his goodes to be sould at An outcrye at his doore' (see M. Eccles, 'Thomas Midelton a Poett', *S.P.*, LIV (1957), 520).

I'll clap up bills this evening.
Touch. Sen. Lady, friends, come!
Lady. If e'er ye lov'd woman, talk not on 't, sir.
What, friends with him! Good faith, do you think I'm mad?
With one that's scarce the hinder quarter of a man? 81
Sir Ol. Thou art nothing of a woman.
Lady. Would I were
Less than nothing! *Weeps.*
Sir Ol. Nay, prithee, what dost mean?
Lady. I cannot please you.
Sir Ol. I' faith, thou art a good soul;
He lies that says it; [*kissing her*] buss, buss, pretty rogue. 85
Lady. You care not for me.
Touch. Sen. [*Aside*] Can any man tell now
Which way they came in? By this light, I'll be hang'd then!
Sir Ol. Is the drink come?
Touch. Sen. Here's a little vial of *Aside*
Almond-milk, that stood me in some threepence.
Sir Ol. I hope to see thee, wench, within these few years, 90
Circled with children, pranking up a girl,
And putting jewels in their little ears;
Fine sport, i' faith!
Lady. Ay, had you been ought, husband,
It had been done ere this time.
Sir Ol. Had I been ought!
Hang thee! Hadst thou been ought! But a cross thing 95
I ever found thee.
Lady. Thou art a grub to say so.
Sir Ol. A pox on thee!

---

78. *clap up bills*] i.e., stick up advertisements for the auction.
85. *He lies that says it*] Anyone lies who says you cannot please me.
89. *stood me in*] cost me: cf. note to II. i. 187.
91. *pranking up*] titivating, decking.
92. *their*] Dyce emends to 'her', but both sexes wore earrings until about 1660.
96. *grub*] (1) 'a person of unpleasant manners' (*O.E.D.*, *sb.* 2b); (2) 'a short, dwarfish fellow' (*O.E.D.*, *sb.* 2a)? Cf. II. i. 149. Probably with a sexual innuendo.

Touch. Sen. [*Aside*] By this light, they are out again
At the same door, and no man can tell which way!
[*To Sir Oliver*] Come, here's your drink, sir.
Sir Ol. I will not take it now, sir,
And I were sure to get three boys ere midnight. 100
Lady. Why, there thou show'st now of what breed thou comest,
To hinder generation. O thou villain,
That knows how crookedly the world goes with us
For want of heirs, yet put by all good fortune.
Sir Ol. Hang, strumpet! I will take it now in spite. 105
Touch. Sen. Then you must ride upon 't five hours.
[*Gives vial to Sir Oliver.*]
Sir Ol. I mean so.
Within there!

Enter a Servant.

Ser. Sir?
Sir Ol. Saddle the white mare: [*Exit* Servant.]
I'll take a whore along and ride to Ware.
Lady. Ride to the devil!
Sir Ol. I'll plague you every way.
Look ye, do you see? 'Tis gone. *Drinks.*
Lady. A pox go with it! 110
Sir Ol. Ay, curse and spare not now.
Touch. Sen. Stir up and down, sir,
You must not stand.
Sir Ol. Nay, I'm not given to standing.

104. put] *Q;* puts *Dyce.*

---

104. *put by*] neglect, set aside.

107. *white mare*] A proverb may be referred to: cf. Robert Tofte, *Ariosto's Satyres* (1608), p. 56, footnote:

Whose horse is white, and wife is faire,
His head is never void of care.

108. *Ware*] a town in Hertfordshire, 20 miles north of London, famous for assignations: cf. *R.G.*, II. ii. 289, III. i. 19. Its 'Saracen's Head' inn was famous for a great bed, ten feet and nine inches square.

111. *Stir*] move.

112. *stand, standing*] The first sense is 'be motionless', the second provides a pun on *penis erectus* (Partridge, p. 194); cf. 'up', l. 133.

Touch. Sen. So much the better, sir, for the——

Sir Ol. I never could stand long in one place yet;
I learn'd it of my father, ever figient. 115
How if I cross'd this, sir? *Capers.*

Touch. Sen. O passing good, sir,
And would show well a-horseback: when you come to your inn,
If you leap'd over a joint-stool or two,
'Twere not amiss;—although you brake your neck, sir. *Aside*

Sir Ol. What say you to a table thus high, sir? [*Capers.*] 120

Touch. Sen. Nothing better, sir; [*Aside*]—if it be furnish'd
With good victuals. [*To him*] You remember how
The bargain runs about this business?

Sir Ol. Or else I had a bad head: you must receive, sir,
Four hundred pounds of me at four several payments: 125
One hundred pound now in hand.

Touch. Sen. Right, that I have, sir.

Sir Ol. Another hundred when my wife is quick;
The third when she's brought a-bed; and the last hundred
When the child cries, for if it should be still-born,
It doth no good, sir.

Touch. Sen. All this is even still: 130
A little faster, sir.

Sir Ol. Not a whit, sir;
I'm in an excellent pace for any physic.

121. furnish'd] *This ed.;* furnished *Q.* 127. wife] *Dyce;* Wifes *Q.*

113.] Cf. similar lacunae at IV. i. 209, 213, and 243. The Master of the Revels may have deleted an obscenity in this example, but it cannot be shown whether the cut was made for the original production or only later for printing. Alternatively, Middleton may have intended the audience to fill in the obvious joke.

115. *figient*] fidgety: cf. Chapman, Jonson, Marston, *Eastward Ho!*, III. ii. 287, E. Guilpin, *Skialetheia* (1598), satire iv.

116. *cross'd this*] i.e., jumped over this (a joint-stool?). Cf. Jonson, *Epicoene*, IV. i. 101–2, V. i. 45–6, and *Epigrams*, CXV. 11, for satire on the fashion for stool leaping. There is a very similar scene between old Lysander and a Dancing Master in *O.L.*, III. ii. 87 ff. (Bullen, II. 183–4).

127. *quick*] pregnant.

130. *even*] exact, just.

Enter a Servant.

Ser. Your white mare's ready.

Sir Ol. I shall up presently.—

[*Exit* Servant.]

[*To Lady Kix*] One kiss, and farewell. [*Kisses her.*]

Lady. Thou shalt have two, love.

Sir Ol. Expect me about three. *Exit.*

Lady. With all my heart, sweet. 135

Touch. Sen. [*Aside*] By this light, they have forgot their anger since,
And are as far in again as e'er they were.
Which way the devil came they? Heart, I saw 'em not,
Their ways are beyond finding out. [*To Lady Kix*] Come, sweet lady.

Lady. How must I take mine, sir?

Touch. Sen. Clean contrary; 140
Yours must be taken lying.

Lady. A-bed, sir?

Touch. Sen. A-bed, or where you will for your own ease,
Your coach will serve.

Lady. The physic must needs please.

Exeunt.

135. S.D.] *So in Q; after* sweet *in Dyce.* 143.1.] *Dyce; Exit Q.*

---

136. *since*] previously.

138. *Which . . . they?*] How the devil did they come into this mood?

143. *coach*] See John Taylor, 'The World runnes on Wheeles,' *Works* (1630), p. 241: '[A coach] is neuer vnfurnished of a bedde and curtaines, with shop-windowes of leather to buckle Bawdry vp as close in the midst of the street, as it were in the Stewes . . .' Cf. *R.G.*, III. i. 58–9, *P.*, II. iii. 17–18.

Act IV

[IV. i]

Enter TIM *and* Tutor.

Tim. *Negatur argumentum,* tutor.
Tut. *Probo tibi,* pupil, *stultus non est animal rationale.*
Tim. *Falleris sane.*
Tut. *Quaeso ut taceas: probo tibi—*
Tim. *Quomodo probas, domine?* 5
Tut. *Stultus non habet rationem, ergo non est animal rationale.*

Act IV] *Dyce; Actus Quartus. Q.*

1–18.] *Tim.* Your proof is denied, tutor.
Tut. I demonstrate it to you, pupil, a fool is not a rational creature.
Tim. You will certainly fail.
Tut. I beg you to be silent: I prove it to you—
Tim. How do you prove it, sir?
Tut. A fool has not the power of reason, therefore he is not a rational creature.
Tim. Thus you argue, sir: a fool has not the power of reason, therefore he is not a rational creature. Your argument is denied again, tutor.
Tut. Again I demonstrate the proof, sir: he who does not share the power of reason, in no wise can be termed rational; but a fool does not share the power of reason, therefore a fool in no wise can be said to be rational.
Tim. He does share it.
Tut. So you argue: who shares it, how does he share it?
Tim. As a man: I will prove it to you by a syllogism.
Tut. Prove this.
Tim. Thus I prove it, sir: a fool is a man just as you and I are; a man is a rational creature, just so a fool is a rational creature.

Latin disputation was still the major teaching device in universities, but this logical exercise is more suited to Middleton's own curtailed career at Oxford than to Tim's status as a bachelor; cf. C. R. Thompson, *Universities in Tudor England* (1959), p. 9: 'In his first two years an undergraduate studied mostly rhetoric and Aristotelian logic'. George (*Middleton's*

Tim. *Sic argumentaris, domine: stultus non habet rationem, ergo non est animal rationale. Negatur argumentum* again, tutor.

Tut. *Argumentum iterum probo tibi, domine: qui non participat de ratione, nullo modo potest vocari rationalis;* but *stultus non participat de ratione, ergo stultus nullo modo potest dici rationalis.* 10

Tim. *Participat.*

Tut. *Sic disputas: qui participat, quomodo participat?*

Tim. *Ut homo, probabo tibi in syllogismo.* 15

Tut. *Hunc proba.*

Tim. *Sic probo, domine: stultus est homo sicut tu et ego sumus; homo est animal rationale, sicut stultus est animal rationale.*

Enter MAUDLINE.

Maudl. Here's nothing but disputing all the day long with 'em!

Tut. *Sic disputas: stultus est homo sicut tu et ego sumus; homo est animal rationale, sicut stultus est animal rationale.* 20

Maudl. Your reasons are both good, whate'er they be;
Pray, give them o'er; faith, you'll tire yourselves;
What's the matter between you?

Tim. Nothing but reasoning
About a fool, mother.

10. *rationalis*] *Dyce; rationalibus Q.* 11. *dici*] *Dyce; dicere Q.* 14. *disputas*] *Dyce; disputus Q.* 17. *sumus*] *Dyce; sum Q.* 20. *disputas*] *Dyce; disputus Q.* *sumus*] *Dyce; sum Q.*

Borrowings, p. 16) suggests that the passage is a reminiscence of the lectures of Richard Crakenthorpe, lecturer in logic and fellow of Queen's College, Oxford, 1591–1605, whose *Introductio in Metaphysicam* (1619) is dedicated to his students and contains an argument 'De Anima Rationali'. The topic seems to have been a commonplace, however: cf. Wye Saltonstall, *Picturae Loquentes* (1613), D1–D1v: '[the student] weares out a great deale of time there to know what kind of Animal he is ...'; *The Ghost* (1640), p. 30:

I remember in my last school disputation
They laught at me for saying *Homo est asinus rationale.*

20–1.] So you contend: a fool is a man just as you and I are; a man is a rational creature, just so a fool is a rational creature. (Cf. *C.* (Revels ed.), I. ii. 156 ff., for a similar irony.) Middleton ponderously repeats the Latin to make sure that the joke is grasped by the audience; this also emphasizes Tim's stupidity, of course.

Maudl. About a fool, son? 25
Alas, what need you trouble your heads about that?
None of us all but knows what a fool is.
Tim. Why, what's a fool, mother? I come to you now.
Maudl. Why, one that's married before he has wit.
Tim. 'Tis pretty, i' faith, and well guess'd of a woman 30
Never brought up at the university;
But bring forth what fool you will, mother, I'll prove him
To be as reasonable a creature as myself
Or my tutor here.
Maudl. Fie, 'tis impossible.
Tut. Nay, he shall do 't, forsooth.
Tim. 'Tis the easiest thing 35
To prove a fool by logic; by logic
I'll prove anything.
Maudl. What, thou wilt not!
Tim. I'll prove a whore to be an honest woman.
Maudl. Nay, by my faith, she must prove that herself,
Or logic will never do 't.
Tim. 'Twill do 't, I tell you. 40
Maudl. Some in this street would give a thousand pounds
That you could prove their wives so.
Tim. Faith, I can,
And all their daughters too, though they had three bastards!
When comes your tailor hither?
Maudl. Why, what of him?
Tim. By logic I'll prove him to be a man, 45
Let him come when he will.

---

28. *come to you*] a disputation term for 'I pose the question to you'.

29.] Mrs Fisher quotes John Manningham, *Diary* (April 1602, p. 52): 'Shee said there was noe greater evidence to prove a man foole than yf he leave the University to marry a wife'.

35–7. *'Tis . . . anything*] Cf. *F.H.T.* (Bullen, VIII. 103): '. . . yet, for all my weighty and substantial arguments, being able indeed to prove anything by logic, I could prove myself never the richer, make the best syllogism I could: . . .'

45.] Cf. proverb 'Nine tailors make but one man' (Tilley, T23): cf. *W.B.W.*, I. ii. 91–3.

Maudl. [*To Tutor*] How hard at first
Was learning to him! Truly, sir, I thought
He would never ha' took the Latin tongue.
How many accidences do you think he wore out
Ere he came to his grammar?
Tut. Some three or four. 50
Maudl. Believe me, sir, some four and thirty.
Tim. Pish,
I made haberdins of 'em in church porches.
Maudl. He was eight years in his grammar, and stuck horribly
At a foolish place there call'd *as in praesenti*.
Tim. Pox, I have it here now. [*Taps his forehead.*]
Maudl. He so sham'd me once 55
Before an honest gentleman that knew me
When I was a maid.

52. haberdins] *Q;* gaberdins *conj. George.*

---

49. *accidences*] books containing the rules for inflexions, here opposed to 'grammar' (l. 50), which is used for syntax.

52.] This is obscure. A *haberdin* is a dried pilchard, often used as a generalized term of abuse (e.g., *S.G.*, IV. iii. 143); in *The Trial of Chivalry*, II. i (ed. Bullen, p. 289), it is associated with 'Yellow-hammer': 'Bowyer a Captayne? a Capon, a button mould, a lame haberdine, a red beard Sprat, a Yellow-hammer ...' Dyce conjectures that the passage may refer to 'some childish sport'; and, though Strutt and Gomme have nothing to the purpose, there is a Christmas game called 'selling of fish' mentioned in Jonson's masque *Love Restored*, l. 52 (unglossed by Herford and Simpson), and in *Shakespeare's England* (II. 481) we find: 'In Selden [whipping of tops] takes a place with the eating of fritters, *the roasting of herrings*, and Jack-a-Lents, which were connected with the beginning of the Lenten season'. Alternatively, perhaps the passage refers to the *foolscap decorated with actual pieces or paper emblems of redherring* which was worn by the Jack-a-Lent (see E. K. Chambers, *The English Folk Play*, 1933, p. 157; Baskervill, *Elizabethan Jig*, p. 93, n. 2; and R. Southern's description of a mummer's 'papers' in *The Seven Ages of Theatre* (1961), pp. 47–8). Tim seems to have some relation to this Lenten scapegoat.

54. as in praesenti] from William Lyly's *A shorte introduction of Latin Grammar* (1567 ed., cvi), in the 'De Verbo' section of Part II, where it begins Lyly's famous didactic poem (see J. D. Reeves, 'Thomas Middleton and Lily's Grammar', *N. & Q.*, CXCVII, 1952, 75). The same pun on 'as' can be found in Dekker, *Satiromastix* (1602), C3, and Nashe, *Works* (ed. McKerrow), I. 282.

Tim. These women must have all out!
Maudl. '*Quid est grammatica?*' says the gentleman to him,—
I shall remember by a sweet, sweet token,—
But nothing could he answer.
Tut. How now, pupil, ha? 60
Quid est grammatica?
Tim. *Grammatica?* Ha, ha, ha!
Maudl. Nay, do not laugh, son, but let me hear you say it now:
There was one word went so prettily off
The gentleman's tongue, I shall remember it
The longest day of my life.
Tut. Come, *quid est grammatica?* 65
Tim. Are you not asham'd, tutor? *Grammatica*:
Why, *recte scribendi atque loquendi ars*,
Sir-reverence of my mother.
Maudl. That was it, i' faith!
Why now, son, I see you are a deep scholar.
And, Master Tutor, a word I pray: [*aside to Tutor*] let us 70
Withdraw a little into my husband's chamber;
I'll send in the North-Wales gentlewoman to him,
She looks for wooing. I'll put together both
And lock the door.
Tut. I give great approbation
To your conclusion. *Exeunt* [MAUDLINE *and* Tutor].
Tim. I mar'l what this gentlewoman 75
Should be that I should have in marriage:

75. S.D.] *Dyce; Exit Q.*

---

57. *must have all out*] 'must tell everything' (cf. Tilley, A179), but with an indecent entendre.

58, 67. Quid est grammatica? ... recte scribendi atque loquendi ars] What is grammar? ... the art of writing and speaking correctly: from the first line of Part II in Lyly's Latin grammar. Cf. *The Wise Woman of Hogsdon*, IV. i (*Thomas Heywood*, Mermaid ed., p. 296), *How to Choose a Good Wife* (Dodsley, IX. 27) for the 'ars' pun, a variant of which is the 'musica est ars' of *Y.F.G.*, II. i. 98.

59. *sweet token*] Maudline's souvenir would appear to be the word 'ars'!

68. *Sir-reverence*] i.e., 'save your reverence', used apologetically in quoting indecency.

She's a stranger to me: I wonder what
My parents mean, i' faith, to match me with a stranger so,
A maid that's neither kiff nor kin to me.
Life, do they think I have no more care of my body 80
Than to lie with one that I ne'er knew, a mere stranger,
One that ne'er went to school with me neither,
Nor ever play-fellows together?
They're mightily o'erseen in 't, methinks.
They say she has mountains to her marriage; 85
She's full of cattle, some two thousand runts:
Now what the meaning of these runts should be,
My tutor cannot tell me; I have look'd
In Rider's Dictionary for the letter R.
And there I can hear no tidings of these runts neither; 90
Unless they should be Romford hogs, I know them not.

Enter Welsh Gentlewoman.

And here she comes. If I know what to say to her now
In the way of marriage, I'm no graduate!
Methinks, i' faith, 'tis boldly done of her
To come into my chamber, being but a stranger; 95

78–81.] Cf. similar clownish objections in *T.C.O.O.*, II. i. 395–6, *W.B.W.*, III. ii. 178 ff.

79. *kiff*] a frequent corruption of *kith*, 'friends, neighbours'.

84. *o'erseen*] mistaken.

85. *to her marriage*] i.e., as dowry.

86. *runts*] a small breed of ox or cow, common to Wales and the Highlands of Scotland: cf. W. Rowley, *Match at Midnight* (1633), II. i, where Randall's fortune includes 'a pair of hundred of seeps, thirty prave cows, and twelve dozen of runts', and Jonson, *Masque for the Honor of Wales*, l. 248.

89. *Rider's Dictionary*] an English–Latin, Latin–English dictionary by John Rider, Bishop of Killaloe, first published in 1589 and often reprinted. It was the subject of a law case in 1613: see C. J. Sisson, 'The Laws of Elizabethan Copyright: the Stationers' View', *Libr.* 5 ser., XV (1960), 8–20. This dictionary, in fact, *does not* contain the word 'runts'.

91. *Romford hogs*] Romford is a town in Essex, 12 miles north-east of London, with a famous hog market every Tuesday (Sugden, p. 442): cf. *R.G.*, V. i. 234–5: 'the gruntling of five hundred hogs coming from Romford market...' It was also a favourite place for illicit assignations: see Jonson, *Bartholomew Fair*, IV. v. 38; *The New Inn*, IV. iii. 71.

She shall not say I'm so proud yet but I'll speak
To her: marry, as I will order it,
She shall take no hold of my words, I'll warrant her.
[*Welsh Gentlewoman curtsies.*]
She looks and makes a cur'sey!—
[*To her*] *Salve tu quoque, puella pulcherrima; quid vis* 100
nescio nec sane curo,—
Tully's own phrase to a heart!

Welsh G. [*Aside*] I know not what he means: a suitor, quoth a?
I hold my life he understands no English.

Tim. Fertur, mehercule, tu virgo, Wallia ut opibus abundas 105
maximis.

Welsh G. [*Aside*] What's this *fertur* and *abundundis*?
He mocks me sure, and calls me a bundle of farts.

Tim. [*Aside*] I have no Latin word now for their runts;
I'll make some shift or other: 110
[*To her*] *Iterum dico, opibus abundas maximis montibus et*
fontibus et, ut ita dicam, rontibus; attamen vero homunculus
ego sum natura simul et arte baccalaureus, lecto profecto
non paratus.

105. *Fertur*] *Dyce; Ferter Q.* *abundas*] *Dyce; abundis Q.* 111. *abundas*] *Dyce; abundat Q.* 112. *homunculus*] *Dyce; homauculus Q.* 113. *simul et arte*] *Dyce; simule arte Q; simul et artis George. lecto*] *Q; lectoque George.* 114. *paratus*] *George; parata Q; parato Dyce.*

100–1.] Save thee also, most beautiful maiden; what you want I do not know, nor truly do I care.

102. *Tully*] i.e., Cicero.

to a heart] exactly (not in *O.E.D.*), apparently from 'learn by heart'.

105–6.] It is said, by Hercules, maiden, that you abound with great wealth in Wales.

110. *shift*] device, expedient, contrivance.

111–14.] The poor Latin may be translated: 'Again, I say, you abound in great riches, in mountains and fountains and, as I may call them, in "runts" [inventing a Latin form *rontibus*]; yet, truly, I am a little man by nature and also a bachelor by training [i.e., Bachelor of Arts], actually not prepared for bed.' Tim's claim to be 'homunculus', with the emphasis on Sir Oliver's 'shortness' (cf. note to 'grub', III. iii. 96), is further evidence that the play was originally designed for the Queen's Revels company: see Intro., p. xxix.

Welsh G. [*Aside*] This is most strange; maybe he can speak
Welsh.— 115
[*To him*] *Avedera whee comrage, der due cog foginis.*
Tim. [*Aside*] *Cog foggin*? I scorn to cog with her; I'll tell her
so too,
In a word near her own language; [*to her*] *Ego non cogo.*
Welsh G. *Rhegosin a whiggin harle ron corid ambre.* 119
Tim. [*Aside*] By my faith, she's a good scholar, I see that already:
She has the tongues plain; I hold my life she has travell'd.
What will folks say? There goes the learned couple!
Faith, if the truth were known she hath proceeded!

Enter MAUDLINE.

Maudl. How now, how speeds your business?
Tim. [*Aside*] I'm glad my mother's come
To part us.
Maudl. [*To Welsh Gentlewoman*] How do you agree, forsooth?
Welsh G. As well as e'er we did before we met.
Maudl. How's that? 126
Welsh G. You put me to a man I understand not;
Your son's no Englishman, methinks.
Maudl. No Englishman!

116. *foginis*] *Q; fogini George.* 119. *ron*] *Q; ren conj. George.* *ambre*] *Q; ambro Dyce.*

116.] Middleton's Welsh is wholly phonetic and unreliable. *Avedera whee comrage* is *A fedrwch chwi Gymraeg*, 'Can you speak Welsh?'; but *der due cog foginis* remains obscure. Wall suggests *er duw, cog fo gennyf*, 'for God's sake, is he pretending with me?'; Bartley (*op. cit.*, p. 278) suggests *dere di . . . o ginio*, 'come . . . of dinner', in which case *cog* is probably related to *cogaf, cogiaf*, 'to cook, prepare a meal'.

117. *cog*] cheat.

119.] Bartley renders this as *Rhyw gosyn a chwigyn ar ôl bod yn cerdedd am dro*, 'Some cheese and whey after taking a walk': i.e., the Welshwoman is trying to get Tim to leave with her for 'dinner' (see his translation of l. 116)? Cheese and whey were popularly supposed to be the favourite Welsh diet: cf. *A.F.Q.L.*, IV. i. 144; *C.* (Revels ed.), I. ii. 206–8.

121. *travell'd*] pun on 'travailed'.

123. *proceeded*] (1) taken a degree (cf. I. i. 148); (2) 'proceeded' beyond virginity; but of course the second meaning is for the audience and is not intended by Tim.

Bless my boy, and born i' the heart of London?

Welsh G. I ha' been long enough in the chamber with him, 130
And I find neither Welsh nor English in him.

Maudl. Why, Tim, how have you us'd the gentlewoman?

Tim. As well as a man might do, mother, in modest Latin.

Maudl. Latin, fool?

Tim. And she recoil'd in Hebrew.

Maudl. In Hebrew, fool? 'Tis Welsh!

Tim. All comes to one, mother.

Maudl. She can speak English too.

Tim. Who told me so much? 136
Heart, and she can speak English, I'll clap to her;
I thought you'd marry me to a stranger.

Maudl. [*To Welsh Gentlewoman*] You must forgive him: he's so inur'd to Latin,
He and his tutor, that he hath quite forgot 140
To use the Protestant tongue.

Welsh G. 'Tis quickly
Pardon'd, forsooth.

Maudl. Tim, make amends and kiss her.—
[*To Welsh Gentlewoman*] He makes towards you, forsooth.

[*Tim kisses Welsh Gentlewoman.*]

Tim. O, delicious!
One may discover her country by her kissing;
'Tis a true saying: 'There's nothing tastes so sweet 145
As your Welsh mutton.'—[*To Welsh Gentlewoman*] It was reported you could sing.

Maudl. O, rarely, Tim, the sweetest British songs.

---

129. *heart of London*] Cf. I. i. 94; *H.E.*, Ent. III, l. 42.

134. *recoil'd*] retorted.

137. *clap*] (1) stick or lie close to: cf. *T.C.O.O.*, II. i. 332; (2) 'catch gonorrhoea' (Farmer and Henley, II. 119): cf. l. 123, n.; again Tim is not aware of the double sense.

138. *stranger*] foreigner.

141. *Protestant tongue*] i.e., English: cf. I. i. 91.

143. *makes towards*] approaches.

146. *mutton*] as usual, a play on the slang for whore.

147. *British*] i.e., Welsh.

Tim. And 'tis my mind, I swear, before I marry,
I would see all my wife's good parts at once,
To view how rich I were.

Maudl. Thou shalt hear sweet music, Tim.—
[*To Welsh Gentlewoman*] Pray, forsooth. 151

Music and Welsh [*Gentlewoman sings*].

The Song

Welsh G. *Cupid is Venus' only joy,*
But he is a wanton boy,
A very, very wanton boy;
He shoots at ladies' naked breasts, 155
He is the cause of most men's crests,—
I mean upon the forehead,
Invisible but horrid;
'Twas he first thought upon the way
To keep a lady's lips in play. 160

Why should not Venus chide her son
For the pranks that he hath done,
The wanton pranks that he hath done?
He shoots his fiery darts so thick,

151.1.] *Wall; Musicke and Welch Song Q.* 152. *Welsh G.*] *not in Q.* 153. *he is*] *Q, MSS;* he's *M.D.B.W.* 158.] *Q, MSS; M.D.B.W. adds two lines* Of the short veluet mask; he was deviser; / That Wiues may kiss, the husband's ne'r the wiser. 159. *thought*] *MSS, M.D.B.W.; taught Q.* 161–9.] *Q, 4175 (viole), 29481; not in M.D.B.W., 4175 (lute).* 162. *pranks*] *Q; trickes MSS.* 163.] *Q, 4175 (viole); not in 29481.*

148–9.] Cf. *W.B.W.*, II. ii. 123 ff. 'Good parts' literally means 'acquirements' but there is a sexual entendre, suggested perhaps by the custom of seeing fiancés naked in More's *Utopia* (ed. 1869), p. 123.

151.1.] Songs were frequently used to characterize Welsh nationality (Bartley, p. 52) but this one is not particularly appropriate. It also occurs in *M.D.B.W.*, and John Cutts argues that it was borrowed from that play because *A Chaste Maid*'s original 'Welsh song' had been lost by 1630. He also considers the third stanza spurious (see Appendix II, p. 128, n. 2).

156. crests] the horns of the cuckold (cf. ll. 157–8).

160. lips] bawdy? Cf. l. 177.

They hurt poor ladies to the quick, 165
Ah me, with cruel wounding!
His darts are so confounding,
That life and sense would soon decay
But that he keeps their lips in play.

Can there be any part of bliss, 170
In a quickly fleeting kiss,
A quickly fleeting kiss?
To one's pleasure leisures are but waste,
The slowest kiss makes too much haste,
We lose it ere we find it. 175
The pleasing sport they only know
That close above and close below.

Tim. I would not change my wife for a kingdom;
I can do somewhat too in my own lodging.

Enter YELLOWHAMMER *and* ALLWIT.

Yell. Why, well said, Tim! The bells go merrily; 180
I love such peals o' life. Wife, lead them in a while;
Here's a strange gentleman desires private conference.—
[*Exeunt* MAUDLINE, Welsh Gentlewoman, *and* TIM.]

165. *hurt*] *Q; wound MSS.* 166. *Ah me*] *Q; Ay mee MSS.* 167. *His*] *Q, 4175 (viole); Thy 29481.* 168. *sense*] *Q; strength MSS.* 169. *he*] *Q; it MSS.* 170–7.] *Q; not in MSS, M.D.B.W.* 175. *We lose it*] *This ed.; And loose it Q; And lost is conj. Dyce.* 179.] *Bullen adds S.D. Sings after* lodging.

165. quick] tenderest part (*O.E.D.*, B4b), but with a sexual implication.

173.] To one bent on pleasure, it seems a waste of time to be leisurely.

175.] Cutts notes that a line seems to have dropped out here.

179.] Bullen adds the direction 'Sings', but Tim's boast is meant to be ambiguous.

179.1.] Though Maudline knows the Allwits, ll. 232–3 suggest that Yellowhammer does not. Otherwise Allwit would have to be disguised in this scene.

180. *The bells go merrily*] proverbial? Cf. *N.W.N.H.*, v. i. 387: 'Why, now the bells they go trim, they go trim'.

181. *peals*] a double pun: (1) noise of bells: cf. III. iii. 72; (2) *peels*, 'matches, equals' (*O.E.D.*, *sb.*[4]); (3) *peels*, 'robberies, pillages' (cf. *O.E.D.*, *vb*[1])?

[*To Allwit*] You're welcome, sir, the more for your name's sake,
Good Master Yellowhammer; I love my name well:
And which o' the Yellowhammers take you descent from,
If I may be so bold with you? which, I pray? 186

Allw. The Yellowhammers in Oxfordshire near Abingdon.

Yell. And those are the best Yellowhammers, and truest bred;
I came from thence myself, though now a citizen:
I'll be bold with you; you are most welcome. 190

Allw. I hope the zeal I bring with me shall deserve it.

Yell. I hope no less: what is your will, sir?

Allw. I understand, by rumours, you have a daughter,
Which my bold love shall henceforth title 'cousin'.

Yell. I thank you for her, sir.

Allw. I heard of her virtues 195
And other confirm'd graces.

Yell. A plaguy girl, sir!

Allw. Fame sets her out with richer ornaments
Than you are pleas'd to boast of; 'tis done modestly:
I hear she's towards marriage.

Yell. You hear truth, sir.

Allw. And with a knight in town, Sir Walter Whorehound. 200

Yell. The very same, sir.

Allw. I am the sorrier for 't.

Yell. The sorrier? Why, cousin?

Allw. 'Tis not too far past, is 't?
It may be yet recall'd?

Yell. Recall'd? Why, good sir?

Allw. Resolve me in that point, ye shall hear from me.

Yell. There's no contract pass'd.

196. confirm'd] Q^b; confir'd Q^a.

---

187. *Abingdon*] actually the capital of Berkshire, on the Thames 5 miles south of Oxford. There were two Lord Mayors of this name in the Middle Ages, hence perhaps the boast (Stow, pp. 452–3).

196. *confirm'd*] firmly established. *plaguy*] troublesome.

199. *towards*] See note to III. ii. 91.

203. *recall'd*] called back, rescinded.

204.] i.e., 'If you can resolve . . .'.

Allw. I am very joyful, sir. 205
Yell. But he's the man must bed her.
Allw. By no means, coz;
She's quite undone then, and you'll curse the time
That e'er you made the match; he's an arrant whoremaster,
Consumes his time and state,—— [*Whispers*]
Whom in my knowledge he hath kept this seven years; 210
Nay, coz, another man's wife too.
Yell. O, abominable!
Allw. Maintains the whole house, apparels the husband,
Pays servants' wages, not so much but—— [*Whispers*]
Yell. Worse and worse! And doth the husband know this?
Allw. Knows? Ay, and glad he may too, 'tis his living; 215
As other trades thrive, butchers by selling flesh,
Poulters by vending conies, or the like, coz.
Yell. What an incomparable wittol's this!
Allw. Tush, what cares he for that? Believe me, coz,
No more than I do.
Yell. What a base slave is that! 220
Allw. All's one to him; he feeds and takes his ease,
Was ne'er the man that ever broke his sleep
To get a child yet, by his own confession,
And yet his wife has seven.
Yell. What, by Sir Walter?
Allw. Sir Walter's like to keep 'em and maintain 'em 225
In excellent fashion; he dares do no less, sir.
Yell. Life, has he children too?
Allw. Children! boys thus high,
In their Cato and Corderius.

209. —] *So Q.* S.D.] *This ed.* 213. —] *So Q.* S.D.] *This ed.*
228. Corderius] *Dyce;* Cordelius *Q.*

209, 213. S.D.] The blanks may merely indicate censorship, but whisperings suit the scene; cf. III. iii. 113, n.

217. *Poulters*] (1) poulterers; (2) pimps.

conies] (1) rabbits; (2) whores.

218. *wittol*] complaisant cuckold.

228. *Cato and Corderius*] i.e., Cato's *Disticha de Moribus* (moral precepts) and the *Colloquia Scholastica* (1564) of Mathurin Cordier, the teacher of

Yell. What! You jest, sir!
Allw. Why, one can make a verse and is now at Eton College.
Yell. O, this news has cut into my heart, coz! 230
Allw. It had eaten nearer, if it had not been prevented:
One Allwit's wife.
Yell. Allwit? Foot, I have heard of him;
He had a girl kursen'd lately?
Allw. Ay, that work
Did cost the knight above a hundred mark.
Yell. I'll mark him for a knave and villain for 't; 235
A thousand thanks and blessings! I have done with him.
Allw. [*Aside*] Ha, ha, ha! This knight will stick by my ribs still;
I shall not lose him yet; no wife will come;
Where'er he woos, I find him still at home. Ha, ha! *Exit.*
Yell. Well, grant all this, say now his deeds are black, 240
Pray, what serves marriage but to call him back?
I've kept a whore myself, and had a bastard
By Mistress Anne, in *anno*——
I care not who knows it; he's now a jolly fellow,
'Has been twice warden; so may his fruit be, 245
They were but base begot, and so was he.

243. —] *Dyce; left blank in Q.*

Calvin: both common schoolbooks of the time, with a puritanical bias.

234. *a hundred mark*] A mark was worth 13s. 4d., so the sum indicated was the equivalent of £66 13s. 4d. M. St C. Byrne, *Elizabethan Life*, 1954, pp. 307–12, estimated that the modern equivalent (at the time she was writing) was £500.

237. *stick by my ribs*] (1) i.e., 'be as close as my skin'? Cf. *O.E.D.*, *sb.*[1], 1, 1a, 1523; (2) often said of a good meal: *ibid.*, 1795; (3) playing on *rib*, 'wife' (*O.E.D.*, *sb*[1], 1, 3)?

241. *call him back*] reform him.

243.] perhaps excised for an indecent play on 'Anne/*anno*', though Dyce suggests it was left blank for the actors to add a date suitable to whenever the play was performed. Unlike the other lacunae, Q leaves this blank, without a dash; cf. III. iii. 113, n., IV. i. 209, 213, n.

245. *warden*] (1) a member of the governing body of one of the City Companies; (2) a kind of pear (hence the play on 'fruit').

his] i.e., Sir Walter's.

246. *They*] i.e., Sir Walter's bastards.

he] i.e., Yellowhammer's bastard.

The knight is rich, he shall be my son-in-law;
No matter, so the whore he keeps be wholesome,
My daughter takes no hurt then; so let them wed:
I'll have him sweat well ere they go to bed. 250

Enter MAUDLINE.

Maudl. O, husband, husband!
Yell. How now, Maudline?
Maudl. We are all undone!
She's gone, she's gone!
Yell. Again? Death! Which way?
Maudl. Over the houses. Lay the waterside;
She's gone for ever, else.
Yell. O vent'rous baggage! *Exeunt.*

[IV. ii]

Enter TIM *and* Tutor.

Tim. Thieves, thieves! My sister's stol'n! Some thief hath got her:
O, how miraculously did my father's plate 'scape!
'Twas all left out, tutor.
Tut. Is 't possible?
Tim. Besides three chains of pearl and a box of coral!
My sister's gone. Let's look at Trig-stairs for her; 5
My mother's gone to lay the common stairs

254. S.D.] *Dyce; Exit Q.*

IV. ii. 4. coral!] *This ed.;* Curral. *Q;* coral. *Dyce;* coral, *conj. Dunkel.*

---

250. *sweat*] Venereal disease was treated by sweating in a steam tub.
253. *Over the houses*] across the roofs.
Lay] search.

IV. ii. 4. *coral!*] Dunkel's punctuation 'coral,' (*Dramatic Techniques of Thomas Middleton*, p. 46) would imply that Moll had taken the pearls and coral with her.

5. *Trig-stairs*] See map, p. lxix, and Intro., p. xlvi. 'Trig' was slang for 'a narrow track or path', 'a hurried walk' (earliest example in *O.E.D.* is 1884, but the verbal form is as early as 1599), and 'coxcomb' (*O.E.D.*, *sb.*[4], 6B).
6. *common*] public.

At Puddle-wharf; and at the dock below
Stands my poor silly father. Run, sweet tutor, run! *Exeunt.*

[IV. iii]

Enter both the TOUCHWOODS.

Touch. Sen. I had been taken, brother, by eight sergeants,
But for the honest watermen; I am bound to them;
They are the most requitefull'st people living,
For as they get their means by gentlemen,
They are still the forwardest to help gentlemen: 5
You heard how one 'scap'd out of the Blackfriars,
But a while since, from two or three varlets came
Into the house with all their rapiers drawn,
As if they'd dance the sword-dance on the stage,
With candles in their hands, like chandlers' ghosts, 10
Whilst the poor gentleman so pursued and banded
Was by an honest pair of oars safely landed.

Touch. Jun. I love them with my heart for 't.

Enter three or four Watermen.

ii. 8. S.D.] *Dyce; Exit Q.*

---

7. *Puddle-wharf*] 'a watergate into the Thames, where horses use to water, and therefore being defiled with their tramplings, and made puddle . . .' (Stow, p. 325). The Mermaid Theatre stands there now.

dock below] i.e., downstream: Dung wharf, where the city refuse was loaded on to barges.

IV. iii. 0.1.] For the locales of IV. iii and IV. iv see Intro., p. xlvi.

2. *watermen*] i.e., boatmen, plying for hire on the Thames.

3. *requitefull'st*] most eager to requite, return favours. For the play's attitude to watermen, see Intro., p. xxxii.

6. *Blackfriars*] Blackfriars Theatre, the 'private house' of the King's Men, was an indoor theatre lit by candles (cf. l. 10).

9. *sword-dance*] In the most common kind of sword dance one man danced in a ring of naked swords held by the other dancers (see J. Strutt, *Sports and Pastimes*, ed. J. C. Cox, 1903, pp. 177–8). Sword dances and ghost impersonations (cf. l. 10) were part of the pre-Christian spring ceremonies, to which the play seems related.

10. *chandlers*] candle-makers.

11. *banded*] bandied, struck to and fro: cf. *Duchess of Malfi*, V. iv. 54.

1 Wat. Your first man, sir.
2 Wat. Shall I carry you gentlemen with a pair of oars?
Touch. Sen. These be the honest fellows. Take one pair 15
And leave the rest for her.
Touch. Jun. Barn Elms.
Touch. Sen. No more, brother.
1 Wat. Your first man.
2 Wat. Shall I carry your worship?
Touch. Jun. Go.
[*Exit* TOUCHWOOD SENIOR *with* First Waterman.]
And you honest watermen that stay,
Here's a French crown for you: [*gives money*]
There comes a maid with all speed to take water, 20
Row her lustily to Barn Elms after me.
2 Wat. To Barn Elms, good, sir.—Make ready the boat, Sam;
We'll wait below. *Exeunt* [Watermen].

Enter MOLL.

Touch. Jun. What made you stay so long?
Moll. I found the way more dangerous than I look'd for.
Touch. Jun. Away, quick! There's a boat waits for you; and I'll
Take water at Paul's-wharf and overtake you. 26
Moll. Good sir, do; we cannot be too safe. [*Exeunt.*]

13, 17. *1 Wat.*] *This ed.;* 1 *Q.* 14, 17, 22. *2 Wat.*] *This ed.;* 2 *Q.* 16.] *Q; Dyce adds Exit.* 22. good,] *Dyce;* good *Q.* 23. *Exeunt* Watermen.] *Dyce; Exit Q.*

---

13. *first man*] trade cry of the watermen; cf. Overbury, 'A Water-man', *Characters* (1615): 'Is one that hath learnt to speake well of himselfe: for alwaies hee names himselfe The first man'.

16. *Barn Elms*] a manor house and park up the Thames on the south bank, opposite Hammersmith; according to Sugden (p. 48), 'a favourite resort of lovers and duellists'. Mrs Fisher cites Otway, *Souldier's Fortune* (1681), p. 29: 'would that *Barn-Elms* was under water too, there's a thousand cuckolds a year made at *Barn-Elms* . . .'

19. *French crown*] the écu, a French silver coin regarded as equivalent to the English five-shilling piece.

21. *lustily*] vigorously, with a good will.

26. *Paul's-wharf*] between Puddle-wharf and Trig-stairs (Stow, p. 325).

[IV. iv]

Enter SIR WALTER, YELLOWHAMMER, TIM *and* Tutor.

Sir Walt. Life! Call you this close keeping?
Yell. She was kept
Under a double lock.
Sir Walt. A double devil!
Tim. That's a buff sergeant, tutor; he'll ne'er wear out.
Yell. How would you have women lock'd?
Tim. With padlocks, father;
The Venetian uses it; my tutor reads it. 5
Sir Walt. Heart, if she were so lock'd up, how got she out?
Yell. There was a little hole look'd into the gutter;
But who would have dreamt of that?
Sir Walt. A wiser man would!
Tim. He says true, father; a wise man for love
Will seek every hole; my tutor knows it. 10
Tut. *Verum poeta dicit.*
Tim. *Dicit Virgilius*, father.
Yell. Prithee, talk of thy jills somewhere else, she's play'd
The jill with me. Where's your wise mother now?
Tim. Run mad, I think; I thought she would have drown'd
herself;

IV. iv. 1. *close keeping*] locking her up securely.

3. *buff sergeant*] The doggedness of sergeants (officers responsible for arresting offenders) was often compared to the durable buff leather of their jerkins.

4–5. *With padlocks . . . The Venetian uses it*] For an elaborate description of a chastity-belt exhibited at St Mark's in Venice, see R. Tofte, *Ariosto's Satyres* (1608), p. 67, sidenote: cf. *M.W.M.M.*, I. ii. 21–3, *W.B.W.*, I. i. 34, 79–80.

my . . . it] i.e., my tutor has told me he has read it somewhere.

9–10. *a wise . . . hole*] perhaps a lewd paraphrase of Ovid, *Ars Amatoria*, II. 243–6; cf. *C.* (Revels ed.), III. iii. 94, 'love creeps in at a mouse-hole'. Tim ludicrously misascribes it to the high-minded Virgil, perhaps remembering the latter's 'Omnia vincit amor' (*Eclogue* x. 69).

11.] The poet speaks the truth. Virgil says it, father.

12–13 *jills . . . play'd / The jill*] wantons; played a scurvy trick. 'To play the jill' is a variant of 'to play the jack' (Tilley, J8).

She would not stay for oars but took a smelt-boat: 15
Sure, I think she be gone a-fishing for her!

Yell. She'll catch a goodly dish of gudgeons now,
Will serve us all to supper.

Enter MAUDLINE *drawing* MOLL *by the hair, and* Watermen.

Maudl. I'll tug thee home by the hair.

1 Wat. Good mistress, spare her!

Maudl. Tend your own business.

2 Wat. You are a cruel mother. 20

Exeunt [Watermen].

Moll. O, my heart dies!

Maudl. I'll make thee an example
For all the neighbours' daughters.

Moll. Farewell, life!

Maudl. You that have tricks can counterfeit.

Yell. Hold, hold, Maudline!

Maudl. I have brought your jewel by the hair.

Yell. She's here, knight.

Sir Walt. Forbear, or I'll grow worse.

Tim. Look on her, tutor; 25
She hath brought her from the water like a mermaid;
She's but half my sister now, as far as the flesh goes,
The rest may be sold to fishwives.

Maudl. Dissembling, cunning baggage!

19. *1 Wat.*] *This ed.; Wat. Q.* 20. *2 Wat.*] *This ed.; Wat. Q; First W. Dyce.* 20.1.] *Dyce; Exit Q.*

---

15. *smelt-boat*] i.e., boat for fishing smelts or sparlings, a kind of small fish used metaphorically for 'fools'.

17. *gudgeons*] 'To gape after, or swallow, gudgeons' was proverbial for being deceived, since they are small fish used as bait (Tilley, G473): cf. *I.T.M.*, ll. 212–13, and the foolish lecher called Gudgeon in *F. of L.* Yellowhammer means that Maudline's gullibility will make them all look foolish.

18. *to*] for.

25. *grow worse*] grow more angry? (cf. l. 30).

26. *mermaid*] slang for whore: cf. *R.G.*, I. i. 339–41, *F.Q.*, IV. iv. 114–15.

28. *fishwives*] 'Fishmonger' was slang for 'procurer, pimp' (Partridge, 113). See Intro., pp. lv–lvi, for the ambiguities of the fish image here.

Yell. Impudent strumpet!
Sir Walt. Either give over, both, or I'll give over!— 30
[*To Moll*] Why have you us'd me thus, unkind mistress?
Wherein have I deserved?
Yell. You talk too fondly, sir:
We'll take another course and prevent all;
We might have done 't long since; we'll lose no time now,
Nor trust to 't any longer. Tomorrow morn, 35
As early as sunrise, we'll have you join'd.
Moll. O, bring me death tonight, love-pitying fates;
Let me not see tomorrow up upon the world.
Yell. Are you content, sir? Till then she shall be watch'd!
Maudl. Baggage, you shall! *Exit* [MAUDLINE *with* MOLL].
Tim. Why, father, my tutor and I 40
Will both watch in armour. [*Exit* YELLOWHAMMER.]
Tut. How shall we do for weapons?
Tim. Take you no care for that; if need be I can send
For conquering metal, tutor, ne'er lost day yet;
'Tis but at Westminster: I am acquainted
With him that keeps the monuments; I can borrow 45

31. S.D.] *This ed.* Thus, unkind] *This ed.;* thus vnkind *Q;* thus unkindly, *Dyce.* 36. sunrise] *Dyce;* Sunne rise *Q.* 38. up upon] *Q;* up on *Dyce.* 40. S.D.] *George; Exeunt Maudline, Moll, and Yellowhammer. after* armour *l. 41 Dyce.*

---

30. *give over . . . give over*] i.e., stop bullying Moll or I'll call the marriage off.

32. *fondly*] (1) indulgently; (2) foolishly.

35. *trust to 't*] i.e., trust our luck, risk delay.

41. *watch in armour*] Londoners were proud of the citizens' watch which kept order through the city and provided a great deal of pageantry: see Stow, pp. 93–5; R. Wilson, *The Three Lordes and three Ladies of London* (1590), F2v:

> Lord Pomp, let nothing that's magnificall,
> Or that may tend to London graceful state,
> Be unperform'd, As showes and solomne feastes,
> Watches in armour, triumphs, Cresset-lightes,
> Bonefiers, belles, and peales of ordinance . . .

Cf. Sir Oliver's methods of celebrating his wife's pregnancy (v. iii. 4, 6–7). See Intro., p. xxxi.

45. *him that keeps the monuments*] Tim means 'master of the monuments',

Harry the Fifth's sword. 'Twill serve us both
To watch with. *Exeunt* [TIM *and* Tutor].

Sir Walt. I never was so near my wish
As this chance makes me: ere tomorrow noon
I shall receive two thousand pound in gold
And a sweet maidenhead worth forty. 50

Enter TOUCHWOOD JUNIOR *with* [First] Waterman.

Touch. Jun. O, thy news splits me!
1 Wat. Half drown'd! She cruelly
Tugg'd her by the hair, forc'd her disgracefully,
Not like a mother.
Touch. Jun. Enough! Leave me, like my joys.
Exit Waterman.

[*To Sir Walter*] Sir, saw you not a wretched maid pass this way?
Heart, villain, is it thou?
Sir Walt. Yes, slave, 'tis I! *Both draw and fight.*
Touch. Jun. I must break through thee, then: there is no stop 56
That checks my tongue and all my hopeful fortunes,

47. S.D.] *Dyce; Exit Q; Exit Tim, Tutor, and Yellowhammer. George.* 50.1. First] *This ed.; a Q.* 51. *1 Wat.*] *This ed.; Wat. Q.* 57. tongue] *Q;* song *conj. George.*

---

the official guide to Westminster Abbey whose doggerel about the tombs is quoted in *Sportive Wit* (1656), pp. 90–102. Cf. Henry Peacham, *Worth of a Penny* (1641), p. 20: 'For a peny you may heare a most eloquent Oration upon our English Kings and Queens, if keeping your hands off, you will seriously listen to *David Owen*, who keeps the monuments in Westminster.'

46. *Harry the Fifth's sword*] probably Edward III's seven-foot sword, mentioned in H.F., *Satyrs and Satyricall Epigrams* (1617), F 6: '*Edward's blade:* with the *Tombes* at Westminster', and in the ballad 'The Tombs in Westminster Abbey' (*Roxburghe Ballads*, 1893, VII. 271)—though one version of the latter calls it 'the sword of *John of Gaunt*'. Henry V comes directly after Edward III in the ballad, and presumably Tim's error would be obvious to the original audience.

51. *splits*] i.e., makes me suffer shipwreck; used figuratively (*O.E.D.*, *vb*, 1b).

57. *checks my tongue*] i.e., 'reduces me to silence'? Dyce conjectures that *tongue* means 'suit': cf. *T.C.O.O.*, I. ii. 30: 'O, 'tis a fine little voluble tongue that wins a widow'. Elsewhere Middleton uses *tongue* to mean 'contract'

That breast excepted, and I must have way.
Sir Walt. Sir, I believe 'twill hold your life in play.
[*Wounds Touchwood Junior.*]
Touch. Jun. [*Counterattacking*] So, you'll gain the heart in my breast at first? 60
Sir Walt. There is no dealing, then? Think on the dowry
For two thousand pounds.
Touch. Jun. O, now 'tis quit, sir. [*Wounds Sir Walter.*]
Sir Walt. And being of even hand, I'll play no longer.
Touch. Jun. No longer, slave?
Sir Walt. I have certain things to think on
Before I dare go further. [*Exit.*]
Touch. Jun. But one bout! 65
I'll follow thee to death, but ha' 't out. *Exit.*

60. So] *This ed.;* Sir *Q.* at first?] *Q;* first. *Dyce.* 66. S.D.] *Q; Exeunt. Dyce.*

(*T.C.O.O.*, IV. iv. 113), and 'sword' (*F. of L.*, I. i. 7, *R.G.*, III. i. 61–2). The General Editor suggests MS. 'Joys', misread by the printer as 'Tõge'.

59. *hold . . . in play*] i.e., make you actively defend your life (*O.E.D.*, play *sb.* 4c).

60. *So*] Q's 'Sir' was probably by eyeskip to the previous line.

at first] (1) 'at once, immediately' (*O.E.D.*, 6b); (2) the name of a particular sword thrust? Cf. *Peace.* (Bullen, VIII. 344) where Middleton condemns the 'schoolmaster of duels' for his 'vainglorious and punctual order of first and seconds'; according to George Silver, *Paradoxes of Defence* (1599), p. 62, the 'first' is one of 'foure offensive actions'. It seems likely, therefore, that at l. 59 Sir Walter thrusts at Touchwood Junior, who escapes with a wound and retaliates by wounding Sir Walter at 'quit' in l. 62. The combat is then pursued off-stage because the surprise of the resurrection scene depends on the audience not knowing the extent of Touchwood Junior's injuries.

61. *dealing*] (1) 'coming to terms': Sir Walter is offering to share the dowry; (2) play on 'dealing of cards'? Gambling terms run throughout the duel: cf. the symbolic duel with law terms in *P.*, II. iii.

62. *quit*] even, requited. Touchwood Junior wounds Sir Walter?

63. *even hand*] (1) 'on equal terms' (*O.E.D.*, even, *a.* 10); (2) another gaming image.

64–5. *I have . . . further*] referring to Sir Walter's religious qualms seen later in V. i? Middleton emphasizes the spiritual dangers of duelling in *F.Q.* (1617), and especially *Peace.* (1618).

Act V

[v. i]

Enter ALLWIT, *his* Wife, *and* DAVY DAHUMMA.

Mrs Allw. A misery of a house!
Allw. What shall become of us?
Davy. I think his wound be mortal.
Allw. Think'st thou so, Davy?
Then am I mortal too, but a dead man, Davy;
This is no world for me whene'er he goes;
I must e'en truss up all and after him, Davy; 5
A sheet with two knots, and away!

Enter SIR WALTER, *led in hurt* [*by two* Servants].

Davy. O, see, sir,
How faint he goes! Two of my fellows lead him.
Mrs Allw. O me! [*Swoons.*]
Allw. Heyday, my wife's laid down too! Here's like to be
A good house kept, when we are all together down:
Take pains with her, good Davy, cheer her up there. 10
Let me come to his worship, let me come. [*Exeunt* Servants.]
Sir Walt. Touch me not, villain! My wound aches at thee,
Thou poison to my heart!
Allw. He raves already,

Act V] *Dyce; Actus Quintus. Q.* 6.1.] *So Q; after* see, sir. *Dyce.* 9. all together] *Dyce;* altogether *Q.*

3. *but a dead man*] a catch-phrase for evil fortune, here taken literally: see J. Crow, 'Some Elizabethan Catch-Phrases', *Elizabethan and Jacobean Studies presented to F. P. Wilson* (1959), p. 261, no. 126.

5. *truss up*] (1) 'pack up', especially with the idea of being wrapped in a shroud (cf. l. 6); (2) possibly 'hang myself'? Cf. II. iii. 0.2, 2.

6. *sheet . . . knots*] i.e., a shroud.

His senses are quite gone, he knows me not.—
[*To him*] Look up, an 't like your worship; heave those eyes,
Call me to mind; is your remembrance left? 16
Look in my face: who am I, an 't like your worship?

Sir Walt. If anything be worse than slave or villain,
Thou art the man!

Allw. Alas, his poor worship's weakness!
He will begin to know me by little and little. 20

Sir Walt. No devil can be like thee!

Allw. Ah, poor gentleman,
Methinks the pain that thou endurest—

Sir Walt. Thou know'st me to be wicked, for thy baseness
Kept the eyes open still on all my sins;
None knew the dear account my soul stood charg'd with 25
So well as thou, yet, like hell's flattering angel,
Wouldst never tell me on 't, let'st me go on,
And join with death in sleep; that if I had not
Wak'd now by chance, even by a stranger's pity,
I had everlastingly slept out all hope 30
Of grace and mercy.

Allw. Now he is worse and worse.
Wife, to him, wife; thou wast wont to do good on him.

Mrs Allw. How is 't with you, sir?

Sir Walt. Not as with you,
Thou loathsome strumpet! Some good pitying man

22. endurest—] *This ed.;* endurest. *Q;* endurest mads thee. *Dyce;* endurest, *Wall.*

---

25. *dear*] costly: cf. v. ii. 51.

28–31.] There is a similar passage spoken by the Cardinal in *W.B.W.*, IV. i. 235–41, which it is interesting to compare for tone:

> . . . O, my brother,
> What were you, if [that] you were taken now!
> My heart weeps blood to think on't; 'tis a work
> Of infinite mercy, you can never merit,
> That yet you are not death-struck, no, not yet;
> I dare not stay you long, for fear you should not
> Have time enough allow'd you to repent in: . . .
> (Bullen, VI. 343.)

Remove my sins out of my sight a little; 35
I tremble to behold her, she keeps back
All comfort while she stays. Is this a time,
Unconscionable woman, to see thee?
Art thou so cruel to the peace of man
Not to give liberty now? The devil himself 40
Shows a far fairer reverence and respect
To goodness than thyself; he dares not do this,
But parts in time of penitence, hides his face;
When man withdraws from him, he leaves the place.
Hast thou less manners and more impudence 45
Than thy instructor? Prithee show thy modesty,
If the least grain be left, and get thee from me:
Thou shouldst be rather lock'd many rooms hence
From the poor miserable sight of me,
If either love or grace had part in thee. 50

Mrs Allw. He is lost for ever!

Allw. Run, sweet Davy, quickly,
And fetch the children hither; sight of them
Will make him cheerful straight. [*Exit* DAVY.]

Sir Walt. [*To Mrs Allwit*] O death! Is this
A place for you to weep? What tears are those?
Get you away with them, I shall fare the worse; 55
As long as they are a-weeping, they work against me;
There's nothing but thy appetite in that sorrow,
Thou weep'st for lust; I feel it in the slackness
Of comforts coming towards me: I was well
Till thou began'st to undo me. This shows like 60
The fruitless sorrow of a careless mother
That brings her son with dalliance to the gallows
And then stands by and weeps to see him suffer.

Enter DAVY *with* [NICK, WAT, *and*] *the* [*other*] Children.

Davy. There are the children, sir; an 't like your worship,

43. parts] *Dyce subs.;* part *Q.* 51. He . . . ever!] *So Q; marked Aside Dyce.*

Your last fine girl: in troth she smiles; 65
Look, look, in faith, sir.

Sir Walt. O, my vengeance!
Let me for ever hide my cursed face
From sight of those that darken all my hopes,
And stand between me and the sight of heaven!
Who sees me now, her too and those so near me, 70
May rightly say I am o'ergrown with sin.
O, how my offences wrestle with my repentance!
It hath scarce breath;
Still my adulterous guilt hovers aloft,
And with her black wings beats down all my prayers 75
Ere they be half way up. What's he knows now
How long I have to live? O, what comes then?
My taste grows bitter; the round world all gall now;
Her pleasing pleasures now hath poison'd me,
Which I exchang'd my soul for: 80
Make way a hundred sighs at once for me!

Allw. Speak to him, Nick.

Nick. I dare not, I am afraid.

Allw. Tell him he hurts his wounds, Wat, with making moan.

Sir Walt. Wretched, death of seven.

Allw. Come, let's be talking
Somewhat to keep him alive. Ah, sirrah Wat, 85
And did my lord bestow that jewel on thee
For an epistle thou mad'st in Latin?

65. smiles] *Q;* smiles on you *conj. Dyce.* 68. darken] *Dyce;* darkens *Q.* 69. stand] *Dyce;* stands *Q.* sight] *Q;* light *George.* 70. her too] *This ed.;* ho to *Q;* O too *Dyce;* O, O *Bullen;* O *Ellis;* go to *George.*

---

66. *my vengeance*] i.e., the children are a sign of God's vengeance on me.

78. *gall*] Cf. 'gall at the end', Crow, 'Catch-Phrases', p. 263, no. 257?

81.] i.e., 'May the hundred sighs that I now breathe clear a path for me (to heaven)'.

84. *death of seven*] The 'seven' are Sir Walter's bastards (cf. IV. i. 224). The phrase means (1) 'I am the (spiritual) death of seven' and also (2) 'my own death is caused by those seven'. Sir Walter's anguish telescopes utterance.

Thou art a good forward boy, there's great joy on thee.

Sir Walt. O sorrow!

Allw. [*Aside*] Heart, will nothing comfort him?

If he be so far gone, 'tis time to moan. 90

[*To him*] Here's pen and ink and paper, and all things ready;

Will 't please your worship for to make your will?

Sir Walt. My will? Yes, yes, what else? Who writes apace, now?

Allw. That can your man Davy, an 't like your worship,

A fair, fast, legible hand.

Sir Walt. Set it down then: [*Davy writes.*] 95

Imprimis, I bequeath to yonder wittol

Three times his weight in curses.

Allw. How!

Sir Walt. All plagues

Of body and of mind.

Allw. Write them not down, Davy.

Davy. It is his will; I must.

Sir Walt. Together also

With such a sickness ten days ere his death. 100

Allw. [*Aside*] There's a sweet legacy! I am almost chok'd with 't.

Sir Walt. Next I bequeath to that foul whore his wife

All barrenness of joy, a drouth of virtue,

And dearth of all repentance: for her end,

The common misery of an English strumpet, 105

In French and Dutch; beholding ere she dies

Confusion of her brats before her eyes,

And never shed a tear for it.

Enter a Servant.

---

93. *will*] pun on *will*, 'lust'? Cf. II. i. 13.

106. *French and Dutch*] venereal diseases: cf. *B.M.C.*, I. ii. 14–16: 'the commodities which are sent out of the Low Countries, and put in vessels called mother Cornelius' dry-fats [i.e., sweating-tubs] are most common in France', and V. ii. 84. 'French' is specifically syphilis (morbus gallicus); cf. *F.Q.*, IV. iv. 145–9.

107. *Confusion*] i.e., incest; cf. I. ii. 111–12: a frequent preoccupation of Middleton (see S. Schoenbaum, '*H.K.K.* and Sexual Preoccupation in the Jacobean Drama', *P.Q.*, XXIX, 1952).

1 Ser. Where's the knight?
O sir, the gentleman you wounded is
Newly departed!

Sir Walt. Dead? Lift, lift! Who helps me? 110

Allw. Let the law lift you now, that must have all;
I have done lifting on you, and my wife too.

1 Ser. You were best lock yourself close.

Allw. Not in my house, sir,
I'll harbour no such persons as men-slayers;
Lock yourself where you will.

Sir Walt. What's this?

Mrs Allw. Why, husband!

Allw. I know what I do, wife.

Mrs Allw. [*Aside to Allwit*] You cannot tell yet; 116
For having kill'd the man in his defence,
Neither his life nor estate will be touch'd, husband.

Allw. Away, wife! Hear a fool! His lands will hang him.

Sir Walt. Am I deny'd a chamber?—[*To Mrs Allwit*] What say
you, forsooth? 120

Mrs Allw. Alas, sir, I am one that would have all well
But must obey my husband.—[*To Allwit*] Prithee, love,
Let the poor gentleman stay, being so sore wounded:
There's a close chamber at one end of the garret
We never use; let him have that I prithee. 125

Allw. We never use? You forget sickness then,
And physic-times; is 't not a place of easement?

Enter a [*second*] Servant.

108, 113. *1 Ser.*] *This ed.; Seru. Q; Third Ser. Dyce.* 127.1] *So Q; after* in me? *l. 129 Dyce.* *second*] *This ed.; fourth Dyce.*

110–11. *Lift . . . lift*] a play on words: (1) 'lift me up' (physically); (2) 'collect', in the sense of 'arrest' (not in *O.E.D.*).

112. *lifting*] (1) helping, assisting; (2) robbing; (3) a sexual innuendo in the case of Mrs Allwit.

on] of.

119. *Hear a fool!*] i.e., 'listen to a fool talking': proverbial, but not in Tilley; cf. 'Take no counsel of a fool' (Tilley, C697)?

124. *close*] hidden, secluded.

127. *place of easement*] 'a privy' (*O.E.D.*, 1c).

Sir Walt. O death! Do I hear this with part
Of former life in me?—What's the news now?
2 Ser. Troth, worse and worse; you're like to lose your land, 130
If the law save your life, sir, or the surgeon.
Allw. [*Aside*] Hark you there, wife.
Sir Walt. Why, how, sir?
2 Ser. Sir Oliver Kix's wife is new quicken'd;
That child undoes you. sir.
Sir Walt. All ill at once!
Allw. I wonder what he makes here with his consorts? 135
Cannot our house be private to ourselves
But we must have such guests? I pray, depart, sirs,
And take your murderer along with you;
Good he were apprehended ere he go,
'Has kill'd some honest gentleman: send for officers! 140
Sir Walt. I'll soon save you that labour.
Allw. I must tell you, sir,
You have been somewhat bolder in my house
Than I could well like of; I suffer'd you
Till it stuck here at my heart; I tell you truly
I thought you had been familiar with my wife once. 145
Mrs Allw. With me? I'll see him hang'd first: I defy him,
And all such gentlemen in the like extremity.
Sir Walt. If ever eyes were open, these are they:
Gamesters, farewell, I have nothing left to play.
Exit [*with* Servants].
Allw. And therefore get you gone, sir.
Davy. Of all wittols 150
Be thou the head!—[*To Mrs Allwit*] Thou, the grand whore
of spittles! *Exit.*

130, 133. *2 Ser.*] *This ed.; Seru. Q; Fourth Ser. Dyce.*

---

133. *quicken'd*] made pregnant.
135. *makes*] does.
consorts] companions, accomplices (i.e., Sir Walter's two servants).
149. *Gamesters*] (1) gamblers; (2) lechers (see Intro., p. lviii): cf. *Y.F.G.*, II. iii. 122, *N.W.N.H.*, II. iii. 175, *Wit.*, II. i. 76, etc.
151. *spittles*] hospitals; cf. note to 'spittlehouses', II. i. 143.

Allw. So, since he's like now to be rid of all,
I am right glad I am so well rid of him.
Mrs Allw. I knew he durst not stay when you nam'd officers.
Allw. That stopp'd his spirits straight. What shall we do now,
wife? 155
Mrs Allw. As we were wont to do.
Allw. We are richly furnish'd, wife,
With household stuff.
Mrs Allw. Let's let out lodgings then,
And take a house in the Strand.
Allw. In troth, a match, wench:
We are simply stock'd with cloth-of-tissue cushions
To furnish out bay-windows; push, what not that's quaint
And costly, from the top to the bottom; 161
Life, for furniture, we may lodge a countess!
There's a close-stool of tawny velvet too,
Now I think on 't, wife.
Mrs Allw. There's that should be, sir;
Your nose must be in everything!

158–60. *Strand ... bay-windows*] 'During the reign of James I the Strand came to be the fashionable residential quarter of London' (Sugden); cf. *F.H.T.* (Bullen, VIII. 77); for the fashion of cushions in parlour windows, cf. *Poetaster*, II. i. 110; *How a Man may choose a Good Wife*, III. iii (1602, F3v). The Strand seems also to have been notorious for courtezans: cf. J. Shirley, *The Lady of Pleasure* (1637), C2v: 'I live i' the Strand, whither few ladies come, To live and purchase more than fame ... my balcony Shall be the courtier's idol'; H. Glapthorne, *The Gamester* (1637), H4v: 'Let her [a frail lady] make the best on 't; set up shop in the Strand or Westminster'; cf. *H.K.K.*, III. i. 143: 'Their birding is at windows', and *W.B.W.*, III. i. 128–31.

158. *a match*] agreed, done; said on concluding an agreement or wager. See Intro., p. lviii.

159. *simply*] absolutely.

cloth-of-tissue] cloth interwoven with gold and silver thread.

160. *push*] Middleton's characteristic form of the interjection 'pish'. Cf. *C.* (Revels ed.), III. iv. 125, etc.

quaint] 'costly, beautiful, fashionable' (*O.E.D.*, *adj.* 4).

163. *close-stool*] commode, portable latrine.

164. *There's ... be*] There's everything necessary.

165. *Your ... everything*] This close-stool joke appears similarly in *R.G.*, III. ii. 21–2.

Allw. I have done, wench; 165
And let this stand in every gallant's chamber:
'There's no gamester like a politic sinner,
For whoe'er games, the box is sure a winner.' *Exeunt.*

[V. ii]

Enter YELLOWHAMMER *and his* Wife.

Maudl. O husband, husband, she will die, she will die!
There is no sign but death.
Yell. 'Twill be our shame then.
Maudl. O, how she's chang'd in compass of an hour!
Yell. Ah, my poor girl! Good faith, thou wert too cruel
To drag her by the hair.
Maudl. You would have done as much, sir,
To curb her of her humour.
Yell. 'Tis curb'd sweetly! 6
She catch'd her bane o' th' water.

Enter TIM.

Maudl. How now, Tim?
Tim. Faith, busy, mother, about an epitaph
Upon my sister's death.
Maudl. Death! She is not dead, I hope?
Tim. No, but she means to be, and that's as good, 10
And when a thing's done, 'tis done; you taught me
That, mother.
Yell. What is your tutor doing?
Tim. Making one too, in principal pure Latin

168. S.D.] *Dyce; Exit Q.*

---

168. *box*] (1) the percentage taken by the house: cf. C. Cotton, *Compleat Gamester* (1674), pp. 11–12, and Tilley, B766; (2) the close-stool of l. 163? (see illustration in Elizabeth Burton, *The Jacobeans at Home*, 1962, p. 165); (3) coffin (Partridge, *Dictionary of Slang*)? See Intro., p. lviii.

V. ii. 11. *a thing's done*] Cf. Jonson, *Cynthia's Revels*, IV. iii. 160 ff.: a childish game rather like the modern 'consequences' (see Nares, p. 876).
13. *principal*] excellent, especially choice.

Cull'd out of Ovid his *de Tristibus*.

Yell. How does your sister look? Is she not chang'd? 15

Tim. Chang'd? Gold into white money was never so chang'd
As is my sister's colour into paleness.

Enter MOLL[, *led in sick*].

Yell. O, here she's brought; see how she looks like death!

Tim. Looks she like death, and ne'er a word made yet?
I must go beat my brains against a bed-post 20
And get before my tutor. [*Exit.*]

Yell. [*To Moll*] Speak, how dost thou?

Moll. I hope I shall be well, for I am as sick
At heart as I can be.

Yell. 'Las, my poor girl!
The doctor's making a most sovereign drink for thee,
The worst ingredients dissolv'd pearl and amber; 25
We spare no cost, girl.

Moll. Your love comes too late,
Yet timely thanks reward it. What is comfort,
When the poor patient's heart is past relief?
It is no doctor's art can cure my grief.

Yell. All is cast away then; 30
Prithee look upon me cheerfully.

Maudl. Sing but a strain or two, thou wilt not think

14. Ovid his] *Bullen;* Ouid *Q;* Ovidius *conj. Dyce;* Ovid's *Wall.* 17.1. *led in sick*] *George.* 25. ingredients] *This ed.;* Ingredience, *Q.*

---

14. de Tristibus] Ovid's *Tristia*, five books of mournful poems, used as a textbook in the third forms of grammar schools (see T. W. Baldwin, *Shakespeare's Small Latine and Lesse Greeke*, 1944, I. 119).

16. *white money*] silver. The same conceit occurs in *P.*, I. iv. 245–6, and with the sense of 'prostituted' in *R.T.*, II. ii. 28. See Intro., p. xlviii, n.4.

20. *beat my brains*] Cf. Tilley, B602: 'to beat one's brains'.

25.] Cf. *M.W.M.M.*, II. vi. 49–50: 'let gold, amber and dissolved pearl, be common ingrediences [*sic*]'. Cf. spelling 'ingredian', *C.* (Revels ed.), I. i. 143–4, and 'performents' (= performances), *G. at C.*, Induction, 62.

27. *timely*] early, in time; antithesis of 'too late' in l. 26.

32–3. *Sing . . . spirits*] For the Renaissance belief in music's therapeutic power, see G. L. Finney, 'Music the Breath of Life', *Centennial Review of Arts and Sciences*, vol. IV (Michigan State University, 1960), 179–205.

How 'twill revive thy spirits: strive with thy fit,
Prithee, sweet Moll.

Moll. You shall have my goodwill, mother.

Maudl. Why, well said, wench. [*Moll sings.*] 35

The Song.

Moll. *Weep eyes, break heart,*
My love and I must part.
Cruel fates true love do soonest sever:
O, I shall see thee never, never, never!
O, happy is the maid whose life takes end 40
Ere it knows parent's frown or loss of friend.
Weep eyes, break heart,
My love and I must part.

Enter TOUCHWOOD SENIOR *with a letter.*

Maudl. O, I could die with music!—Well sung, girl.

Moll. If you call it so, it was.

Yell. She plays the swan 45
And sings herself to death.

Touch. Sen. By your leave, sir.

Yell. What are you, sir? Or what's your business, pray?

Touch. Sen. I may be now admitted, though the brother
Of him your hate pursu'd: it spreads no further;
Your malice sets in death, does it not, sir? 50

Yell. In death?

Touch. Sen. He's dead: 'twas a dear love to him,
It cost him but his life, that was all, sir;
He paid enough, poor gentleman, for his love.

Yell. [*Aside*] There's all our ill remov'd, if she were well now.—

36. *Moll.*] *not in Q.* 41. *parent's*] *Dyce; parents Q.* 43.1.] *So Q; after* death. *l. 46 Dyce.*

---

33. *fit*] (1) attack of melancholy; (2) stave of music.
34. *You . . . goodwill*] i.e., 'I'll do the best I can'.
45–6. *swan . . . death*] (1) proverbial: cf. Tilley, S1028; (2) possibly a reference to the decline of the Swan theatre? See Intro., p. xxxiii, n.3.
50. *sets*] subsides, abates, declines; for a similar idea, cf. *F.Q.*, III. i. 180.
51. *dear*] (1) sweet; (2) costly: cf. V. i. 25.

[*To Touchwood Senior*] Impute not, sir, his end to any hate 55
That sprung from us; he had a fair wound brought that.

Touch. Sen. That help'd him forward, I must needs confess;
But the restraint of love, and your unkindness,
Those were the wounds that from his heart drew blood;
But being past help, let words forget it too: 60
Scarcely three minutes ere his eye-lids clos'd
And took eternal leave of this world's light,
He wrote this letter, which by oath he bound me
To give to her own hands: that's all my business.

Yell. You may perform it then; there she sits. 65

Touch. Sen. O, with a following look!

Yell. Ay, trust me, sir,
I think she'll follow him quickly.

Touch. Sen. Here's some gold
He will'd me to distribute faithfully
Amongst your servants. [*Gives gold to Servants.*]

Yell. 'Las, what doth he mean, sir?

Touch. Sen. [*To Moll*] How cheer you, mistress?

Moll. I must learn of you, sir.

Touch. Sen. Here's a letter from a friend of yours, 71
[*Giving letter to Moll*]
And where that fails in satisfaction,
I have a sad tongue ready to supply.

Moll. How does he, ere I look on 't?

Touch. Sen. Seldom better;
'Has a contented health now.

Moll. I am most glad on 't. [*Reads.*] 75

Maudl. [*To Touchwood Senior*] Dead, sir?

Yell. He is. [*Aside*] Now, wife, let's but get the girl
Upon her legs again, and to church roundly with her.

72. fails . . . satisfaction,] *Dyce;* fails, . . . satisfaction *Q.*

---

66. *following*] about to follow (i.e., die). Cf. *O.E.D.*, *vb*, 8b: 'resemble, take after'.

70. *How . . . you*] how do you feel?

75. *'Has . . . now.*] a commonplace for death: cf. Tilley, H347.

77. *roundly*] promptly.

Moll. O, sick to death he tells me: how does he after this?
Touch. Sen. Faith, feels no pain at all: he's dead, sweet mistress.
Moll. Peace close mine eyes! [*Swoons.*]
Yell. The girl! Look to the girl, wife! 80
Maudl. Moll, daughter, sweet girl, speak! Look but once up,
Thou shalt have all the wishes of thy heart
That wealth can purchase!
Yell. O, she's gone for ever!
That letter broke her heart.
Touch. Sen. As good now, then,
As let her lie in torment and then break it. 85

Enter SUSAN.

Maudl. O Susan, she thou loved'st so dear is gone!
Sus. O sweet maid!
Touch. Sen. This is she that help'd her still.—
I've a reward here for thee. [*Gives Susan a note.*]
Yell. Take her in,
Remove her from our sight, our shame and sorrow.
Touch. Sen. Stay, let me help thee; 'tis the last cold kindness 90
I can perform for my sweet brother's sake.
[*Exeunt* TOUCHWOOD SENIOR, SUSAN, *and* Servants, *carrying* MOLL.]
Yell. All the whole street will hate us, and the world
Point me out cruel: it is our best course, wife,
After we have given order for the funeral,
To absent ourselves till she be laid in ground. 95
Maudl. Where shall we spend that time?
Yell. I'll tell thee where, wench:
Go to some private church and marry Tim
To the rich Brecknock gentlewoman.
Maudl. Mass, a match!
We'll not lose all at once, somewhat we'll catch. *Exeunt.*

99. S.D.] *Dyce; Exit Q.*

98. *a match*] (1) agreed (cf. v. i. 158); (2) a wedding.

[v. iii]

Enter SIR OLIVER *and* [*four*] Servants.

Sir Ol. Ho, my wife's quicken'd; I am a man for ever!
I think I have bestirr'd my stumps, i' faith.
Run, get your fellows all together instantly,
Then to the parish church and ring the bells.

1 Ser. It shall be done, sir. [*Exit.*]

Sir. Ol. Upon my love 5
I charge you, villain, that you make a bonfire
Before the door at night.

2 Ser. A bonfire, sir?

Sir Ol. A thwacking one, I charge you.

2 Ser. [*Aside*] This is monstrous! [*Exit.*]

Sir Ol. Run, tell a hundred pound out for the gentleman
That gave my wife the drink, the first thing you do. 10

3 Ser. A hundred pounds, sir?

Sir Ol. A bargain! As our joy grows,
We must remember still from whence it flows,
Or else we prove ungrateful multipliers: [*Exit* 3 Servant.]
The child is coming and the land comes after;
The news of this will make a poor Sir Walter. 15
I have struck it home, i' faith!

v. iii. 0.1. *four*] *This ed.* 3. all together] *Dyce;* altogether *Q.* 5. *1 Ser.*] *Dyce subs.; Seru. Q.* 7, 8. *2 Ser.*] *Dyce subs.; Seru. Q.* 11. *3 Ser.*] *Dyce subs.; Seru. Q.* joy] *Dyce;* ioyes *Q.*

---

v. iii. 1.] Lady Kix's pregnancy seems to telescope time; Dunkel gets all the other events into a time-chart of a week (*Dramatic Technique of Thomas Middleton*, pp. 44–7), but see Intro., p. xxxi.

2. *bestirr'd my stumps*] (1) been busy: cf. Tilley, S946, *B.M.C.*, I. ii. 76; (2) bawdy innuendo: cf. Webster, *Appius and Virginia*, III. i. 3–4.

6–7. *bonfire . . . night*] See note to IV. iv. 41.

8. *thwacking*] large, jam-packed.

9. *tell*] count.

13. *multipliers*] (1) breeders; (2) 'false coiners' (*O.E.D.*, 3); reflecting the play's 'counterfeit' theme?

14–15. *after . . . Walter*] a rhyme: cf. Shakespeare's 'halter . . . after', *Lr.*, I. iv. 321–2 (discussed Kökeritz, p. 183), *Eastward Ho!*, V. v. 78–9: 'after . . . daughter'.

16. *struck it home*] metaphor from duelling, playing on *strike*, 'copulate' (Partridge, p. 196).

4 Ser. That you have, marry, sir;
But will not your worship go to the funeral
Of both these lovers?
Sir Ol. Both? Go both together?
4 Ser. Ay, sir, the gentleman's brother will have it so;
'Twill be the pitifullest sight. There's such running, 20
Such rumours, and such throngs, a pair of lovers
Had never more spectators, more men's pities,
Or women's wet eyes.
Sir Ol. My wife helps the number then?
4 Ser. There's such drawing out of handkerchers;
And those that have no handkerchers, lift up aprons. 25
Sir Ol. Her parents may have joyful hearts at this!
I would not have my cruelty so talk'd on
To any child of mine for a monopoly.
4 Ser. I believe you, sir.
'Tis cast so too, that both their coffins meet, 30
Which will be lamentable.
Sir Ol. Come, we'll see 't. *Exeunt.*

[V. iv]

Recorders dolefully playing, enter at one door the coffin of the Gentleman [TOUCHWOOD JUNIOR], *solemnly decked, his sword upon it, attended by many in black* [*among whom are* SIR OLIVER KIX, ALLWIT, *and a* Parson,] *his brother* [TOUCHWOOD SENIOR] *being the chief mourner; at the other door the coffin of the virgin* [MOLL], *with a garland of flowers, with epitaphs pinned on 't, attended by maids*

16, 19, 24, 29. *4 Ser.*] *Dyce subs.*; *Seru. Q.* 31. S.D.] *Dyce; Exit Q.*

---

23. *helps the number*] increases the number (of mourners).
28. *monopoly*] (1) a reference to James I's notorious grants of exclusive commercial rights (see G. Unwin, *The Gilds and Companies of London*, 1938, pp. 309–11, for monopolies in 1613); (2) ironic, considering Sir Oliver's cuckoldom.
30. *cast*] 'arranged' (*O.E.D.*, 45).

V. iv. 0.1–0.10.] The pantomime here is discussed by D. Mehl, *The Elizabethan Dumb Show* (1965), pp. 148–9.

and women [among whom are LADY KIX, MRS ALLWIT, *and* SUSAN]. *Then set them down one right over-against the other; while all the company seem to weep and mourn, there is a sad song in the music-room.*

Touch. Sen. Never could death boast of a richer prize
From the first parent; let the world bring forth
A pair of truer hearts. To speak but truth
Of this departed gentleman, in a brother
Might, by hard censure, be call'd flattery, 5
Which makes me rather silent in his right
Than so to be deliver'd to the thoughts
Of any envious hearer, starv'd in virtue,
And therefore pining to hear others thrive;
But for this maid, whom envy cannot hurt 10
With all her poisons, having left to ages
The true, chaste monument of her living name,
Which no time can deface, I say of her
The full truth freely, without fear of censure:
What nature could there shine, that might redeem 15
Perfection home to woman, but in her
Was fully glorious? Beauty set in goodness

15. shine] *Q;* shrine *conj. Dyce.*

0.8. over-against] alongside.

0.9. sad song in the music-room] Cf. Beaumont and Fletcher, *The Captain*, III. iv (ed. Glover and Waller, v. 273):

... bid the boy go sing
That song above, I gave him: the sad song.

For a discussion of the Swan's music-room see Intro., pp. lxii–lxiii.

2. *From the first parent*] i.e., since Adam's death.

5. *censure*] judgment.

7. *to be deliver'd*] (1) 'to speak' (*O.E.D.*, 10); (2) to be made vulnerable to, to be surrendered up to.

8. *starv'd*] famished, lacking.

15–16. *What ... woman*] what nature could make shine in a woman, bringing to her the perfection lost at the fall. Cf. *W.B.W.*, III. ii. 23–8:

... come Bianca,
Of purpose sent into the world to show
Perfection once in woman; I'll believe
Henceforward they have everyone a soul too,
'Gainst all the uncourteous opinions
That man's uncivil rudeness ever held of 'em.

Speaks what she was: that jewel so infix'd,
There was no want of anything of life
To make these virtuous precedents man and wife. 20

Allw. Great pity of their deaths!

All. Ne'er more pity!

Lady. It makes a hundred weeping eyes, sweet gossip.

Touch. Sen. I cannot think there's anyone amongst you
In this full fair assembly, maid, man, or wife,
Whose heart would not have sprung with joy and gladness 25
To have seen their marriage day.

All. It would have made
A thousand joyful hearts.

Touch. Sen. [*To Touchwood Junior and Moll*] Up then apace,
And take your fortunes, make these joyful hearts;
Here's none but friends.

[*Touchwood Junior and Moll rise out of their coffins.*]

All. Alive, sir? O sweet, dear couple!

Touch. Sen. Nay, do not hinder 'em now, stand from about 'em;
If she be caught again, and have this time, 31
I'll ne'er plot further for 'em, nor this honest chambermaid
That help'd all at a push.

Touch. Jun. [*To Parson*] Good sir, apace!

Pars. Hands join now, but hearts for ever,
Which no parents' mood shall sever:— 35
[*To Touchwood Junior*] You shall forsake all widows, wives, and maids;—
[*To Moll*] You, lords, knights, gentlemen, and men of trades;—

21. *All.*] *Q; First Mour. Dyce.* 26. day.] *Dyce;* day? *Q.* *All.*] *Q; Sec. Mour. Dyce; 1 Mour. George.* 29. *All.*] *Q; Dyce gives* Alive, sir? *to Third Mour.*, O . . . couple! *to Fourth Mour.* 33. *Touch. Jun.*] *So Dyce subs.; T.S. Q.*

---

18. *Speaks*] 'expresses, shows' (*O.E.D.*, 29).
20. *precedents*] exemplars.
33. *at a push*] (1) when things were at the most critical; (2) playing on *push*, 'copulate' (Farmer and Henley, v. 331)?
34.] See note to III. i. 13–14.
35. *mood*] 'anger' (*O.E.D.*, *sb.*[1], 2b).

And if in haste any article misses,
Go interline it with a brace of kisses.

Touch. Sen. Here's a thing troll'd nimbly.—Give you joy,
brother; 40
Were 't not better thou shouldst have her than
The maid should die?

Mrs Allw. To you, sweet mistress bride.

All. Joy, joy to you both.

Touch. Sen. Here be your wedding sheets
You brought along with you; you may both go to bed
When you please to.

Touch. Jun. My joy wants utterance. 45

Touch. Sen. Utter all at night then, brother.

Moll. I am
Silent with delight.

Touch. Sen. Sister, delight will silence
Any woman, but you'll find your tongue again
Among maid servants now you keep house, sister.

All. Never was hour so fill'd with joy and wonder. 50

Touch. Sen. To tell you the full story of this chambermaid,
And of her kindness in this business to us,
'Twould ask an hour's discourse; in brief, 'twas she
That wrought it to this purpose cunningly.

All. We shall all love her for 't.

Enter YELLOWHAMMER *and his* Wife.

43. *All.*] *Q; First Mour. Dyce; Allw. conj. Dyce.* 45. to] *This ed.;* too *Q.* 50. *All.*] *Q; Sec. Mour. Dyce.* 55. *All.*] *Q; Third Mour. Dyce.* 55.1.] *So Q; after* now! *Dyce.*

---

40. *troll'd*] 'uttered rapidly' (*O.E.D.*, 12).

43–5. *Here* ... *to*] referring to their shrouds: cf. v. i. 6 (a favourite Middleton image): cf. *Wid.*, I. ii. 186–99, *C.* (Revels ed.), v. iii. 83–4, *W.B.W.*, I. i. 20–4.

45. *wants utterance*] is past speech.

46. *Utter*] (1) speak; (2) ejaculate, in sexual sense (not in *O.E.D.*, though see *vb*[1], 3b).

55.] Since Q gives both halves the separate speech head '*All.*', presumably they are spoken by different people: cf. l. 33 s.h. for a similar confusion.

Allw. See who comes here now! 55
Touch. Sen. A storm, a storm, but we are shelter'd for it
Yell. I will prevent you all and mock you thus,
You and your expectations: I stand happy
Both in your lives and your hearts' combination!
Touch. Sen. Here's a strange day again!
Yell. The knight's prov'd villain:
All's come out now, his niece an arrant baggage; 61
My poor boy Tim is cast away this morning,
Even before breakfast, married a whore
Next to his heart.
All. A whore?
Yell. His 'niece', forsooth!
Allw. [*Aside to his Wife*] I think we rid our hands in good time
of him. 65
Mrs Allw. I knew he was past the best when I gave him over.—
[*To Yellowhammer*] What is become of him, pray, sir?
Yell. Who, the knight?
He lies i' th' knight's ward.—[*To Lady Kix*] Now your belly,
lady,
Begins to blossom, there's no peace for him,
His creditors are so greedy.
Sir Ol. [*To Touchwood Senior*] Master Touchwood, 70
Hear'st thou this news? I am so endear'd to thee
For my wife's fruitfulness, that I charge you both,
Your wife and thee, to live no more asunder

55. *Allw.*] *George; All. Q; Fourth Mour. Dyce.* 68. ward.—Now] *Dyce;* ward now. *Q.*

---

57. *prevent*] anticipate.
64. *Next to his heart*] (1) closest to affection (*O.E.D.*, 10.4); (2) 'fasting' (*O.E.D.*, 4).
His] i.e., Sir Walter's.
68. *knight's ward*] In the London 'counters' (or debtors' prisons) there were four 'wards' or divisions, in descending order of comfort and cost: the master's, the knight's, the twopenny, the hole: cf. *P.*, IV. iii. 18–22. There was a convenient Counter for Sir Walter in Poultry and another off Wood-street (see map).

For the world's frowns: I have purse, and bed, and board
for you:
Be not afraid to go to your business roundly; 75
Get children, and I'll keep them.

Touch. Sen. Say you so, sir?

Sir Ol. Prove me with three at a birth, and thou dar'st now.

Touch. Sen. Take heed how you dare a man, while you live, sir,
That has good skill at his weapon.

Enter TIM, Welsh Gentlewoman[, *and* Tutor].

Sir Ol. Foot, I dare you, sir!

Yell. Look, gentlemen, if ever you say the picture 80
Of the unfortunate marriage, yonder 'tis.

Welsh G. Nay, good sweet Tim—

Tim. Come from the university
To marry a whore in London, with my tutor too!
O tempora! *O mores*!

Tut. Prithee, Tim,
Be patient!

Tim. I bought a jade at Cambridge; 85
I'll let her out to execution, tutor,

79.1.] *So Q; after* you, sir! *Dyce.* 80. say] *Q;* saw *Dyce.* 82. Tim—] *Dyce; Tim. Q.* 84. *mores*] *Dyce; Mors Q.*

---

75. *roundly*] thoroughly; with a quibble on *round*, 'pregnant' (Partridge, p. 181).

77. *Prove*] try, test.

80. *say*] obsolete past tense of 'to see' (*O.E.D.*).

84. O ... mores!] O times, O manners (Cicero, *Catiline*, I. i).

85. *jade*] (1) ill-conditioned horse; (2) a whore: cf. *R.G.*, II. i. 295, Nashe, *A Choise of Valentines*, 24–8 (ed. McKerrow, III. 404–5).

86–7.] Tim implies that he will act as the Welsh-woman's pander: cf. *Y.F.G.*, III. ii. 110–11: 'he has a nag can run for nothing, has his choice, nay, and gets by the running of her', T. Lupton, *All for Money* (1577), D2v (about a young wife):

A tired Jade by thee I think she hath not ben,
For she is properly a Jade that hath bene ouer ryden:
And therefore thou hast spared her nowe she is freshe and lustie.
Therefore hyer her out for a hacknie, and she wil bring thee money.

86. *to execution*] i.e., to pay off her debt to me (*O.E.D.*, 7).

For eighteen pence a day, or Brainford horse-races,
She'll serve to carry seven miles out of town well.
Where be these mountains? I was promis'd mountains,
But there's such a mist, I can see none of 'em. 90
What are become of those two thousand runts?
Let's have a bout with them in the meantime;
A vengeance runt thee!

Maudl. Good, sweet Tim, have patience.

Tim. *Flectere si nequeo superos, Acheronta movebo*, mother.

Maudl. I think you have marry'd her in logic, Tim. 95
You told me once by logic you would prove
A whore an honest woman; prove her so, Tim,
And take her for thy labour.

Tim. Troth, I thank you:
I grant you I may prove another man's wife so,
But not mine own.

Maudl. There's no remedy now, Tim; 100
You must prove her so as well as you may.

Tim. Why then, my tutor and I will about her
As well as we can.
Uxor non est meretrix, ergo falleris.

Welsh G. Sir, if your logic cannot prove me honest, 105
There's a thing call'd marriage, and that makes me honest.

Maudl. O, there's a trick beyond your logic, Tim.

94. *nequeo*] *Dyce; neguro Q.* *movebo*] *Dyce; mourbo Q.* 95. marry'd] *This ed.;* maried *Q.* 104. *falleris*] *Dyce; falacis Q.*

---

87. *Brainford*] Brentford (see note to II. ii. 174), a favourite spot for assignations (cf. *R.G.*, II. i. 289) where 'Entertainments for the visitors were provided in the shape of horse-races, puppet-shows, etc.' (Sugden).

93. *runt*] 'reprove, rate' (*O.E.D.*'s sole example is 1440).

94.] If I cannot move the gods, I will appeal to the lower world (Virgil, *Aeneid*, VII. 312).

98. *for thy labour*] for the pains you have taken; but cf. Goneril's pun in *Lr.*, IV. vi. 267–8: 'supply the place for your labour'.

102. *about*] i.e., set about, deal with; possibly 'turn her about, change her course' (*O.E.D.*)?

104.] A wife is not a whore, therefore you lie.

106.] Cf. similar solutions in *T.C.O.O.* and *M.W.M.M.* and the main situation of *The Honest Whore*.

Tim. I perceive then a woman may be honest
According to the English print, when she is
A whore in the Latin; so much for marriage and logic! 110
I'll love her for her wit, I'll pick out my runts there;
And for my mountains, I'll mount upon—

Yell. So Fortune seldom deals two marriages
With one hand, and both lucky; the best is,
One feast will serve them both! Marry, for room, 115
I'll have the dinner kept in Goldsmiths' Hall,
To which, kind gallants, I invite you all. [*Exeunt.*]

FINIS.

108–10. *honest ... Latin*] playing on 'meretrix' (l. 104) and merry 'trick' (l. 107): cf. W. Bullein, *A Dialogue bothe plesaunt and pitiefull* (1573), p. 26: 'a kinde hearted woman, and full of meretrix, ha, ha, ha', J. Heywood, *Woorkes* (1562), Oij:

> Madame, ye make my hert lyght as a kyx,
> To see you thus full of your *meretrix*.
> This tricke thus well tricked is the latine phrase...;

and Barry's *Ram Alley, or Merry Tricks*.

109. *print*] spelling.

112.] censored for indecency, or cut short by Yellowhammer?

113–14. *deals ... hand ... lucky*] again the gaming imagery.

116. *Goldsmiths' Hall*] Cf. Stow, p. 273: 'On the east side of this Foster lane [north of Cheapside] ... is the Goldsmiths' Hall, a proper house, but not large.'

APPENDIX I

Lineation

All departures from the quarto are recorded here, together with all Dyce's alterations which have not been accepted in the present text. If Dyce is not specifically mentioned, his lineation agrees with that of the quarto. Later editors are noticed when the present text adopts one of their innovations but not otherwise. See Intro., p. xxii, for a comment on Middleton's blank verse.

[I. i]

1–15. Have . . . week.] *This ed.; prose in Q.*
15–19. Last . . . company;] *This ed.; prose in Q;* Last . . . board / He . . . at it; / I . . . me; / Pretty . . . company: *Dyce.*
20–36.] *Dyce; prose in Q.*
38–9. Sir . . . company] *Q;* Sir . . . met / At . . . company *Dyce.*
46–7.] *Dyce; prose in Q.*
53.] *Dyce;* But . . . Cambridge, / (has . . . an't ?) *Q.*
54–6.] Had . . . commoners.] *Dyce; prose in Q.*
58–9.] *Dyce; prose in Q.*
62–4. Nay . . . witch.] *This ed.; prose in Q;* Nay . . . me: / He's . . . witch. *Dyce.*
64–5. Pray . . . him.—] *This ed.; prose in Q.*
80–1. If . . . you.] *This ed.; prose in Q.*
82–3.] *This ed.; prose in Q.*
84–5. How . . . Tim ?] *Dyce; prose in Q.*
86–8. What's . . . else.] *This ed.; prose in Q.*
88–90. Go . . . Latin.] *This ed.;* Goe . . . Court. / Fye . . . Latine. *Q.*
91–2.] *This ed.; prose in Q;* Nay . . . disclaims it, / Calls . . . with it.— / What . . . gentleman ? *Dyce.*
93–4. Now . . . London.] *Dyce; prose in Q.*
97–103. 'Twill . . . word !] *Dyce; prose in Q.*
105–6.] *Dyce; prose in Q.*
107–8. I have . . . years.] *Dyce; prose in Q.*
110–11. A hundred marks . . . Whorehound ?] *Dyce;* A hundred . . . else. / What . . . *Whorehound* ? *Q.*
112.] *Dyce;* O Death. / Why Daughter. / Faith . . . Baggage *Q.*
118–21. *This ed.; prose in Q;* Why . . . caught you. / What . . . stray / Thus . . . servant ? / Pish . . . else, — *Dyce.*

122–9.] *Dyce; prose in Q.*
131–4. Higher . . . right.] *Dyce; prose in Q.*
135–6.] *Dyce;* is . . . Mutton, / to . . . it, *Q.*
139–45. Turn . . . it.] *This ed.; prose in Q;* Turn . . . heart. (*prose*) / Read, and . . . words; / I'll . . . it. *Dyce.*
151–2.] *Dyce; prose in Q.*
166–7. We . . . lack ?] *Dyce; one line in Q.*
171–3. Of . . . grace.] *This ed.;* Of . . . ounce, / stand . . . Diamond. / Sir . . . grace. *Q;* Of . . . fair / And . . . diamond; / Sir . . . grace. *Dyce.*
173–4. Pray . . . one.] *Dyce; one line in Q.*
181–2. I protest . . . alike;] *Dyce; one line in Q.*
185–7. Say . . . gentlewoman ?] *Dyce;* Say . . . Girle. / Shall . . . Gentlewoman ? *Q.*
190–1.] *Dyce; one line in Q.*
196–7.] *Dyce;* Doe . . . I / wonder . . . carried, *Q.*
200–2. Tomorrow . . . gentlewoman.] *Dyce; prose in Q.*

[I. ii]

2–3. What . . . come ?] *Dyce;* What . . . Wales / I faith . . . come ? *Q.*
4–8. In . . . boy.] *Dyce; prose in Q.*
19–20.] *Q;* Monthly . . . rent, / Nor . . . scavenger: *Dyce.*
61–2. O . . . husband.] *Dyce; one line in Q.*
63–6. *Negatur* . . . him.] *Dyce; prose in Q.*
68–9. E'en . . . meets.] *This ed.;* Eene . . . Sir, / She's . . . meets. *Q.*
72–3. Slippers . . . sleepy!] *This ed.; one line in Q.*
74–6. Now . . . observing—] *This ed.; prose in Q;* Now . . . now, / As . . . bidding; / 'Tis . . . observing, *Dyce.*
77–8.] *Dyce; prose in Q.*
91–5. Of . . . her.] *Dyce; prose in Q.*
97–8. That . . . awe.] *Dyce; prose in Q.*
104–6. Peace . . . there.] *Dyce; prose in Q.*
107.] *Dyce;* Oh . . . Schoole, / Ply . . . ha ? *Q.*
108–9. Where's . . . prayers.] *Dyce; prose in Q.*
114–17. I'll . . . i' faith.] *Dyce;* I'le . . . *Yellowh.* / As . . . Goldsmith / And . . . I faith. *Q.*
120–3.] *This ed.; prose in Q.*
126–8. No . . . fear,] *This ed.; prose in Q;* No . . . swear / It's . . . it!— / Thus . . . fear, *Dyce.*

[II. i]

17–18. Sir . . . house,] *Dyce; one line in Q.*
65–6.] *Dyce;* Doe . . . workemanship, / Nay . . . doe, *Q.*
68–72. Your . . . churchwardens.] *This ed.;* Your . . . you, / You . . . me, / I . . . it, / From . . . Church-Wardens. *Q;* Your . . . you! / You . . . me: / I . . . certificate / For . . . churchwardens. *Dyce.*
72–6. I'll . . . thee.] *This ed.; prose in Q;* I'll have / The . . . to't. / Thou . . . me / But . . . Derbyshire; / Thou'st . . . thee. *Dyce.*

78–80. True . . . husband.] *Dyce;* True . . . doe, / And . . . Husband, *Q.*
84–5. Of . . . two.] *Dyce;* Of . . . wants / A . . . two. *Q.*
102–3. And . . . myself.] *Dyce; prose in Q.*
125–6. With . . . me.] *Dyce; prose in Q.*
133–4. To . . . child!] *Dyce; one line in Q.*
146.] *Dyce;* Giue . . . find / Children, *Q.*
157.] *Dyce;* They . . . deceiued, / Be . . . Wife. *Q.*
158–9. Suffer . . . thee!] *Dyce; one line in Q.*
160–1. Come . . . child?] *Dyce;* Come . . . done, / You'le . . . Child? *Q.*
167–8. O . . . harmony!] *This ed.;* O . . . rayling, / That's . . . harmony. *Q.*
170–1.] *This ed.;* Throw . . . Drugges, / They're . . . remedy *Q.*
184–5. But . . . dear.] *This ed.; one line in Q.*
186–7. There's . . . pint,] *This ed.;* There's . . . me / In . . . pint, *Q.*

[II. ii]

4–6.] *Dyce;* And . . . nothing / In . . . recreation, / Not constraint. *Q.*
13–15.] *Dyce;* She . . . portion / And . . . slut, / Vnder . . . Sir, *Q.*
18.] *This ed.;* Giue . . . thou, / Come . . . hither, *Q;* Give . . . hither, / Come hither: *Dyce.*
27–8. I . . . sir.] *Dyce; one line in Q.*
28–9. Here . . . -meat.] *Dyce; prose in Q.*
30–1. Get . . . myself.] *Dyce; one line in Q.*
44–6. A . . . living?] *Dyce; prose in Q.*
74.] *Dyce;* How . . . *Dicke,* / A . . . Bird. *Q.*
77–8. I . . . admitted.] *Dyce; prose in Q.*
89–90.] *Dyce;* This . . . vp the / Bottome . . . Apron, *Q.*
95–6. That . . . us.] *Dyce; prose in Q.*
97–8. I . . . busy.] *Dyce; prose in Q.*
100–5. No? . . . smocks?] *This ed.; prose in Q;* No . . . lump / Stick . . . sir. / What . . . sir? / A . . . smocks / Going . . . washers. / O . . . well! / You . . . us? / Call . . . smocks? *Dyce.*
110.] *This ed.; prose in Q;* All veal? / Pox . . . faithfully *Dyce.*
111–13.] *Dyce; prose in Q.*
118–19. A rack . . . diet.] *Dyce;* A Racke . . . Lambe, / You . . . dyet. *Q.*
130.] *Dyce;* Looke . . . Foole, / She . . . too, *Q.*
133–5. O . . . us.] *Dyce;* O . . . Seruant, / Let . . . goe. / You . . . vs. *Q.*
146–8. A politic . . . made.] *This ed.;* A politike Baggage, / She . . . it, / I . . . made. *Q;* A politic . . . it: / I . . . made. *Dyce.*
148–50. *Imprimis* . . . lamb.] *This ed.;* Imprimis . . . Mutton, / What . . . Cloath? / Now . . . Lambe. *Q;* Imprimis . . . mutton. / What . . . quarter / Of lamb. *Dyce.*
154–5. No . . . wager.] *Dyce;* No . . . Head, / I . . . wager. *Q.*
161–5. Half . . . candles.] *This ed.;* Halfe . . . -sops, / And . . . Sope, /

And . . . still, / To . . . Candles. *Q;* Half . . . gettings / Must . . . now, / Besides . . . tallow; / We've . . . save / Suet . . . candles. *Dyce.*

166–7.] *This ed.; prose in Q;* Nothing . . . me / But . . . felt it: / She . . . us. *Dyce.*

168–9.] *This ed.;* Prethe . . . on't, / There's . . . come / To . . . yet. *Q.*

170.] *Q;* I . . . angry, / I'll . . . to-day. *Dyce.*

172–4. Let's . . . Branford.] *This ed.; prose in Q;* Let's . . . Queen-hive, / And . . . flood; / Then . . . Branford. *Dyce.*

[II. iii]

3–4. How . . . Davy?] *This ed.; one line in Q.*

4–6. Excellent . . . know.] *Dyce; prose in Q.*

9–10.] *This ed.;* O . . . quicke, / Quicke . . . faith, / Your . . . here? *Q;* O . . . youth! / In . . . faith. / Your . . . here? *Dyce.*

11–13. Here . . . faith.] *This ed.; prose in Q;* Here . . . have / Such . . . Underman, / Welcome, i' faith. *Dyce.*

16–17. Thanks . . . Underman.] *This ed.; one line in Q.*

28.] *Dyce;* I . . . get, / And . . . Master. *Q.*

29–31.] *This ed.;* They . . . things, / Put . . . minutes, / I . . . 'em, / Will . . . Wenches? *Q;* They're . . . minutes, / I . . . wenches? *Dyce.*

33–4.] *Dyce; prose in Q.*

36–7. Mistress . . . cup.] *Dyce; prose in Q.*

[II. iv]

3–4. So . . . forsworn.] *Dyce;* So . . . company / And . . . forsworne. *Q.*

5–7. Before . . . place.] *Dyce; prose in Q.*

7–8. Your . . . wife?] *Dyce; prose in Q.*

10–12. Come . . . spirit.] *This ed.; prose in Q;* Come . . . go / In . . . peace, / Like . . . spirit. *Dyce.*

[III. i]

1–2. O . . . me!] *Dyce; prose in Q.*

6–8. The ring . . . together.] *This ed.;* The Ring . . . hither. / She . . . long / A clapping . . . together. *Q.*

10–12. You . . . have.] *This ed.;* You . . . can, / For . . . shift / For . . . haue. *Q.*

21–2.] *Dyce;* Thou . . . strumpet, / And . . . end, *Q.*

24–5. And you . . . more.] *Dyce; prose in Q.*

28–9. I . . . for 't.] *Dyce; one line in Q.*

36–7.] *Dyce; one line in Q.*

41–4. As . . . me!] *Dyce;* As . . . Sunne / If . . . on't. / O . . . me. *Q.*

44–5. Farewell . . . comfort:] *Dyce;* Farewell . . . thee, / And . . . comfort, *Q.*

48–9. Your . . . soon;] *Dyce;* Your . . . lately, / Yet . . . soone, *Q.*

52–4. Like . . . sir.] *Dyce; prose in Q.*

[III. ii]

8–9.] *Dyce; prose in Q.*
15–16. No ... heart,] *Dyce; one line in Q.*
19–20. She ... neighbour.] *Dyce; prose in Q.*
21–2.] *Dyce;* We ... once, / But ... againe, / 'Tis ... faith, *Q.*
31–2. I would ... children.] *Dyce; prose in Q.*
33–5. Children ... home.] *Dyce;* Children ... zeale, / By ... home. *Q.*
35–6. The worst ... gossip ?] *This ed.; one line in Q.*
40–1. Look ... gossip ?] *This ed.; prose in Q.*
42–3.] *Dyce; prose in Q.*
45–8. I would ... colour.] *This ed.; prose in Q;* I would ... feed / My ... world, / For ... hair / The ... much; / 'Tis ... colour. *Dyce.*
54–5. Now ... end!] *Dyce;* Now ... pocketing, / See ... end. *Q.*
58–60.] *George; prose in Q;* A pox ... purity / Loves ... together. / Had ... beggar'd; *Dyce.*
61–70.] *Dyce; prose in Q.*
74–9. They ... payment.] *Dyce;* They ... strength, / And ... forward, / To ... such, / Like ... bearing. / Now ... whistles / It ... payment. *Q.*
87–8.] *Dyce; prose in Q.*
99–100. A gentleman ... forsooth.] *Dyce;* A gentleman ... Cambridge, / I ... forsooth. *Q.*
101–2.] *Dyce;* 'Tis ... faith, / Prethe ... Women, / 'Twill ... well, *Q.*
104–5. Would ... now.] *This ed.; one line in Q.*
107–8. There's ... for him.] *Dyce; one line in Q.*
108–9. Yes ... mountains,] *Dyce;* Yes ... Wales, / At ... Mountaines, *Q.*
127–8. Come ... plums!] *Dyce; one line in Q.*
131–3. You'll ... church-yard ?] *Dyce; prose in Q.*
136–7.] *Dyce;* Let ... you, / 'Twould ... Vniversitie, / No ... Mother. *Q.*
138–40. Yes ... to him.] *This ed.; prose in Q;* Yes ... lady, / I ... logic, / And ... him. *Dyce.*
141–5. That ... sir.] *This ed.; prose in Q;* That ... mother; / But ... pate, / And ... he, / Mistress ... him. / I ... sir. *Dyce.*
146–7.] *This ed.;* True ... indeed, / When ... mended, *Q.*
152–3.] *Dyce; prose in Q.*
154–6. O ... come on.] *Dyce;* O ... kisses, / Your ... come on (*prose*) *Q.*
157–64. This ... brethren.] *Dyce; prose in Q.*
167–9. I'm ... me.] *Dyce;* I'me ... sure, / It ... me. *Q.*
169–73. Here's ... show!] *This ed.;* Here's ... yet ? / Hyda ... Plate, / That ... Vessels, / Yonder's ... Shew. *Q;* Here is ... hoida, / A ... plate, / That ... vessels.— / Yonder's ... shew! *Dyce.*
173–5. Come ... bearer.] *This ed.;* Come ... -conduit, / With ... -bearer. *Q.*

184–5. Nothing . . . belike.] *Dyce; prose in Q.*
196.] *Q;* Marriage, Davy ? / Send . . . rather. *Dyce.*

[III. iii]

3–8.] *Dyce;* For . . . me, / Then . . . vow, / E'ne . . . none / Else . . . gamefull / To . . . brother, *Q.*
14–15. Prithee . . . blood] *Dyce; one line in Q.*
26–7. Why . . . brother.] *Dyce;* Why . . . right, / I . . . Brother. *Q.*
34–5. I care . . . yours.] *Dyce; one line in Q.*
56–7.] *Dyce;* That . . . thee: / I . . . destiny, *Q.*
68.] *This ed.;* Singlenesse . . . her, / I . . . Smocke. *Q.*
69–70.] *This ed.;* But . . . single, / When . . . Shipboard. *Q;* But . . . you / Came . . . shipboard. *Dyce.*
71.] *Dyce;* Heart . . . there, / Prethe . . . friends. *Q.*
76–8. Good . . . evening.] *Dyce;* Good . . . House, / Which . . . Euening. *Q.*
82–3. Would . . . nothing!] *This ed.; one line in Q.*
84–5. I' faith . . . rogue.] *This ed.;* I faith . . . it, / Busse . . . Rogue. *Q.*
86–7. Can . . . then!] *This ed.;* Can . . . in ? / By . . . then. *Q.*
88–9. Here's . . . threepence.] *This ed.;* Here's . . . -milke / That . . . pence. *Q.*
94–6. Had . . . thee.] *Dyce;* Had . . . ought, / But . . . thee. *Q.*
97–8. By this . . . way!] *Dyce;* By this . . . dore, / And . . . way, *Q.*
106–7. I . . . there!] *Dyce; one line in Q.*
111–12. Stir . . . stand.] *Dyce; one line in Q.*
116–19. O passing . . . neck, sir.] *Dyce; prose in Q.*
121–3.] *This ed.; prose in Q;* Nothing . . . victuals. / You . . . business ? *Dyce.*
124–6. Or . . . hand.] *Dyce; prose in Q.*
127–30. Another . . . good, sir.] *Dyce; prose in Q.*
130–1. All . . . faster, sir.] *Dyce; one line in Q.*
133–4. I shall . . . farewell.] *Dyce; one line in Q.*
140–1. Clean . . . lying.] *Dyce; one line in Q.*

[IV. i]

24–5. Nothing . . . mother.] *Dyce; one line in Q.*
25–7. About . . . fool is.] *Dyce; prose in Q.*
28.] *Dyce;* Why . . . Mother ? / I . . . now. *Q.*
30–4. 'Tis . . . here.] *This ed.; prose in Q.*
35–7. 'Tis . . . anything.] *This ed.;* 'Tis . . . Logicke, / By . . . any thing. *Q.*
39–40. Nay . . . do 't.] *Dyce; prose in Q.*
41–4. Some . . . hither ?] *Dyce; prose in Q.*
46–50. How . . . grammar ?] *Dyce; prose in Q.*
51–2. Pish, . . . porches.] *This ed.; one line in Q.*
53–4.] *Dyce; prose in Q.*
55–7. He so . . . maid.] *Dyce; prose in Q.*
58–61. '*Quid . . . est grammatica ?*] *Dyce; prose in Q.*

62–5. Nay, ... life.] *Dyce; prose in Q.*
66–8. Are ... mother.] *Dyce; prose in Q.*
68–75. That ... conclusion.] *This ed.; prose in Q;* That ... son, / I ... tutor, / A ... little / Into ... in / The ... wooing: / I'll ... door. / I ... conclusion. *Dyce.*
75–8.] *This ed.;* I mar'le ... be, / That ... me: / I ... faith, / To ... so: *Q.*
81.] *Dyce;* Then ... knew / A ... stranger. *Q.*
88–9.] *Dyce;* My ... me, / I ... *R*, *Q.*
91.] *Dyce;* Vnlesse ... Hogges, / I ... not, *Q.*
92.] *Dyce;* And ... comes, / If ... now *Q.*
96–7.] *This ed.;* She ... her, / Marry ... order it, *Q; She* ... but / I'll ... order it, *Dyce.*
100–1.] *Dyce; Salue ... pulcherima, / Quid ... curo, Q.*
103.] *Dyce;* I ... meanes, / A ... quoth a? *Q.*
105–6.] *Dyce; Ferter ... virgo, / Wallia ... maximis. Q.*
109–10.] *Dyce; prose in Q.*
117–18.] *This ed.; prose in Q.*
124–5. I'm ... us.] *This ed.; one line in Q;* I'm glad / My ... us. *Dyce.*
128–9. No ... London?] *Dyce;* No ... Boy, / And ... London? *Q.*
141–2. 'Tis ... forsooth.] *This ed.; one line in Q.*
143–6. O ... sing.] *Dyce; prose in Q;* O ... Country / By ... saying, / There's ... Mutton. / It ... sing. *conj. George.*
187.] *Dyce;* The ... Oxfordshiere, / Neere Abbington. *Q.*
188–9.] *Dyce; prose in Q.*
195–6. I heard ... graces.] *Dyce; one line in Q.*
202–3. 'Tis ... recall'd?] *Dyce; one line in Q.*
206–10. By ... years;] *Dyce;* By ... then, / And ... match, / He's ... state, / — ... yeres, *Q.*
219–20. Tush, ... do.] *Dyce;* Tush, ... that? / Beleeue ... doe. *Q.*
229.] *Dyce;* Why ... Verse, / And ... Colledge. *Q.*
233–4. Ay ... mark.] *Dyce; prose in Q.*
251–2. We ... gone!] *Dyce; one line in Q.*
253–4. Over ... else.] *Dyce;* Ouer ... Houses: / Lay ... else. *Q.*

[IV. ii]

1.] *Dyce;* Theeues ... stolne, / Some ... her: *Q.*

[IV. iii]

7–8.] *Dyce;* But ... Varlets / Came ... drawne, *Q.*
15–16. These ... her.] *Dyce;* These ... Fellowes, / Take ... her. *Q.*
17–18. Go ... stay] *This ed.; one line in Q.*
19–23. Here's ... below.] *Q;* Here's ... maid / With ... lustily / To ... sir.— / Make ... below. *Dyce.*
25–6.] *Dyce;* Away ... for you, / And ... you. *Q.*

[IV. iv]

1–2. She . . . lock.] *Dyce; one line in Q.*
4–5. With . . . reads it.] *Dyce;* With . . . vses it, / My . . . reads it. *Q.*
9–10.] *Dyce; prose in Q.*
12–16.] *Dyce; prose in Q.*
21–2. I'll . . . daughters.] *Dyce; prose in Q.*
25–8. Look . . . fishwives.] *Dyce; prose in Q.*
32–6. You . . . join'd.] *Dyce; prose in Q.*
40–1. Why . . . armour] *Dyce; prose in Q.*
42.] *This ed.; prose in Q;* Take you / No . . . send *Dyce.*
43–7. For . . . with.] *Dyce; prose in Q.*
47–8. I . . . noon] *Dyce;* I . . . chance / Makes . . . noone, *Q.*
50.] *Dyce;* And . . . Mayden-head / Worth fourtie. *Q.*
51–3. Half . . . mother.] *This ed.;* Halfe . . . Hayre, / Forc't . . . Mother. *Q.*
61–2. There . . . pounds.] *Dyce; prose in Q.*

[V. i]

28–9.] *Dyce;* And ioyne . . . wak't / Now . . . pittie, *Q.*
59–61.] *Dyce;* Of . . . me, / I . . . me, / This . . . mother *Q.*
66–7. O . . . face] *Dyce; one line in Q.*
84–6. Come . . . thee] *Dyce;* Come . . . aliue / Ah . . . thee, *Q.*
87–8.] *Q;* For . . . thou / Art . . . thee. *Dyce.*
97–8. All . . . mind.] *Dyce; one line in Q.*
101.] *Dyce;* There's . . . Legacie, / I . . . with't. *Q.*
109–10. O . . . departed!] *Dyce; one line in Q.*
120.] *Dyce;* Am . . . Chamber? / What . . . forsooth? *Q.*
155.] *Dyce;* That . . . straight, / What . . . Wife? *Q.*
156–7. We . . . stuff.] *Dyce; one line in Q.*

[V. ii]

6–7. 'Tis . . . water.] *Dyce; one line in Q.*
11–12. And . . . mother.] *This ed.;* And . . . 'tis done, / You . . . Mother. *Q; one line in Dyce.*
22–3. I . . . be.] *Dyce;* I . . . Heart, / As . . . be. *Q.*
45–6. She . . . death.] *Dyce; one line in Q.*
66–7. Ay . . . quickly.] *Dyce; one line in Q.*
68–9. He . . . servants.] *Dyce; one line in Q.*
74–5. Seldom . . . now.] *Dyce; one line in Q.*
78.] *Dyce;* O sicke . . . me: / How . . . this? *Q.*
81–2.] *Dyce;* Moll . . . speake, / Look . . . hart *Q.*
83–4. O . . . heart.] *Dyce; one line in Q.*
84–5. As . . . it.] *Dyce;* As . . . torment, / And . . . it. *Q.*
96–8. I'll . . . gentlewoman.] *Dyce;* I'le . . . Church, / And . . . Gentlewoman. *Q.*

[V. iii]

5–7. Upon . . . night.] *Dyce; prose in Q.*

[v. iv]

26–9. It . . . friends.] *Dyce;* It . . . Hearts. / Vp . . . fortunes, / Make . . . Friends. *Q.*

41–2. Were't . . . die?] *This ed.;* Were't . . . her, / Then . . . dye? *Q; one line in Dyce.*

43–5. Here . . . please to.] *This ed.; prose in Q;* Here . . . with you; / You . . . please too. *Dyce.*

46–9. I . . . sister.] *This ed.;* I . . . delight. / Sister . . . Woman, / But . . . Seruants, / Now . . . Sister. *Q.*

67–9. Who . . . him,] *Dyce;* Who . . . now. / Your . . . him *Q.*

70–4. Master . . . you:] *Dyce;* M^r . . . newes? / I . . . fruitfulnesse, / That . . . thee, / To . . . frownes, / I . . . you: *Q.*

84–5. Prithee . . . patient!] *George; one line in Q.*

108–12. I . . . upon—] *Dyce; prose in Q.*

APPENDIX II

The Music for *A Chaste Maid in Cheapside*

by John P. Cutts

Music is used on the following occasions:

I. ii. 56. The contented cuckold, Allwit, sings an indelicate burden of dildoes '*La dildo, dildo la dildo, la dildo dildo de dildo*' (STC 17877, sig. C)[1] at the thought of his wife being laboured over by Sir Walter Whorehound.

IV. i. 152–77. The supposed Welsh heiress, Sir Walter's whore, woos Tim Yellowhammer with an indelicate song which is introduced specifically as: *Musicke and Welch Song* ... CVPID *is* VENVS *onely Ioy* (sigs. H–H^{v}). Three verses are given but the third lacks a line.[2] The music for this song is extant in two seventeenth-century manuscripts:

A British Museum Additional MS. 29481, fol. 6^{v} (*circa* 1630). Vocal part only with first verse underlaid and second verse given at the foot of the folio.[3]

B New York Public Library, Drexel MS. 4175 (*circa* 1620–30).[4]

[1] See J. H. P. Pafford, ed., *The Winter's Tale* (New Arden Shakespeare, 4th ed., 1963), IV. iv. 197, for a good note on dildoes and fadings.

[2] See my *La musique de scène de la troupe de Shakespeare, The King's Men, sous le règne de Jacques Ier* (Paris, 1959), pp. 145–6, for suggestions regarding the text, the puzzle of the *Welch* song, and the use of this song in Middleton's *More Dissemblers Besides Women*.

[3] See my 'Two Jacobean Theatre Songs', *Music & Letters*, XXXIII. 4 (Oct. 1952), 333–4.

[4] See my '"Songs vnto the violl and lute"—Drexel MS. 4175', *Musica Disciplina*, XVI (1962), 73–92, for a description of the MS. and *Musique de scène* for a transcription of both items.

Item XXIIII: Treble and Bass with first verse underlaid and second verse given at the foot of the folio;

Item LVI: Treble and Lute tablature with first verse underlaid.

The music given now (by courtesy of the Music Department of the New York Public Library) is a transcription of item XXIIII with first and second verses underlaid and a suggestion of how the third verse might be used. There are no important variants in the music of the vocal line in all three versions; occasionally the barring is different in item LVI from item XXIIII; *A* is entirely unbarred. For variants in the text of the extant versions, see the collation notes.

V. ii. 36–43. Now that her love for Touchwood Junior is hopeless Moll 'sings her selfe to death' (sig. K)[1] with 'a straine or two' (sig. I4^{v}) of the swan song '*Weepe Eyes, breake Heart*' (sig. I4^{v}). 'Weep eies, break hart' occurs as the burden of a song 'Faire are those eies' by Michael Cavendish in '14. Ayres in Tabletorie to the Lute expressed with two / *voyces and the base Violl or the voice & Lute only.* / 6. more to 4 voyces and in Tabletorie, / And / 8. MADRIGALLES *to* 5. *Voyces.*' 1598 (STC 4878):

Item X: Cantus and Lute tablature with Bassus given separately;

Item XVI: Cantus and Lute tablature with Altus, Tenor, and Bassus (for XVII) given separately.

Fellowes[2] correctly pointed out that there are several interesting variants in item XVI in the voice part but neglected to say that there are also important variants in the lute tablature.

[1] Her mother's remark 'O, I could die with Musicke' (sig. K also) and her father's 'She playes the Swan, and sings her selfe to death' may possibly reflect the immediate influence of Gibbons's 'The silver swan, who living had no note, / When death approached unlocked her silent throat ... O death, come close mine eyes', *The First Set of Madrigals* ... 1612, item i.

[2] See E. M. Fellowes, ed., *The English School of Lutenist Song Writers*, Second Series, 1925—Songs Included in Michael Cavendish *Booke of Ayres and Madrigalles*, 1598. Fellowes edited item X without printing the tablature.

1. Cu - pid is Ve - nus on - ly ioy, but he
2. Why should not Ve - nus chide her sonne? for the
[3. Can there be a - ny part of blisse, in a
is a wan-ton boy a ve - ry ve - ry wan-ton
trickes yt hee hath donne? the wan-ton trickes yt he hath
qui - ckly flee-ting kisse, a qui - ckly flee - ting
boy, hee shootes at la - dyes na - ked
donne hee shootes his fi - rie darts soe
kisse to ones plea - sure, lea - sures are but
brests, hee is the cause of most mens crests
thicke, they wounde poore la - dyes to the quicke
wast, the slow - est kisse makes too much hast,

I meane v - pon the fore - heade,
ay mee with cru - ell woun - dinge,
and loose it ere we find
in - ui - si - ble, but hor - rid twas hee
his darts are soe con - foun - dinge that life
.... the plea -
first thought v - pon the way, to
and strength would soone da - caye but
- sing sport they one - ly know that
keepe a la - dyes lippes in playe.
that it keepes theyre lippes in playe.
closae a - boue and closae be-low.]

Weep eies weep eies, break hart, break
break break hart [My Loue and

Fine
I must part and I must part
Cru - e - ll Fates, trew-loue doe

soo - nest seuer. O, I shall
see thee, ne - uer, ne - uer, neuer.

O hap - py is the
Mayd, whose life takes end. Ere it knowes

D.C. al Fine
Pa - rents frowne, or losse of friend.]

The music now given is basically a literal transcript of item XVI but set forth differently so that the burden which is marked to be repeated at the end by Cavendish is here put at the beginning and marked for repeat just as the text calls for in the play. I think the play's calling for a 'straine or two' is sufficient warranty for this editorial licence, and for omitting two bars 'But if my faith cannot his merit gain' for which there is no correspondence in the play's text. I have given the vocal line in notes of half the original value. The Lute part is scanty, but I have thought it better to present it as such rather than attempt to fill out or justify the bars other than by using appropriate rests.

V. iv. 0.1, 0.9. Stage-directions '*Recorders dolefully playing*' (sig. K2) while the funeral processions of Moll and Touchwood are progressing and for a '*sad Song in the Musicke-Roome*' (sig. K2v) make it abundantly clear that another song was used in the play, but there is as yet no way of tracing it. The reference to the '*Musicke-Roome*' is very important. Not one of the King's Men plays from 1603 to 1625 contains such an explicit reference.[1]

[1] See *Musique de scène*, pp. xxix–xxx.

APPENDIX III

Lenten Documents

1. After many years' laxity, restrictions began to be seriously re-imposed in Lent 1607/8. See Robert Steele, *Bibliography of Royal Proclamations of the Tudor and Stuart Sovereigns* ... (1910), I, 22 January 1607/8 [BM 506. h. 10. (84)]. Eight butchers in Eastcheap, four in St Nicholas Shambles, and ten in the suburbs were licensed to sell during Lent. This order was repeated in 1608/9 and 1609/10.

2. Restrictions tightened up in 1610/11. See letters of 14 and 28 January 1610 from the Privy Council to the Lord Mayor (W. H. and H. C. Overall, *Analytical Index to Remembrancia of the City of London* (1878), III. 397–8).

3. There was further tightening up in 1611/12. See a Privy Council letter to the Lord Mayor requiring more vigilance, 19 February 1611 (Overall, III. 398), and the Lord Mayor's letter to the Privy Council agreeing to limit the number of butchers licensed to sell during Lent, with marginal note that only eight were actually licensed (Overall, III. 398–9).

4. Extraordinary measures were taken for 1612/13:

(*a*) The reasons are explained by John Stow (J. Stow and E. Howes, *Annales or A Generall Chronicle of England*, 1631, p. 1004a.):

> The last Sommer through want of raine, both grane and hay waxed very scant in most shires of this Kingdome, so as such persons as had not extraordinary meanes of provision of winters food for their Cattell, were extreamly dismayd and perplexed, lest the ensuing winter should prove hard like as did this Sommer ... [They feared starvation of the cattle and unscrupulous speculation.] But it pleased Almighty God to send a mild open winter, and a forward spring, which releeved the whole kingdome, ... Also the King in his prudent care for the better prevention of the great feared famine ... to command his subjects in generall that all the time of Lent they should utter-

ly abstain from eating all manner of Butchers flesh, and that no Butcher should bee suffered to kill flesh within London nor neere the Citie, as had bin used in many late yeeres (which restraint ... had not bin in the memory of man)... by this means all sorts of cattell were preserved & encreased, and at Easter all manner of flesh [was] very plenteous... The Lords of the Privy Council incessantly sent word to the L. Maior & Sheriffs to look and search diligently that no flesh should be kild or sold within London and their liberties: in which service they used all diligence & strictnes, committing the offenders to the gaole, and gave their meat to prisoners.

(*b*) There was a more stringent Privy Council order, 'made by the King's special direction', with 'No licence for killing in Lent to be given to any butcher'. See Steele, 5 February 1612/13, and *State Papers, Domestic*, LXXII, at the same date.

(*c*) A Privy Council letter to the Lord Mayor, 9 February 1612/13, in *Remembrancia of the City of London*, III, No. 72 (Overall, III. 399), gives the following order:

So greate hath bene the abuse and contempte of those Orders and directons which by his Maiesties expresse Commaundement in former yeares have bene published for the orderlie keepinge of Lent ... as his maiestie is is [*sic*] nowe informed insteede of the late dispensations and qualifications of the ancient severitie and strictnes where with that time hath bene observed in former Ages ... to resolve nowe absolutelie to prohibite the killinge and utteringe of fflesh by any Butcher or other person in the Cittie of London or in anie other partes of the kingdome duringe Lent ... [The Lord Mayor is warned that he will be held personally responsible and that King James is directly interested in the prohibition.]

(*d*) This stringency is objected to in a letter of the Lord Mayor to the Privy Council, 18 February 1612/13 (Overall, III. 399).

(*e*) The Privy Council replied to the Lord Mayor, 25 February 1612/13 (Overall, III. 399), authorizing him to license as many *poulterers* as he sees fit for relief of the infirm and sick.

(*f*) A letter from the Lord Mayor and Aldermen to the Privy Council, 11 March 1612/13 (Overall, III. 399), objects to the Privy Council licensing its own 'messengers' to spy on city butchers without consulting the Lord Mayor.

(*g*) A letter of the Privy Council to the Lord Mayor and Aldermen, 16 November 1613 (*Acts of the Privy Council 1613–14*, ed. H. C. Maxwell Lyte, 1921, pp. 271–2), reaffirms the order:

> Although it might be easilie discerned ... what good effectes were produced by the generall prohibicion of killing of flesh ... this last Lent, upon soe short and suddaine warning ... yet to thende all persons may take notice of his Maiesties' express pleasure and resolucion not to give way to any such dispensacion or qualification, as hath of late yeeres bin admitted in killing and uttering of flesh ... his Highnes hath commaunded that the orders which we send you herewithall be forthwith published...

(*h*) A Privy Council warrant, 16 November 1613 (*Acts of the Privy Council*, p. 273), to Evan Birch and Nicholas Stott, 'messengers of his Maiesties Chamber', directed them to 'make diligent search and enquiry ... for all such butchers and graysiers as kill or sell flesh ... and to bring them and every of them fourthwith and in your companie before us, to answere their contemptes...'

5. The strictness was somewhat relaxed in 1614:

(*a*) A Letter of the Privy Council to the Lord Mayor, 12 March 1613/14 (Overall, III. 400), authorizes him to license 'some one Butcher whome you shall thinck fittest' for the 'vse of Embassadors and sicke persons onelie'.

(*b*) But the licence was extended to several other butchers: see the Privy Council letter to the three Chief Justices, 13 May 1614 (Overall, III. 400), defending certain butchers who had been informed against and imprisoned for selling in Lent.

6. Strictness finally dropped after a letter from the Lord Mayor to the Privy Council, 26 January 1615, complaining that the severe orders against licensed butchers during the last three years had merely encouraged open flouting of the law.

APPENDIX IV

Source Materials

1. *The Second Maiden's Tragedy* (1611), ed. W. W. Greg (Malone Soc., 1909), p. 2:

> . . . I allowe her her owne frend, to stop her mouth
> and keep her quiet, gi' him his table free,
> and the huge feeding of his great stone horse
> on wch he rides in pompe about the Cittie
> only to speake to gallants in bay-windowes;
> marry his lodging he paies deerly for,
> he getts me all my children, there I save by'te,
> Besides I drawe my life owt by the bargaine
> some twelve yeres longer than the tyme appointed, . . .
> Tis the right waie to keep a woman honest
> one frend is Baracadoe to a hundred
> & keepes em owte, nay more, a husbandes sure
> to have his children all of one mans getting,
> & he that performes best can have no better,
> I'me eene as happie then that saue a labour.

(Act I, ll. 42–50, 54–9)

2. Anon., *The Batchelars Banquet* (London, 1603), sig. B4:

CHAP. III.

The humour of a woman lying in Child-bed.

There is another humor incident to a woman, when her husband sees her belly to grow big (peraduenture by ye help of some other friend) yet he perswades himselfe, it is a worke of his owne framing: and this breeds him new cares & troubles, for then must he trot vp & down day & night, far, & neere, to get with great cost that his wife longs for . . . he poore soule takes all the care, rising earely, going late to bed, and to be short, is faine to play both the husband and the huswife. But when the time drawes neere of her lying downe, then must he trudge to get Gossips, such as shee will appoint, or else all the fatte is in the fire. Consider then what cost and trouble it will bee to him, to haue all things fine against the Christ-

ening day, what a store of Sugar, Biskets, Comphets, and Carowayes, Marmilade, | [B4v] and marchpane, with all kind of sweete suckets, and superfluous banqueting stuffe, with a hundred other odde and needlesse trifles, which at that time must fill the pockets of daintie dames: Besides the charge of the Midwife, she must haue her nurse to attend and keepe her, who must make for her warme broaths, and costly caudels, enough both for her selfe and her mistresse, being of the minde to fare no worse then she: ... putting the poore man to such expence, that in a whole yeare he can scarcely recouer that one moneths charges. Then euery day after her lying downe will sundry dames visit her, which are her neighbours, her kinswomen, and other her speciall acquaintance, whom the good man must welcome with all cheerefulnesse, and be sure there be some dainties in store to set before them: where they about some three or foure houres (or possible halfe a day) will sit chatting with the Child-wife, and by that time the cups of wine haue merily trold about, and halfe a dozen times moystned their lips with the sweet iuyce of the purple grape: ... [A passage of malicious chat between the gossips follows, like in kind to that in *A Chaste Maid* but with no resemblance in detail.] |
[C3] Well wife, said the good man, you must remember that this night is our Gossips supper, and they will come hither with many other of our friends, therefore we must prouide something for them, especially since it is your upsitting, and a fortnight at the least since you were brought to bed: but good wife, let us goe as neere to the world as we may, seeing that our charge doth euery day increase, and money was neuer so ill to come by. [The wife then nags him for niggardliness, demanding not only an expensive entertainment for the gossips but a new dress for herself, threatening to risk her life by getting out of bed. The husband gives in.] |
[C4v] ... hee in the meane while is double diligence, to prouide all things against their comming, according to his abilitie, and by reason of his wiues words, he buyes more meate, and prepares a great deale better cheare then he thought to haue done. At their comming he is readie to welcome them with his Cap in his hand, and all the kindness that may be shewed. Then doth he trudge bare-headed vp and downe the house, with a cheareful countenance, like a good Asse, fit to bear the burthen, he brings the Gossips vp to his wife, and comming | [D] first to her himself, he tels her of their comming. Iwis (quoth she) I had rather they had kept at home, and so they would too, if they knew how litle pleasure I tooke in their comming. Nay I pray you wife (saith he) giue them good countenance, seeing they be come for good will: with this they enter, & after mutuall greetings, with much gossips cere-

monies, downe they sit and there spend the whole day, in breaking their fasts, dining, and in making an after-noones repast: besides their petty suppings at her beds side, and at the cradle, where they discharge their parts so well, in helping him away with his good Wine and Sugar, that the poore man comming oft to cheare them, doth well perceiue it, and greeues inwardly thereat, howsoever he couers his discontent with a merrie countenance. But they not caring how the game goes, take their peniworths of that cheare that is before them, neuer asking how it comes there, and so they merily passe the time away, pratling and tatling of many good matters . . . [Finally the husband gets into debt for his wife's new dress, wears old clothes himself to economize, and is troubled by the child crying, and his wife and the nurse nagging.]

3. Cf. three verses of a ballad 'The Batchelor's Feast, or, the difference betwixt a single life and a double; being the Batchelor's pleasure, and the married Man's trouble', *The Roxburghe Ballads*, ed. Charles Hindley (1873), I. 61–2:

> No cradle have wee to rocke,
> nor children that doe cry,
> No land-lords rent to pay,
> no nurses to supply:
> No wife to scould and brawle,
> now we still keep good company
> With them that take delight
> to live at liberty:
> *With hie dilldo dill,*
> *hie ho dildurlie:*
> *It is a delightfull thing*
> *to live at liberty.*
> While married men doe lie
> with worldly cares opprest,
> Wee Batchelors can sleepe,
> and sweetly take our rest:
> O, married men must seeke
> for gossips and a nurse,
> Which heavie makes the heart,
> but light it makes the purse.
> *With hie dilldo, etc.*
> For candell and for soape
> and many knacks beside,
> For clouts and swaddling bands,
> hee likewise must provide,

To pay for sops and wine
hee must also agree,
O 'tis a delightfull thing
to live at liberty:
With hie dilldo, etc.

4. 'The Country Girl's Policy: Or, the Cockney Outwitted', *The Roxburghe Ballads*, ed. J. W. Ebsworth (1893), VII. 286–7:

All you that are to mirth inclin'd, come tarry here a little while:
Pray read it once, and I do not fear, but soon it will make you to smile.
The *Londoners* call us 'Country Fools', and laugh at us every day;
But I'll let them see, before I have done, we know as good things as they.

A jolly young girl in *Hertfordshire*, who lately had learn'd to dance;
In less than the space of one whole year she light of a Child by chance.
Being very poor this cunning whore, upon a certain day,
Resolved was she the City to see, so to *London* she took her way.

With an old straw hat, and her tail pinn'd up, and with Dirt instead of fringe,
Not long ago this cunning slut did come to the *Royal Exchange*;
With the Child in a basket under her arm, close covered, as it is said,
With a clean white cloth, and at each end hung out a Goose's head.

She saw two Stock-jobbers standing by, she unto one did say,
'Gaffer, what stately Church is this ? come tell me now I pray!'
The other [one] to her smiling said, 'How like a fool you talk!
This is no church, it is the '*Change*, where all the Merchants walk.'

'Is this the '*Change*, good Sir ?' she said, 'a glorious place it be;
A finer place in all my life, I never before did see:
I'll warrant you there's fine chambers in't, as you and I do live!
Now if you'll let me go and see, a penny to you I will give.'

The one said, 'Your basket I will hold, and tarry here below,
Whilst my Consort goes up with you, the Chambers for to show.'
She answered, 'I am afraid, that when I do come down,
You will be gone, and I would not lose my basket for a crown.'

'I am not such a man,' the [Jobber] cry'd, 'and that I'd have you know;'
She gave it [to] him, and with her guide she up the stairs did go;
She view'd the pictures very fine, and did them much admire;
He soon dropp'd her, she down stairs run, and after him did enquire.

She runs straight up to a Merchant, 'Good honest man,' said she,
'Did not you see a thick tall man that had two Geese of me?'
'Alas!' said he, 'poor country girl, our Cocknies are too quick;
Go home and tell your Country Girls of this fine *London* trick.'

She stamp'd and cry'd, 'Thus to be bit, would make a body swear.
I'll never come to the *Royal Exchange* any more to sell my ware;
For by a couple of cheating knaves, alas! I am undone.'
She gave a stamp, and laugh'd aloud, and then away she run.

But now we will to the Jobbers turn, who thought they had got a Prize;
They stept into an Ale-house, and sent for both their wives.
They told [to] them the story, with hearts both merry and light,
Said they, 'We'll have a Frolick on't, and roast them both at night.'

The women cryd, 'No, one at a time, the further they will go;
The other we'll have at another house, and order the matter so.'
Thus they began to jangle, and got on either Side;
But all the while this Basket stood, without ever a knot unty'd.

Then opening of the basket, as I the truth unfold,
There did they find a curious Boy, just about five weeks old.
The women flew into a damnable rage; O how they did scold and curse!
'Instead of a Cook, ye rogues,' said they, 'you must run and call a Nurse.'

The one said, 'This is your bastard, sirrah, you have had by some common whore.
If these be your Geese, ye Rogues!' she said, 'I never shall love Geese more.'
The one she kick'd the drink all down, the other whipp'd up the glass,
And after she had drunk the Beer, she threw it and cut his face.

There was helter-skelter, the Devil to pay, oh how the pots did fly!
Just as they were in the midst of the fray, the child began to cry:
There were clouts and blankets all bes[poil]t, such sights are seldom seen;
I hope it will learn them both more wit, how they meddle with Geese again.

They put it out for three shillings a week, which is eighteen-pence a piece,
Which they pay every Saturday night, in remembrance of the Geese.
Come, here's a health to the Country Lass, I think she was not to blame;
If she has but wit to take care of her[self], she may pass for a Maid again.

Ebsworth notes that one of the copies (Roxburghe Collection, III. 302) has the imprint '*Newcastle-upon-Tyne*. Printed and sold by *John White*.' and that another (Douce, III. 17 *verso*) is a London copy of about 1765.

5. Thomas Jordan, 'The Cheaters Cheated. *A Representation in four parts to be Sung*, Nim, Filcher, Wat, *and* Moll, *made for the Sheriffs of London*', *A Royal Arbor of Loyal Poesie* (1664), pp. 34–53.

Summary:

Two thieves, *Nim* and *Filcher*, lament their poverty; when *Wat*, a west-country clown, enters, they distract his attention with a coloured glass and pick his pockets—only to find nails in one purse and bread and cheese in the other. *Moll Medlar* enters with a basket; meeting *Wat*, she persuades him to dance with her, handing him the basket and then dancing off. *Wat* finds a child in the basket and, lamenting '*Water Gruel* [his full name] must now veed the childe,' tries to hand it over to the audience. *Filcher* and *Nim* determine to get the better of *Wat*; he enters with a trunk which he says is full of rich clothes, and they take it from him by force. Then they quarrel about shares, but are parted by *Moll*, who opens the trunk and finds her child. She accuses *Filcher* of being the father, and he agrees to marry her. All three vow to give up evil courses in the future, and the jig ends with *Wat* praising country guile over city shrewdness.

The set used in the Royal Court Production, 1966

APPENDIX V

The Royal Court Production of *A Chaste Maid in Cheapside*, London 1966

Until William Gaskill directed it for the English Stage Company in 1966, Thomas Middleton's *A Chaste Maid in Cheapside* seems never to have been performed professionally[1] since it was 'often acted at the Swan' around 1613. This circumstance alone would make the production of more than ordinary interest, and William Gaskill's inventive and controversial direction is worth attention in its own right.

Gaskill says he has always liked Middleton's work because of its clarity of style. Compared to the other great Jacobeans—Jonson, Webster, Marston, and the later Shakespeare—Middleton is sparing of figurative expressions and his syntax is straightforward, neither 'metaphysically' contorted nor too pastorally mellifluous. Thus the Royal Court actors found no difficulty in delivering his verse naturalistically, without the ululation to which English actors are prone when faced with something which looks like Shakespeare. Nor were there many alterations needed to update the text. This was done by Edward Bond, whose own play, *Saved*, was the *succès de scandale* of the same season. He worked from the Mermaid text and his alterations are roughly of two kinds: cuts and rewordings to avoid the obscurity of contemporary references and Jacobean vocabulary, and cuts and transpositions made in order to streamline the plot. The two kinds tend to overlap.

The first category needs little illustration. It is largely made up of changes of simple words or phrases—'Curzon Street' for 'Turnbull Street' (the prostitute area), 'informers' for 'promoters', or a 'Virgil–virgin' pun for the original 'Virgil–jill' of IV. iv. 11–12. It would be tedious to list them in detail. The only passage of any length which required rewriting because of obscurity was Allwit's aside explaining the promoters and Lent (II. ii. 53 ff.). Gaskill felt, however, that the

[1] If we except a much condensed version, called *A Posy on the Ring*, put on for only one performance at the 'Shakespeare's England' exhibition at Earl's Court in 1912. See Intro., p. lxvii.

whole Lenten situation was too removed from modern experience and that, in spite of the rewriting, it never quite got across.

Of the passages rewritten in order to simplify the plot, the longest is a rewording of the latter part of IV. iii, the scene in which Touchwood Senior, Moll, and Touchwood Junior embark successively for Barn Elms. Middleton seems to have rendered the confusion and haste of this elopement deliberately in the writing, but since the events are crucial for understanding what follows—Moll's capture and the fight between Touchwood Junior and Sir Walter Whorehound—it was thought wise to simplify it.

For the most part alterations to the plot took the form of cuts and transpositions rather than wholesale rewritings. The large number of characters in *A Chaste Maid* strained the acting resources of the English Stage Company to its limit, so the excision of certain minor characters was as much for economic as for aesthetic reasons. The first cut was the Porter in I. i and with him went the whole business of Tim's Latin letter and its comic construe. A disadvantage of this was that Tim then turned up in III. ii unheralded, and, since his Tutor was also cut, he tended to seem extraneous throughout, memorable only for a very funny wooing scene with the Welshwoman (played by an actress who was able to reply to his Latin with floods of improvised Welsh). With the Tutor gone, the Latin logic passage which begins IV. i was avoided, the scene commencing instead with Tim's 'I mar'l what this gentlewoman / Should be' (ll. 75–6). The Tutor's lines in III. ii were cut, and those in IV. ii, IV. iii, and V. iv given to Tim. Each time Tim intoned one of the few Latin tags which were left, everyone on stage froze to listen politely; then his mother boxed his ears and the chatter started off again.

Another minor character who was cut was the Maid who tells the Kixes of Touchwood Senior in II. i. She was replaced by Touchwood Senior himself, who intervened in the Kixes' quarrel with the invented lines:

> I have overheard—nay, nay, pardon me—
> The matter of your quarrel. I have
> A certain remedy. . .

and then took over the Maid's original lines. In II. ii the Dry Nurse was cut, and 'Mr. Oliver' whom the promoters allow to smuggle meat was replaced by Sir Oliver Kix; in II. iii the comfit-maker's man was cut; in II. iv the fourth and fifth Gossips disappeared; and, finally, Susan was cut from V. ii and the comments about her from V. iv. These were the major excisions. There were also minor ones to remove inessential elaborations of language, such as Touchwood Senior's running commentary about the Kixes in III. iii or Tim's comparison of his new wife to a hack at the end, but these are comparatively unimportant.

Besides cuts, the plot was also streamlined by transpositions. III. i (Moll's first elopement) was presented without a scene change as though the attempted marriage actually took place at Allwit's christening. This was prepared for by Moll asking Touchwood Junior 'Is the Parson ready?' at II. ii. 34, and in III. i, instead of complaining of the 'hard shift' she had to get away, she reminds Touchwood Junior that 'even now the christening waits for us.' The christening scene which follows (III. ii) brought the first half of the production to a close with a company ensemble scene, the curtain falling on an improvised coo from Mrs Allwit: 'Little baby Whorehound'. In the second half, the scene of Sir Oliver Kix's jubilation at his wife's pregnancy (V. iii) was brought forward between IV. iii and IV. iv. The 4th Servant's news of the double funeral, which ends the original V. iii, thus became premature and was cut, and Sir Oliver was given a separate entry in the final scene just before he speaks (V. iv. 70). This transposition certainly streamlined the finale, though it ran the risk of emphasizing the impossibly short stage interval between Lady Kix's 'physicking' and the announcement of her pregnancy. On the whole, Bond's alterations are few, deft, and successful, the only real objection being the isolation of Tim. The controversial part of the production was not here but in the costuming and direction.

The main difficulty facing Gaskill, as Ronald Bryden pointed out in *The New Statesman*,[1] was how to update so densely Jacobean a work. The very brilliance of *A Chaste Maid*'s contemporary reference makes it at times impenetrable for a modern audience. Gaskill was fully aware of this difficulty. One of the main attractions of the play for him was its shrewd observation of the social relationships analysed in Tawney's *Religion and the Rise of Capitalism*. He believed that most of these relationships are still applicable to English life and could be readily grasped by a modern audience, provided that their permanent characteristics were emphasized more strongly than the Jacobean setting. He decided, therefore, to abandon any attempt at historical realism, and to use music-hall and Commedia dell' arte techniques instead, to make a more generalized statement. His model here was Brecht. However, his interest was divided between presenting a social parable and exploiting the techniques for entertainment. And, in effect, whatever his social intentions may have been, they were soon submerged by exuberant theatricalism.

This theatricalism was most strikingly seen in the costumes. Though their general effect was Edwardian, there was no attempt at historical consistency. Gaskill explains that to set the play in any

[1] 'Fornication Street', *New Statesman* (21 Jan. 1966), p. 99.

other particular period would be to invite direct comparison with the Jacobean references. Instead, the designer, John Gunter, was asked to costume the characters by the most immediately recognizable image of their type, irrespective of period. The result was a fascinating collection of caricatures. Sir Walter Whorehound appeared as a Wodehousian squire in plusfours and deerstalker, with monocle, handlebar moustache, and port-flushed wattles (port was brought to him immediately he arrived at the Allwits in I. ii). The plump, peroxided Mrs Allwit spent the whole play in a cantaloupe negligé, ready for action, while Allwit was given a checked three-piece suit, a self-satisfied little paunch, and a red polka-dot handkerchief with which he persistently wiped his brow. The social and sexual precariousness of Sir Oliver ('looking like a young T. S. Eliot', Bernard Levin, *Daily Mail*, 14 January 1966) was distinguished from Sir Walter's assurance by dressing him in a grey double-breasted pinstripe of 1930's looseness, with a grey bowler, a monocle, and a stick which he flourished phallically on such lines as 'I have stirred my stumps,' 'I have struck it home.' Lady Kix was Victorian in long gaunt dress, boa, parasol, and garden party hat, and Maudline Yellowhammer a frump in long greeny-brown dress, Edwardian saucepan hat, and ratty fur. Moll Yellowhammer, on the other hand, wore a modern summer dress and a chic raincoat for the river. Her brother had a brown duffle coat and college scarf, with spectacles which he constantly pushed up; while their father Yellowhammer was dressed in an ill-fitting second-hand business suit with eight-inch shirt cuffs and two watch chains. He peered myopically to the right or left of whoever was speaking, failed to see the lovers kiss right under his nose, actually donned two pairs of spectacles at Touchwood Junior's gibe in III. i. 25, and hovered with his jeweller's eyeglass over the exposed bosom and beauty spot of the Welsh Gentlewoman. The Touchwoods were faintly sporty, the elder in a suède bowler and stovepipe trousers like a bookie, the younger 'dashing' in an ascot; Davy was in hunting breeches; and the servants all had a tapster appearance in bowler hats and cream waistcoats. The watermen wore tarpaulins and sou'westers.[1]

The distancing nature of these costumes reached its apogee in the children and the gossips. Wat and Nick were played by adults dressed in sailor suits, while the gossips were not only played like pantomime dames by men but in addition wore masks. Gaskill explains that the first reason for these peculiarities was economic: his company did not include enough actresses to play all the female rôles, nor could he

[1] There are pictures of the production in *Plays and Players* (March 1966) and in *Life*, LX (20 May 1966), 92–3. Some costume designs are reproduced in the *Times* review of the play, 14 Jan. 1966.

afford extra child actors. However, he decided to exploit this very weakness for Commedia dell' arte effects. What he probably had in mind can be seen from Keith Johnstone's 'Note on Clowning' in the season's *Programme 3*.[1] Johnstone singles out two aspects of the Commedia dell' arte: its concern for basic social relationships, especially master–servant ones (and we have said that this was one of the things which Gaskill saw in *A Chaste Maid*); and, secondly, its subordination of narrative to improvisation. Gaskill had earlier used *A Chaste Maid* for improvisational exercises with the students of the Royal Court Workshop and the Theatre Centre. And it was this aspect of the play, its important non-narrative scenes with the promoters and gossips, which stimulated him most.

Gaskill, in fact, considers the promoters' scene the central scene of the play, a key statement of the lust–greed theme on which the other scenes are all variations. It was one of his headaches that this particular scene was among the hardest to put over because of modern unfamiliarity with the customs and attitudes associated with Lent. He tried it first by costuming the promoters as private detectives in raincoats and snapbrim trilbies; and, when this failed, fell back on memories of the Blitz by dressing them in tin hats and blue-serge uniforms with the arm-band 'Meat-warden'. It never really worked to his satisfaction, however. The drunken gossips' scene, on the other hand, worked marvellously well, masks and all, and was one of the scenes picked out for special comment by the critics. The improvisational approach produced some very funny business, but inevitably it tended to isolate particular scenes into self-contained units.

Another Commedia influence may perhaps be seen in the set. Gaskill rejected any idea of trying for a Jacobean 'open stage' effect. Quite apart from the difficulty of such an effect at the Royal Court, he had decided after directing *The Dutch Courtezan* at Chichester that the open stage was not suited to a play which relied on asides to the audience. For *A Chaste Maid*, therefore, he used a modification of the late seventeenth-century proscenium stage with a type of set which goes back to the Latin Renaissance comedy. In front of the proscenium was a shallow apron with a door at either side; behind the proscenium the stage was raked steeply upwards (about three feet) to within a yard or so of the backdrop; and between the edge of the rake and the backdrop was the 'Thames', a sunken traverse which carried the actors laterally across stage so that from the front they looked as though they were being borne along in boats on the river. The set, in greens and browns, consisted mainly of two 'houses', each standing with a corner to the audience so that two outside walls of each could be seen. The one on stage right was Yellowhammer's

[1] pp. 23–4.

with a door on the centre-facing wall; the other was Allwit's with a window on the centre-facing wall and a door on the other wall. On the backdrop between the houses was an impressionist blow-up of an early engraving of London showing St Paul's, with a sign on it saying 'London'. It was in front of this that the various groups of watermen and passengers were carried on the traverse, poling vigorously with only their upper halves visible. The set tended to focus on the Thames, therefore, and one of the biggest laughs of the production came when Sir Walter threw Touchwood Junior into the river at the climax of their quarrel in IV. iv—a piece of business which was necessary to explain Touchwood Junior's 'death' from a mere fist-fight ('The gentleman you pushed into the Thames has caught an ague and died'). This was accompanied by a sound-effects 'splash' and a shower of rice thrown all over Sir Walter to suggest spray, a clever effect which Gaskill found in a letter by Bernard Shaw about *Caesar and Cleopatra*. The ingenuity of the river tended, perhaps, to attract too much attention to itself; but Gaskill justifies it by saying that he considered it a central factor in the characters' experience.

It was compensated for, moreover, by the rake of the stage. This was introduced partly because the auditorium at the Royal Court is too flat, but mainly so that the action could be thrown forward. The main acting area became the middle of the apron, where both exterior and interior scenes were played, with necessary props carried on or let down from the flies (Mrs Allwit's bed coming up by trapdoor between the houses) and the view of London hidden for interior scenes by a curtain. This, combined with the large number of openings available for exits and entrances, let Gaskill move the action very fast and fluidly, with a vivacity which even unsympathetic critics applauded.

The director and actors took every opportunity for bawdry and farce. The constant *double entendres* were hammered home as intentional word-plays of which the characters were quite conscious. Thus, when Sir Oliver was called 'brevity', he delicately placed his hat over his 'brevity'—a joke duplicated by the Welshwoman in her song about hurting poor ladies to the 'quick'. Lascivious eating was comically exploited by having the pregnant Mrs Allwit wolf pickles as she welcomed Sir Walter, and again in the christening scene with the 'mouthing' of comfits. The Second Puritan seems to have made a strong impression in the latter scene, since she is mentioned by several critics. She was acted as a nymphomaniac, kissing Allwit like a suction pump, drawling out 'I *love* lowliness,' and eventually chasing Tim offstage. The bawdy exit was a bit overplayed, perhaps, and sexual innuendoes read sometimes into unsuitable lines. It is just possible that Allwit might carry his wife off lustfully at the end, but it is uncharacteristic of Tim to chase the Welshwoman offstage or of Sir Oliver to say 'I mean so' lecherously when he is told to ride five hours after his medicine. And the eructations of the christening scene were a *very* free adaptation of 'lurch [i.e., steal] at the lower end'. The most outrageously funny invention of all, however, was the birth of Mrs Allwit's seventh bastard on stage behind a curtain, mimed to a musical chorus of moans and cries. This was inserted between II. i and II. ii.

This scene, the Thames scenes, the fight, the wooing scene, the christening scene, and Sir Oliver's shrill caperings to fizz up his aphrodisiac ('like a pair of animated compasses') were so hilariously inventive that they tended rather to stand out as separate 'turns', contrasting strongly with the more static scenes in which characters explained their point of view and moralized. For some critics this contrast seemed a weakness, and the feeling was either that Gaskill was trying to galvanize a rather dull play or that he had oversimplified a subtle play into farce. The *Times* reviewer was closest to Gaskill's intention, however, when he commented:

> In style, the production is cunningly detached, varying between breakneck comedy (with fights and dives into the Thames) and moments when the characters step forward to comment on it as a passing show. This also helps to punctuate the intrigue and give separate scenes a clearly defined shape.[1]

What Gaskill was aiming for, in fact, was a Brechtian mixture of discrete scenes and detached commentary. This he seems to have achieved, although the effect was not generally appreciated. The majority of the audience merely accepted the play as a risqué farce with occasional regrettable soliloquies.

The reason for Gaskill's partial failure here seems to lie in the nature of the moral commentary offered by the production, and is directly related to the director's interpretation of the play. Gaskill believes that *A Chaste Maid* is Brechtian not only in its episodic, theme-and-variation structure, but also in its attitude to life. He sees this attitude as an unsentimental, cheerfully materialistic 'realism' like Azdak's in *The Caucasian Chalk Circle*, and believes that Middleton approved of the Allwits and accepted everyone in the play except Sir Walter, whom he condemned not for moral but for social reasons. Gaskill sees no 'black' side in the comedy and no foreshadowings of *The Changeling* or *Women Beware Women*.

Any suspicion of sentiment or serious moralizing was briskly undercut in the Royal Court production, therefore. The romantic appeal of Moll was destroyed by having her greet each setback with a banshee wail which made the audience roar with laughter. The

[1] *The Times* (14 Jan. 1966), p. 13b.

funeral was elaborately Victorian, which was funny in itself, and all thoughts of sentiment or morality were dissipated by business with the parson's vestments and the fact that both he and the 'corpses' smiled all through the ceremony. Sir Walter Whorehound's eloquent crisis of conscience was particularly guyed: he entered in bandages after his fight with Touchwood Junior, was given medicine and promptly belched, was shown the baby and belched again at the sight of it, started to rant and belched again; the grotesquely adult 'children' fell off his knee and were knocked down by a sweep of his arm; when he belched yet again, Mrs Allwit held out a basin for him to be sick into, and, when Allwit suggested he may have been 'familiar' with his wife, she innocently placed the same basin over her 'quick'; finally, when Davy called her a whore, Mrs Allwit gave him a withering look and handed him the basin as he walked out.

The elaborateness of the by-play, however, is a witness to the fact that this scene gave Gaskill more trouble than any other in the play. He admits that Sir Walter's verse here struck him as 'Shakespearian' and says he was able to incorporate it into his interpretation only by supposing it must be a parody of Claudius' repentance in *Hamlet*. He also found Touchwood Senior's moralizings an embarrassment and did not quite know how to handle them. He was unwilling to accept their seriousness at face value, however, and to this unwillingness can be traced the main weakness of his production. The original intention to combine theatricalism with social criticism, to balance farcical action scenes with scenes of detached comment, in the Brechtian manner, foundered because the kind of comment he wished to make was not the kind which Middleton in fact offers. To maintain tone, half of the commentary scenes had to be guyed or played so flatly that they seemed irrelevant, and, not surprisingly, the clever farcical invention then took over and unbalanced the production.

The idea was nonetheless bold and imaginative, and the revival must be considered as largely a success. It was universally praised for its pace and vivacity; in places it was outrageously funny; and Gaskill proved his point that the play is about relationships which are not exclusively Jacobean. Few who saw the production came away indifferent, though foyer opinion varied all the way from the Cambridge undergraduate who proclaimed that *A Chaste Maid in Cheapside* was better than anything Jonson ever wrote, to the Chelsea matron who objected, 'This play is *disgustingly* filthy.'

Glossarial Index to the Annotations

An asterisk indicates that the annotation referred to contains information as to sense or usage not provided by the *Oxford English Dictionary*; where more than one reference is given for a word, the asterisk refers to the first reference, unless otherwise noted. When a gloss is repeated in the annotations, only the first occurrence is indexed.